LOVE
WITH NO
TOMORROW

Mindelle Pierce has dedicated over fifteen years of her career to studying and teaching the history of the Holocaust. As a child of Holocaust survivors herself, she has a personal connection and insight into this history. Mindelle continues to contribute her knowledge and research to many renowned organizations, including the Museum of Jewish Heritage, which acts as a living memorial to the Holocaust, and Manhattan College.

Dr Michael Berenbaum is a Professor of Jewish Studies at American Jewish University in Los Angeles who has previously served as Deputy Director of the President's Commission on the Holocaust, Project Director of the United States Holocaust Memorial Museum (USHMM), and Director of the USHMM's Holocaust Research Institute.

Dr Miriam Klein Kassenoff acted as an educational consultant for this book. She is the director of the Holocaust Teacher Institute at the University of Miami and has studied at Yad Vashem. Dr Kassenoff is a film critic, author and lecturer who has appeared at conferences and workshops across the United States. She is a survivor of the Holocaust, having escaped Nazi Europe as a small child in 1941.

LOVE
WITH NO
TOMORROW

TALES OF ROMANTIC LOVE
DURING THE HOLOCAUST

MINDELLE PIERCE

AMBERLEY

TESTIMONIALS

Love at first sight. During the Holocaust. Bonds as strong as steel, forged in the flames of hate. These are extraordinary stories of love affairs during the most dangerous, degrading, and deadly conditions of genocidal persecution. The extreme lengths to which two people will go to express their love, and the superhuman strength that is derived from such love, is the stuff of miracles and endless inspiration. This little known aspect of the Holocaust, seen through the eyes of those in love, is a unique contribution to our understanding of the best and the worst qualities of human nature. This book must be read by everyone who wants to know more about life and love, beyond the most horrendous conditions one could imagine.

Ira Brenner, MD
Editor, *Handbook of Psychoanalytic Holocaust Studies –
International Perspectives*
(Routledge, 2020)

The Holocaust involved the murder of millions, the destruction of entire communities and their ways of life, as well as the theft of unimaginable potential – lives to be lived, creativity to be expressed, battles to be won for humanity. Yet, despite its vastness – or perhaps because of it – the Holocaust is too often conceived of as a single event in history and not what it was: the combined histories of all who were affected by it. *Love With No Tomorrow*, through its compelling stories of love and affirmation in the darkest of contexts, relates important history about individual lives. It confirms that there is a strength and power in the human spirit that, even in the most inhuman of circumstances, can animate and ennoble. It is a testament to the exponential power of survival.

David G. Marwell, PhD, Director Emeritus of the Museum of
Jewish Heritage, A Living Memorial to the Holocaust in New
York City, and author of *Mengele: Unmasking the 'Angel of
Death'* (W. W. Norton & Company. 2020)

The memory of the six million has now become enshrined in everything from museums and college courses, to poetry and cookbooks. The only problem with this is that we recall the death of six million victims, but know nothing about their individual lives. It was Josef Stalin who said: 'The death of one man is a tragedy ... the death of millions is a statistic.' Mindelle Pierce is much to be applauded for making the story of six million a story of individuals who had their own challenges and struggles, but also their hopes, dreams and love In painful detail she tells the story from a very unique perspective; from the perspective of love John Updike wrote: 'We are most alive when we are in love.' Mindelle Pierce does the impossible: she makes the six million come alive in our hearts ... with love.

Mitchell Wohlberg, Senior Rabbi, Beth Tfiloh Congregation, Baltimore MD

Love during the Holocaust: How can that be during a time of violence, destruction and mass murder? This topic, rarely dealt with in Holocaust studies, is the focus of Mindelle Pierce's book, which contains twenty-seven riveting, well-researched stories of relationships developed in all parts of Nazi-occupied Europe. There are fascinating details of how men and women fell in love and how their relationship persisted for decades after the war and genocide. This perspective does not diminish the horror of the Nazi years, but highlights how bonds between men and women helped them find strength and courage during the terrifying times and reminds us how humans preserved their humanity despite all efforts to dehumanise them.

Mary Johnson, Ph.D. Affiliate and Adjunct Professor, Stockton University Holocaust and Genocide Studies and Adjunct Professor, Kean University Holocaust Resource Center

I dedicate this book to my parents, Jacob and Reisel Najman, who both, with God's help, lived nearly 100 years. They used these years to impart their beliefs, love and stories on how they transcended the trauma of the Holocaust to their children, grandchildren and great-grandchildren. I am forever grateful to them. Their story is the first one I wrote for this book.

This edition published 2023

Amberley Publishing
The Hill, Stroud
Gloucestershire, GL5 4EP

www.amberley-books.com

Copyright © Mindelle Pierce, 2021, 2023

The right of Mindelle Pierce to be identified as the Author of this work has been asserted in accordance with the Copyright, Designs and Patents Act 1988.

Chapter 16 written by Alvin Lewis, son of Victor and Regina Lewis. © 2017 Alvin Lewis. All rights reserved.

ISBN 978 1 3981 1547 7 (paperback)
ISBN 978 1 3981 0831 8 (ebook)

British Library Cataloguing in Publication Data. A catalogue record for this book is available from the British Library.

1 2 3 4 5 6 7 8 9 10

Typesetting by SJmagic DESIGN SERVICES, India. Printed in India.

CONTENTS

Timeline of the Holocaust   9

Foreword by Dr Michael Berenbaum   14

  1 Joseph and Rebecca Bau   20
  2 Sally and Charles Bedzow   33
  3 Isadora and Joshua Szereny   41
  4 Max and Toby Berger   47
  5 Murray and Fruma Berger   53
  6 Daniel and Lucyna Berkowicz   61
  7 Herman Shine and Max Drimmer   71
  8 Henny Durmashkin and Simon Gurko   81
  9 Lillie Burstyn and Simcha Fogelman   90
 10 Peska and Wolvie Friedman   104
 11 Nardus and Sipora Groen   117
 12 Dina and Frank Kabak   125
 13 Chaim Joseph and Hanka Kempner   130
 14 Chaim Kleinberg and Nechama Baum   139
 15 Judith and Gus Leiber   147

16 Victor and Regina Lewis   162
17 Henry and Lydia Lilienheim   172
18 Manya Hartmayer and Ernst Breuer   181
19 Jacob and Reisel Najman   192
20 Ernest and Sara Paul   213
21 Rabbi Salomon and Henrietta Rodrigues Pereira   222
22 Jack and Ina Soep Pollack   229
23 Rosi and Fritz Schleiermacher   237
24 Sala and Sidney Garncarz   244
25 Lunia and Leo Weiss   253
26 Rose Weisz and Joska Cseh   265
27 Heniek Greenspan, Millie and Jack Werber   272

Acknowledgements   282

TIMELINE OF THE HOLOCAUST

1933

30 Jan.	Hitler appointed Chancellor of Germany
23 Mar.	First concentration camp established at Dachau
	German parliament empowers Hitler to enact all laws on its behalf
1 Apr.	Hitler proclaims one-day boycott of all Jewish shops/businesses
26 Apr.	Establishment of the Gestapo
10 May	Public burning of books written by Jews and opponents of Nazism
Spr./Summ.	Jewish professors are expelled from Universities; Jewish writers and artists are prohibited from pursuing their work
14 Jul.	Nazi Party proclaimed by law to be only legal political party in Germany
19 Oct.	Germany withdraws from League of Nations

1934

2 Aug.	Hitler named Fuhrer and Reich Chancellor after the death of von Hindenburg

1935

16 Mar.	Compulsory military service reinstated in Germany in violation of Treaty of Versailles
31 May	Jews barred from military service
14 Sept.	Nuremberg Laws passed depriving Jews of German citizenship

1936

7 Mar.	Nazi Army occupies the Rhineland
17 June	Himmler appointed Chief of Nazi Police
25 Oct.	Hitler and Mussolini form Rome-Berlin Axis
25 Nov.	Germany and Japan sign military pact

1937

16 Jul.	Buchenwald Concentration Camp is opened

1938

13 Mar.	Germany annexes Austria
6 Jul.	Evian Conference produces no result in helping provide refuge for Jews
29–30 Sept.	Munich Conference, England and France turn over part of Czechoslovakia to Germany
5 Oct.	Jewish passports are marked with a 'J'
28 Oct.	Approximately 15,000 Polish citizens living in Germany are resettled in Poland. Poland refuses to admit them and they are stranded on the border
9–10 Nov.	*Kristallnacht* (Night of Broken Glass) pogrom against Jews in Germany and Austria; Jewish shops and businesses are burned, looted, and synagogues are destroyed
12 Nov.	Jews are forced to turn over all retail businesses to Aryans
15 Nov.	Jewish students are expelled from schools in Germany
3 Dec.	Jews must hand in their drivers' licenses and car registrations
8 Dec.	Jews can no longer attend universities

1939

30 Jan.	Hitler threatens that if war erupts the Jews will be exterminated
15 Mar.	Nazi troops occupy part of Czechoslovakia
13 May	The *St. Louis* sets sail from Hamburg for Cuba
23 Aug.	Soviets and Germans sign pact of nonaggression
1 Sept.	Poland is invaded; World War II begins
17 Sept.	Soviets invade and occupy Eastern Poland
23 Sept.	Jews must turn in all radios
28. Nov	First ghetto established in Poland

1940

12 Feb.	German Jews begin to be deported to concentration camps
9 Apr.	Germany invades Denmark and Norway
7 May	Lodz ghetto established
10 May	Germany invades Holland, Belgium, and France
20 May	Auschwitz Concentration Camp is established
22 Jun.	France surrenders to Nazis
15 Nov.	Warsaw Ghetto is established

1941

22 Feb.	Deportation of Dutch Jews begins; Holland's workers strike in sympathy for Jews
March	Adolf Eichmann made head of Gestapo section for Jewish affairs
6 Apr.	Germany occupies Greece and Yugoslavia
22 Jun.	Germany invades Soviet Union
June–Dec.	Nazi *Einsatzgruppen* (special mobile killing units) carry out mass murder of Jews in areas of Soviet Union occupied by Nazi Army
31 Jul.	Heydrich appointed by Göring to carry out 'Final Solution'
1 Sept.	Every Jew in areas occupied by Nazis must wear yellow Star of David
28. Sept.	Massacre of Jews at Babi Yar

14 Oct.	Large-scale deportations of Jews to concentration camps begin
Oct.	Establishment of Birkenau
7 Dec.	Japan attacks Pearl Harbor
8 Dec.	Chelmno concentration camp begins operation
11 Dec.	Germany and Italy declare war on the United States

1942

20 Jan.	Wannsee Conference-plans for 'Final Solution' are made
17 Mar.	Extermination by gas begins in Belzec
Mar.	Deportations to Auschwitz begin
April	Extermination by gas begins in Sobibor; Summer Deportation of Jews to extermination camps from Holland, Poland, France, Belgium, Croatia; armed resistance by Jews in several ghettos
22 Jul.	Large-scale deportation of Jews from Warsaw Ghetto
23 Jul.	Treblinka is established
28 Jul.	Jewish Fighting Organization (Z.O.B.) organised in Warsaw Ghetto
4 Oct.	Jews still in concentration camps in Germany to be transferred to Auschwitz for extermination

1943

18–21 Jan.	Armed Jewish resistance to Nazi attempt to liquidate Jews in Warsaw Ghetto
2 Feb.	Germany's Sixth Army surrenders at Stalingrad
March	Liquidation of Krakow Ghetto
19 April	Warsaw Ghetto revolt begins
11 June	Himmler orders liquidation of all ghettos in Poland and Soviet Union
Aug.	Revolt in Treblinka
14 Oct.	Revolt in Sobibor

1944

| 19 Mar. | Germany invades Hungary |
| 15 May | Nazis begin deporting Hungarian Jews |

6 Jun.	Allied invasion of Normandy, D-Day
20. Jul.	Attempt to assassinate Hitler fails
24 Jul.	Russian troops liberate Majdanek death camp
6 Aug.	SS begins to drive concentration camp prisoners into Germany in advance of Soviet troops
25 Aug.	Paris is liberated
Nov.	Last deportation from Theresienstadt to Auschwitz
8 Nov.	Beginning of death march of Jews from Budapest to Austria
24 Nov.	Himmler orders destruction of Auschwitz crematoriums to hide evidence of death camps

1945

17 Jan.	Evacuation of Auschwitz; beginning of death march from there
27 Jan.	Soviet troops liberate Auschwitz/Birkenau
4–11 Feb.	Yalta Conference
11 Apr.	American troops liberate Buchenwald
15 Apr.	British troops liberate Bergen-Belsen
29 Apr.	American troops liberate Dachan
30 Apr.	Hitler is believed to have committed suicide
7 May	Germany surrenders, the Third Reich is over; World War II ends in Europe
15 Aug.	Japan surrenders; World War II is over
22 Nov.	Nuremberg Trials begin

FOREWORD

I have been waiting for a book like this for a long time, and here's why.

Thirty or so years ago, a prestigious university press asked me to referee a draft book on women and the Holocaust. The author argued, most properly and cogently, that historians had not paid sufficient attention to gender issues as they pertained to the Holocaust. For example, more women were killed than men. In the early years of the war, men were perceived as more vulnerable to arrest than women, so they often escaped, leaving their families behind, and assumed that the civilized Germans would not murder women and children. Men could be accepted into partisan units in the forests, but women were rarely accepted, and those who were, were mostly expected to sexually service the fighters – as well as take care of cooking and washing. If a woman did join a group, she discovered that her only protection was to find a strong and feared fighter who would become her lover and protect her from the rest of the men.

During the *selektions* in Birkenau, men and women were separated. Mothers who stayed with their children were marched directly to the gas chambers. Fathers stood a chance – albeit a slim one – of surviving. Yet women were not just victims, they were also protectors.

On the night of the November Broken Glass pogroms in 1938, 30,000 Jewish men aged between sixteen and sixty were arrested, but could free themselves from concentration camps if they could prove they would leave Germany within a fortnight. In retrospect, they were lucky because women – mothers, wives, sisters and daughters – did everything imaginable to free their men. This was a chapter in women's ingenuity and empowerment that was rarely told.

The author of the book wrote tellingly about what had been a taboo subject in the Holocaust – sexual violation and exploitation, everything from rape to brothels, sexual slavery and sexual favours. She had broken barriers and had advanced the field. And yet something was missing. Every relationship between men and women was marked by exploitation and violence. But when survivors told me their stories, I also heard about love fused in the flames of horror.

This book is a corrective to that oversight.

Let me be clear. Sexual abuse, exploitation and rape are an under-researched and very significant part of the history of women during the Holocaust, but they are not the *only* narrative.

While working at the United States Holocaust Memorial Museum in the 1980s, I grew close to Vladka and Ben Meed, revered leaders in the Holocaust survivor movement. When they met, Vladka was a courier for the Warsaw Ghetto Resistance and Ben was a red-headed Polish-speaking Jew hiding with his parents on the Aryan side. From time to time, I would hear parts of their story.

Vladka talked about how she said to Ben, 'I am going somewhere, and I do not know if I will return.' Ben knew that her parents and brother were already dead and that she was alone in the world. Then she told him, 'If I do not return, I want someone to miss me, someone to care. You can be my boyfriend.' And that is how their relationship began.

When they married – for the first time – they had been spending time together, late into the evening and early morning, something Ben's religious mother found unacceptable. Yet how could she tell the young couple to wait for tomorrow when looming death was a daily reality? Ben's mother took off her ring, gave it to Ben and said, 'Give it to Vladka.' She lifted a cup of water and said. '*Zol zein mit mazel,* let it be with good fortune.' Fused in the fires of Warsaw, their love was born of desperation and deep loneliness, but it was love nonetheless.

Other relationships were formed in Europe's living hell. Helen K. was a beautiful young woman, also in the Warsaw Ghetto, whose parents suggested that she take advantage of her beauty and marry the 'richest man in the ghetto'. The 'richest man' was the baker. After all, if bread was to be gotten in the ghetto, he was indispensable, central to its baking and essential to its distribution. She listened to her mother and married him. Her husband protected her in the ghetto and provided for her. A marriage of protection became a marriage. Later, after the war, Helen thought her husband was gone forever, lying dead in a mass grave or buried in a pile of ashes. Still young, she fell in love with a French doctor, but when she heard a rumour that her husband, the baker, might still be alive, she followed every lead she could find until they were reunited. That marriage of convenience was a love-filled marriage for the rest of their lives.

Survivors were scandalised when Fanya Gottesman Heller told her story. As a beautiful teenager she had a romantic relationship with a Ukrainian policeman who saved her parents. He was of a different religion, ethnicity, educational background and class – and she was totally dependent upon him for survival. Yet she refused to claim exploitation or coercion. She explained, explicitly, that her 'proper' parents encouraged the relationship, which she contended – even after years of psychoanalysis – was loving and enjoyable. She, too, had broken a taboo, spoken the unspoken, and later in her life her children did not want her to reveal that part of her story. I knew her well and do not believe she was being provocative – she insisted on telling the truth as she lived it.

Some couples married for protection. Fanya was also quite candid about how, after the Holocaust, she married a man who would protect her and provide her with safety and security, the kind of relationship that was not uncommon among survivors after the war. After what they had been through, and even in the post-war period, protection was all important.

Reading these stories of diverse forms of love and differing relationships, some that endured and others that did not, I was struck by several observations. The intensity of the relationships was directly related to the turbulence of those times. When tomorrow is uncertain at best, today is all there is. These survivors were young, most often alone and desperately so. The potential for love was a source of vitality and energy, a gift of meaning in a world devoid of almost all meaning. One recalls Viktor Frankl's *Man's Search for Meaning*, an autobiographical account of his time in concentration camps – primarily in Theresienstadt and not, as commonly assumed, in Auschwitz. Love, real or imagined – and even real love can be imagined – is a source of meaning, energy and comfort. In almost all these stories, love was indispensable to survival, and either provided the couple with desperately needed aid and resources or with a reason to endure what had to be endured in order to survive.

Some marriages survived; others did not or could not. There is a debate as to what to make of the lessons learned in the Holocaust. Some argue that *in extremis veritas*, the extreme reveals the deepest truth, yet others see the distorting role that extreme circumstances can play. I was impressed by the stories of survivors who, in the desperation of war, could thrive and survive. Yet after the war, many found it difficult to transition to a world where laws and norms prevail, where stability is sought and the thrill from dangers and perpetual crises removes the frisson of a relationship. When you read the story of Rose Weisz and Joska Cseh, you catch a glimpse at what he could do during the war and what he could not do thereafter.

It is fascinating how some of these couples came together and how quickly their relationships developed. We read of civil weddings, improvised weddings, a couple – Jacob and Reisel Najman (the author's parents) – stopping a religious Jew on the street to ask him to bless their marriage and only afterwards being able to get a *Chuppah* and make the blessings. The nature of the formalities did not matter; what was urgent was the relationship and giving it the stamp of permanence in a world where everything and every moment was fragile.

'War was the great *shadchan* (matchmaker),' Anne Weiss wrote. People who would have never met each other, who would never have been allowed to meet each other, overcame barriers that normally divide future mates – class, wealth, religion and education.

Some were bound together because the man had saved the woman, or the woman had saved the man. Owing your life to another person is a bond of power and depth. The traditional secular vow is 'for better, for worse, for richer, for poorer, in sickness and in health'; having experienced what they experienced, it seemed as if anything would be better, any circumstances would be richer and healthier. If you were able to hold it together then, the future beckoned.

In reading these accounts we realise a difference between marriages today and then. Our children take their time, perhaps too much time. They deliberate, they hesitate, they live with uncertainty until they finally commit. Living together is an option – you can have friends with benefits. But among the Holocaust survivors, one was able to sense the loneliness of these couples, the immediacy of attraction, the need for commitment, for emotional stability in a world that was still so unstable. Couples settling for marriage was the norm and one gambled on an attraction that might lead to love. Think of the pious woman, Peska, sister of a Rebbe, daughter of a Rebbe, who travelled alone to meet her Wolvie knowing only of her interest and his attraction. She gambled it all, went against the norms of her community, and won.

We don't have much of a description of the weddings. Survivors are always conscious of who was there and often, more importantly, who could not be there to walk one down the aisle. Memorial prayers were recited under the *Chuppah* and when they were not recited the missing figures hovered over the wedding. But even a funeral procession must stop for a wedding procession and so it did, again and again.

Rabbi Arthur Hertzberg told a story of what happened to him in the early years of his Rabbinate soon after the Holocaust. A survivor bride and groom came to see him to plan their wedding. All went well and when the groom left, the bride remained behind. 'Rabbi,' she said, 'I cannot marry.' She opened her blouse and revealed a tattoo between her breasts. She had been used as a sexual slave and the Nazis tattooed her to make sure that she bore an external, indelible mark of her degradation. Hertzberg was stunned and then, in a moment of inspiration, he answered, 'You must get married and on your *ketubah,* the religious marriage contract, I will write *betultah* (virgin).' He then offered to speak to the groom. I always wondered what could not be said between man and wife, even among those most intimate. What could not be said about a murdered spouse, children who were killed in the innocence of their youth? The unspoken was always there in the marriage, the unspoken and the unseen.

Survivors are not random samples of the victims. They tended to be younger, but not too young. And though some survived with luck, few survived without some skill and cunning or without the ability to make decisive, life-and-death decisions in the moment. We see this when trust is quickly developed, in the experience of love at first sight. Even after more than seventy-five years, we can still feel the magnetism of the initial attraction and the decisive resolve that led to love in the telling of these stories.

These narratives, important as they are, cannot be considered the whole of the story, but they are *part* of the story, even if not a major part. Yet they merit a place in our history as we recount the experiences of women and men during the Holocaust.

Michael Berenbaum
American Jewish University
Los Angeles, CA

I

JOSEPH AND REBECCA BAU

In the 1960s, when Joseph and Rebecca Bau's youngest daughter, Clila – a kindergartner – met Oskar Schindler, the German industrialist who saved thousands of Jews during the Holocaust, he introduced himself as her grandfather. She was confused, because she knew her grandparents had been murdered in the camps. Schindler explained, 'I am responsible for saving your father's life.' Today, thanks to *Schindler's List*, the book and the movie, everyone knows how Schindler became a hero and saved Jews, risking his own life to do it.

Joseph and Rebecca were both born in Poland between the two World Wars. Joseph was born into a secular Jewish family in Krakow in 1920. His father collected Judaica and helped his wife run her chocolate shop. In addition to running a retail business, she also was a hat designer and an artist. In 1938, pursuing his own artistic inclinations, Joseph enrolled in the Academy of Fine Arts at the University of Krakow to study calligraphy and graphic arts.

Less than a year later, Joseph's education was cut short by the Nazi invasion of Poland. He and his family were forced into the Krakow ghetto, where prisoners were allowed to bring only a limited number of personal items with them. Joseph brought his drafting table, art supplies and family photos, which were hidden in a compartment he created in his art supply case.

Rebecca Tannenbaum was a descendant of a long line of doctors and pharmacists on both sides of her family. Her father, who owned a farm, was a veterinarian as well as a physician. Her mother was a homemaker who died when Rebecca was just seven years old, and so she was raised by her aunt and uncle. She wanted to study medicine and become a doctor, but by the time she was old enough to begin her studies, the Nazis had prevented Jews from attending university. Instead, she studied to be a beautician; and when her family was forced into the Krakow ghetto, she worked in the hospital and trained to become a nurse.

Joseph, desperate to save Jews from disease, starvation and death in the camps, used his artistic skills to forge documents to save hundreds of Jews. A member of the Jewish underground asked Joseph, 'Why don't you make yourself papers? Why don't you save yourself?' He answered, 'If I run away, who will save the others?' As it turned out, his calligraphic skills did save him. The Nazis needed him to draw plans, maps and signs, so they were reluctant to send him to hard labour or the gas chamber.

In 1941, Joseph and his family were transferred to Plaszow, the forced labour camp made famous in *Schindler's List*. Joseph had suffered the loss of his brother in the ghetto. In Plaszow, he was forced to watch a camp guard named Green execute his father. After the war, Joseph testified against Green at a war crimes trial held in Vienna.

Because of his skills, Joseph worked for the camp's Commandant, the notorious Amon Goeth – a vicious, sadistic Nazi commander known for brutally torturing his victims to death. Every day, Joseph shook with fear and dread as he worked in the same office with this mercurial monster, never knowing what the next moment would bring. Yet despite the chaos, Joseph also had privileges which allowed him to walk through the camp and sometimes get extra food rations.

For one of his assignments, Joseph was ordered to draw a detailed map of the camp and used Gothic script for its legends. When Goeth saw the map, he demanded Joseph make a copy for him. In those days, copies were made on a wooden frame using heat and sunlight-sensitive paper. That day it was -4 deg. F. (-20 deg. C.) and the sky was overcast, so Joseph tried to explain why it would therefore be impossible to make a good copy. Goethe gave him a choice. 'Make that copy today or get a bullet in the head. You decide.'

In despair, shivering in the cold, knowing his life was over if the sun did not come out, Joseph set up the wooden frame and the paper, praying the entire time. Like a penitent, he held the frame in his outstretched arms, lifting it to face the dead grey sky. But the sun stayed hidden. There was no break in the clouds. His life was over, he thought!

As he stood there contemplating his last day on earth, frozen and holding up the frame, out of nowhere a young, beautiful prisoner came by and asked Joseph what he was doing. She wanted to know if, maybe, he was sending signals to American airplanes.

A man appreciates a pretty woman. Dead man or not, he answered with a smile, 'I'm waiting for the sun, but today, she doesn't want to come out. Will you be my sunshine?' And he aimed the frame at her.

She blushed, smiled and then laughed before walking away. Her name was Rebecca, and though Joseph did not know it, she had just laughed for the first time since she had arrived in the living nightmare that was Plaszow.

But Joseph still was quaking. The sun had not come out, and so he stayed outdoors as long as he could. He was stunned, late in the day, when a print of the map appeared on the copy paper. He attributed that miracle to the beautiful passerby who had been his 'sunshine'. He gave Goeth the map and was permitted to continue living.

The next day, Joseph gathered a handful of wildflowers near the barbed wire fence at the edge of the camp. He found out that Rebecca worked in the same building as he did. He decided to give them to her for saving his life. When he got to her office, a Jewish worker looked at him in amazement.

'Are you crazy? Walking in the camp office with flowers? The Commandant is sitting right here. If he sees you with flowers, he'll kill you!'

Quickly, he ripped the flowers from Joseph's hand, threw them in the garbage, covered them up with some papers, and instructed Joseph to get out of there – fast. He did!

While waiting on the soup line a few days later, Joseph spotted Rebecca and went over to speak with her. He was thrilled when he heard that the man who trashed the flowers told her how Joseph had risked his life to bring them to her.

Neither of them ever imagined they would find love in such a hell hole. They were thrilled to find each other. They wanted to touch and hug and kiss, but that could lead to a death sentence. They were so much in love that they did take risks to meet secretly. Two months later, Joseph proposed marriage. Rebecca was taken aback. 'Married? In a concentration camp? Who gets married like this?'

'Tell me,' Joseph responded, 'Who promises us that tomorrow we will be alive?'

And with that, she agreed to marry him.

Taking four portions of his bread ration, he traded them with one of the other prisoners for a silver teaspoon. Then he took four more rations and gave them to a prisoner who used to be a jeweller and asked him to fashion two rings out of the spoon. When the rings were finished, Joseph gave them to his mother for safekeeping; she happened to live in the same barracks as Rebecca.

The day they planned to marry finally arrived. It was a day on which the women prisoners were assigned to work outside the camp and were scheduled to return late at night. As always, women who could not keep pace or meet the demands of the work were killed on the spot and left where they fell. Many never came back.

When the women who survived the day returned to the camp and wanted to communicate with the men in the barracks – to let loved ones know they were still alive – they did so as they entered the camp. The Nazis kept the lights off to prevent men and women from finding each other, because all contact was forbidden. The inmates risked their lives under the blackness of night as they walked along a path separating the women's barracks from the men's, each woman whistling her own code.

Rebecca whistled and Joseph whistled in response. The back-and-forth of their music continued until, at last, they found each other in the darkness. He pulled a white kerchief from his pocket and covered his head to disguise himself as a woman. Walking between his mother and his bride, he was smuggled successfully into Women's Bunk 13.

On 13 February 1944, inside a barrack at Plaszow, a Jewish woman, Joseph's mother, performed the wedding ceremony for her son and new daughter-in-law. There was no rabbi, and unlike what was shown in the movie *Schindler's List*, no *Chuppah* (wedding canopy) and no *ketubah* (marriage contract). Time and secrecy were of the essence.

Joseph pulled the rings out of his pocket, gently sliding one band onto Rebecca's finger while betrothing her with the ancient words of the Jewish tradition, 'Behold, you are consecrated to me with this ring according to the laws of Moses and Israel.'

Traditionally, the Jewish wedding ceremony ends with the breaking of a glass to commemorate the destruction of the Holy Temples in Jerusalem, a sad note for a joyous occasion. There was no need to break a glass in Plaszow, a place that was sadder than sad. Besides, they didn't have a glass to break. Joseph and Rebecca were bound by love and the passion to survive in a place where people were sent to die.

In the barracks, ten women slept on rows of wooden slabs designed to hold two women. To honour the new couple, Rebecca's bunk mates joined already overcrowded bunks, allowing the newlyweds a brief honeymoon.

Moments later the sirens and whistles went off and dogs barked. The Nazis were hunting for men who had smuggled themselves into the women's barracks that night. Quickly, Rebecca covered Joseph with rags and used him as a mattress. Her bunkmates joined her on the 'mattress' and they hid him successfully by pretending to be asleep. All of them could hear screams as the Nazis dragged two other men out of the barracks and executed them on the spot.

Joseph knew that if he did not return to his barracks immediately, the Nazis would discover he was missing and kill his friends. Then they would find him and kill him, too. He put the white kerchief back on his head, jumped off the bunk and ran to the gate for the men's section, only to find it locked.

He was left with two options. He could stay where he was and be killed, or he could climb the electrified fence and die. Either way, he was as good as dead. Better to have loved and lost than never to have loved at all, he thought. He could die a happy man having found Rebecca, his soul mate for eternity.

Deciding to deny the Nazis the satisfaction of killing him, he climbed the fence, ready to die by his own hand. Imagining this act of rebellion, of jumping over the fence and boldly advertising his last night in the women's barracks in defiance of the Nazis, gave him the strength to throw himself onto the wire. He climbed the 9-foot (3-metre) fence, feeling the electricity vibrate through the metal. He heard the hum, and yet, somehow, nothing happened to him. He jumped to the other side. Just as he approached the rows of men waiting to be counted, a trumpet blast signalled the cancellation of the *Appel*, the head count. And once again, Joseph lived to see another day.

While separated from Rebecca, Joseph began collecting paper from the Nazis' discarded cigarette butts. He created a tiny 3-inch-by-3-inch artist's notebook, wherein he sketched the life around him and wrote love poems, including a dedication to his beloved bride. (After the war, the volume, *The World and I*, was translated into several languages and published.)

One morning, a Nazi who had nothing better to do confronted Rebecca when he saw her limping. Having no use for a damaged Jew, he took out his gun, pointed it at her head and prepared to shoot. In fluent German, she said, 'You want to kill me because I'm limping. I'm limping because you gave us wooden shoes and I have calluses on my toes.'

As a trained nurse and beautician, she explained she could fix her toes if he gave her a knife. Inexplicably, he did, and she kept it after she fixed her feet. And because she kept the knife, she helped other prisoners suffering from the same issues – including the Nazi who gave her the knife in the first place.

Eventually, word of her skill reached Commandant Goeth, and he ordered her to manicure his nails nightly. Sometimes his hands were covered in blood, likely the blood of her tortured and dead fellow Jews. It was her duty to wash the blood from his murdering hands before she could begin his manicure. Before she would begin, he would place his gun under her elbow and say, 'If you so much as scratch me, I will kill you on the spot.'

Rebecca worked in an office filled with Nazis and did what she could to resist. A polyglot, Rebecca spoke nine languages including perfect German, and eavesdropped on conversations in the office, later relaying the information to other prisoners. When she heard that Goeth planned to kill twelve men from a town near Krakow, she warned them and bought them time to hide.

Goeth realised Rebecca was the source of the leak and whipped her until her back was flayed raw. Then, in sub-zero weather, he forced her to stand in a pit of frozen mud for five days. Rebecca expected to die, but somehow found the strength and the will to survive. The beautician who replaced her did not have Rebecca's skills and was caught stealing food, so Rebecca was brought back and continued to risk her life by sharing information.

Rebecca was in the courtyard one morning when an SS officer walked over to an older woman who was limping, drew his gun, and aimed for her head. Rebecca boldly walked up to the Nazi, looked him straight in the eye and, said, in perfect German, that his target was the mother of the Commandant's Jewish secretary. She warned that if he killed her, the Commandant would be furious with him. After thinking it over for a moment, the Nazi put his gun back in his holster and walked away.

Later, when Rebecca learned that Oskar Schindler was compiling a list of Jews to work in his factory in Czechoslovakia, she went to see Goeth's Jewish secretary. She asked him, 'Do you know I saved your mother's life? You owe me!' He did – and added her name to Schindler's list, but she asked that Joseph's name be placed on the list instead. She kept this selfless act of love a secret for many years.

Schindler, a businessman, started out by supporting the Nazis, but had a change of heart. He helped workers in his factory sabotage the bullets they were making, and said he was lucky the war ended after seven months – if he had shipped those flawed munitions and they were discovered, all of them would be dead, including him.

As a result of Rebecca's sacrifice, Joseph went to work for Schindler while she was transferred to Auschwitz. Her innate ability to survive, plus her skills as a nurse and linguist, enabled her to save herself and many others in Auschwitz, as well as Plaszow.

Joseph was moved to Schindler's labour camp in Czechoslovakia. When Schindler heard he was an artist, he asked him to make a sign. Joseph said his art supplies were confiscated when the Nazis closed Plaszow. He was surprised when Schindler went to a storage room and found the case with Joseph's initials. When Joseph opened his case, he found his supplies and the precious pictures, paintings, and poems he had hidden in the secret compartment all intact.

After he was liberated by the Russians, Joseph assumed that Rebecca and his family would return to Krakow. Crossing borders via freight trains and by foot, eventually he found the house where his family resided. It was occupied by a man who threatened him with a knife. Joseph had to find a place to live elsewhere, and he spent time visiting the Jewish Joint Committee office, which posted updates on survivors and those who died. He completed his arts degree and drew caricatures for Polish newspapers. Still, he had the tiny journal he had made from discarded cigarette papers, full of poems and etchings. It recalled an innocent world before the Nazis destroyed European Jewry. When he went through the former ghetto in Krakow, he found his old beloved drafting table, which he rescued and kept with him for the rest of his life.

Driven by his love for Rebecca, Joseph continued his search, following a trail of clues until he found that she had survived. He also discovered that she and a few other women were involved in an accident – a wagon they were in overturned, and they were hospitalised in the small city of Freudenthal, Czechoslovakia. He set off to find them by train, but little did he know that he was about to experience several other hardships, followed by incredible miracles.

Joseph fell asleep on the train and missed his connection. After being drenched from heavy rain and hail while lying on top of the overcrowded train going back to the transfer point, he was able to catch the connecting train. There he thought he was lucky to find a seat, upon which he fell asleep. Suddenly, he was awakened when all passengers were instructed to leave the train due to a nearby accident. He discovered that the train he had missed earlier had crossed a bridge damaged by the war and plunged into a river; had he been on board, he would have probably drowned or been crushed to death.

While waiting at the river crossing, amazed at what had happened, Joseph was singled out by a hysterical woman who accused him, still wearing his striped prisoner shirt, of being a Nazi criminal. He was taken to the local police station in the town of Opawa, where he explained that he was on a journey to find his wife who had been in an accident where a wagon overturned; and he was able to show documents proving who he was. The police took pity on him and told him a similar accident had occurred in their town, and that the young women involved still were in the town's hospital. Joseph had information that his wife's accident did not take place in Opawa. Nonetheless, he went along with the policeman to the hospital. There he whistled the special notes they used to locate one another in the camp. One can imagine what happened next!

There they were reunited, and he presented her with the little book that described everything that was in his heart. The inscription read, 'After seven months of separation and six years of slavery.'

The couple returned to Krakow to search for their families. Rebecca believed that everyone in her family was murdered, and it took until 1975 before she discovered one of her brothers was living in Israel. They found Joseph's only surviving brother, Marcel, and years later discovered that Joseph's mother died two weeks after the British liberated Bergen-Belsen – a hell hole mishandled by the rescuers. Thousands died daily of over-eating and/or disease.

In 1946, two years to the day after their wedding in Plaszow, the couple renewed their vows in Krakow, with a *Chuppah*, a *ketubah*, a rabbi and a broken glass. They celebrated with food and music. For the rest of their lives, Joseph and Rebecca celebrated two anniversaries every year: the date of their wedding in Plaszow and their post-war 'official' wedding in Krakow.

In 1950, penniless and unable to speak Hebrew, the Baus moved to Israel with Hadas, their three-year-old daughter. Despite hardships and challenges, they loved their new life in Israel, a beautiful dream from which they never wanted to wake.

Joseph became a successful commercial and graphic artist. By 1956, he had his own studio in Tel Aviv and launched Israel's animation industry. He was known as Israel's Walt Disney. In addition to his artistic successes, he wrote several books, including one called *Circumcision/Brit Milah*, about the peculiarities, humour and logic of the Hebrew language. Bau liked to play with words. Brit Milah has two meanings: circumcision and covenant. What he wanted was a covenant with the Hebrew language, and not a circumcision. In 1982, he published his memoir, *Dear God, Have You Ever Gone Hungry?* In the 1960s and 70s he became known for designing Hebrew fonts and titles for Israel's movie industry.

But his most vital work was top secret. Joseph was chief forger for the Mossad, Israel's vaunted intelligence agency. He created the documents for Operation Eichmann, where a team of agents led by Isser Harel, Peter Z. Malkin and Rafi Eitan smuggled Adolf Eichmann, one of the world's most notorious escaped Nazi war criminals, out of Argentina to bring him to trial in Israel.

Recently, after an intense lobbying effort by the authors of this story, the espionage artifacts of Mr Bau's work in Operation Eichmann were declassified by career Mossad agent and curator of the program Avner Avraham. They now are included in the travelling exhibit 'Operation Finale: The Capture and Trial of Adolf Eichmann', which until recently was housed at the headquarters of Mossad.

In the early 1990s, there was a flurry of interest in tracking down people who were on Schindler's list in Plaszow, because the fictionalised book by Thomas Keneally was being made into a movie by Steven Spielberg. Reporters wanted to know what happened to the people on the list after the war. A few reporters tracked down Joseph and interviewed him. There was one journalist who asked him how he had gotten on the list, and Joseph had to admit he was clueless. But the reporter saw a small smile flit across Rebecca's face when he asked the question. He turned and asked her why she was smiling. That was when, for the first time, Rebecca revealed the secret of trading her life for his. According to the Bau's younger daughter, Clila, her father was 'flabbergasted ... We were in shock and my father was crying.' He could not believe that Rebecca did that, particularly since they had known one another only for a few months.

Joy and laughter were a key to the Baus' lives. Joseph always sought to make Rebecca smile and laugh. He was fond of telling his daughters, 'Your mother's laughter is like the most beautiful opera.' Their years in the camps taught Joseph and Rebecca the power of humour to heal, to strengthen and to inspire. With a joke, Joseph could lift the spirit of a hopeless prisoner. A chuckle could give someone the strength to endure another day. After witnessing and surviving the darkest of humanity, they made it a priority to laugh every day as a tribute to their survival, their future, and the good that remained in the world. They refused to live in the dark past, and looked forward to light and laughter, appreciating wholeheartedly the miracle of their survival and the circumstances that brought them together.

Their two daughters, Hadasa and Clila, travelled to Plaszow to see the camp where their parents lived through those terrible years. An architect took them on a tour of the grounds, though no structures remained intact. They did find a small section of the concrete foundation for Bunk 13 – the bunk where their parents were married and which was portrayed in *Schindler's List*, the movie.

Before Rebecca was deported to Auschwitz, Joseph slipped one of his poems, 'The Parting', into his beloved's hand. She carried it around with her always, reading it over and over again for inspiration and in the hope that they would reunite one day. It survived Auschwitz. After the war, it was Joseph who carried it with him, always, in his tiny book of poems which he wrote on the paper of cigarette butts.

The Parting, by Joseph Bau

Though our life together was so short, I must leave now.
Sad and forlorn, I am going
to a fate ordained by these desperate times, by a road
  unmarked by any signs,
to a mocking destiny, all set to welcome me.

I am going, but when the gate closes behind me and a
  momentary silence reigns,
when time erodes my footprints,
don't think of me with sorrow
because I leave behind so little of myself: the heart of a mad
  poet,

a few letters, a few odes dedicated to you,
a withered flower and the dreams we dreamt of our future
together,
and plans that alas! could not come true. Do you remember
our dream house,
That was not to be,
your workroom and my workroom?

Dear God, why can't you be kind?

But if things change, as I foretold,
And if the memory lives on in your mind, think of me often,
without the despair that is our lot now. Our roads will yet
meet again!
Then... but why are you crying? Cry no more, don't be sad...
Because, you see, I am holding back too...

Well, good-bye, I will see you again!
Give me another kiss and a hug and take care of yourself,
my dear and sacred love.

This is the last poem in the tiny book that the Nazis could not destroy. 'Father, who fought for love, didn't agree to let the Nazis take it away from him,' said his daughter, Hadas. 'Just because men and women weren't allowed to be together, just because they took his property and almost took his life as well, he refused to give up love.'

His relationship with his wife was 'supreme happiness, like light,' she said. 'Every day when he came home, he hugged and kissed her, saying: "Look how we defeated Hitler with all his army, his tanks and his evil – with love, kisses and a wedding."'

Clila, her sister, added, 'The Nazis wanted all the Jews dead. The Plaszow concentration camp was, in fact, built on a cemetery. It was a place of death. Joseph and Rebecca Bau had a love that shone even in the face of death, a love that saved the Jewish world.'

The Joseph and Rebecca Bau House is located in his original studio, at 9 Berdichevsky St., Tel Aviv. His daughters have turned it into a museum dedicated to their parents, their lives and their work. Learn more at www.josephbau.com

Hadas and Clila Bau were interviewed by Mindelle and Ira Pierce at the Jewish Community Center (JCC) in Margate City, NJ on 22 March 2015, prior to the Bau sisters' talk to the community on the lives of their parents.

2

SALLY AND CHARLES BEDZOW

Sally Golcman was born in 1926 in the small town of Ryky, Poland, not far from Warsaw. There, she lived with her parents, four sisters, four brothers and grandmother, until the autumn of 1941, when the Nazis relocated the Jews of Ryky to the neighbouring town of Demblin.

Before the start of the Second World War, Ryky had been a very nice town with a large, vibrant Jewish community. In the mid-1930s, Jews fleeing Nazi Germany sought refuge with families in Ryky, and Sally's family took in a couple and their two children. But on 1 September 1939, when the Nazis invaded Poland, Ryky was enveloped in a cloud of fear, violence and terror. That year, ten-year-old Sally witnessed the death of her uncle at the hands of Polish anti-Semites. While walking on the streets of the town, he was attacked in the street by men wielding axes. He managed to stumble back home and into their house before dying on the floor, in front of his family. By this time, hatred and death had become a way of life for the Jews.

The Nazis turned Demblin into a ghetto in 1941 and then mandated that each family send two representatives into forced labour. Sally, fourteen years old, and her sister, Gittel, twelve, reported for work with a group of young girls and were forced to endure back-breaking labour every day, ranging from digging ditches and graves to picking potatoes.

On the morning of 6 May 1942, as Sally and her sister were dressing for work, their mother gave them vests to wear under their clothing. She had heard rumblings that the ghetto was going to be liquidated and had sewn some valuables into the lining of the vests, hoping to give her daughters every opportunity to survive.

That day, as the girls worked nearby, they saw their families forcibly expelled from the ghetto. Sally and Gittel watched in horror as their mother, father and six-year-old sister were loaded onto a horse and buggy and taken away. Though the girls wanted desperately to run to their families, the Nazi soldiers warned that anyone who moved would be killed immediately. Having no idea about the concentration camps or the Nazis' Final Solution, the girls assumed their families were being relocated to another town. In fact, this was the first of two transports of the Demblin Jews. This first group was taken to Sobibor, a Nazi extermination camp in Nazi-occupied Poland. In the autumn of that year, the Jews left behind after the first transports were sent to Treblinka.

That evening, the Nazis locked Sally and the other girls in an unroofed barn. In the middle of the night, Sally seized the rare opportunity to escape. In the darkness, Sally climbed out of an opening in the wall of the barn, unlocked the barn doors from the outside and freed the girls, who quickly dispersed into the blackness of the night. Despite Sally's best efforts, she was unable to convince her sister, Gittel, to escape with her. With time running out, Sally fled the barn without her sister. Eventually, she made her way to the farm of her father's friend, in accordance with their family's plan. This friend, a non-Jewish man who served in the First World War with Sally's father, had promised to help the family. Sally arrived to find her brothers, Josef and Harry, already in hiding there, having escaped the ghetto before the deportation. The three siblings squeezed into a small hiding place below the floorboards in the horse barn. After six months in hiding, Josef and Harry emerged to join a small partisan group living in the forest. Two girls quickly took their places under the floorboards with Sally.

Months later, in February 1943, the family's stable boy ran to the barn to warn the girls that nearby fighting had ignited the barn, which was now becoming engulfed in flames. He told the girls to run, fearful they would die in the fire. Sally and the other girls sprinted through a snow-covered field into the freezing winter night, barefoot, wearing only thin nightgowns. As Sally ran ahead, she heard the blast of gunshots and turned in horror to see the other girls shot dead in the snow. She dropped into the drifts and lay there, completely still, for over an hour until it was quiet, before dragging her near-frozen body into the woods. After the fighting ended, Sally's brothers found her in the forest, nursed her back from hypothermia and inducted her into their partisan group. The group was focused on survival, hiding in the forest and foraging for food, though some participated in anti-Nazi activities. At just sixteen years old, she was one of only three women in their 120-person group.

In June 1944, when the Russians liberated that part of the country, the partisans left the cover of the forest and travelled to Lublin, one of the main hubs where Jews convened to exchange information and try to determine the fate of their loved ones. Here, Sally, Harry and Joseph learned that the other members of their family had all been killed. They were the only three survivors of the Golcman family. Though devastated, they knew they had to move forward. While in Lublin, they crossed paths with two sisters whom they had known before the war, Bronya and Saba, and Saba's three-year-old son. Josef married Bronya and in the autumn of 1944 the families travelled together to Zelechov, another hub of post-war Jewish activity.

By January 1945, they had relocated to Lodz, where the Hebrew Immigrant Aid Society (HIAS), a Jewish refugee resettlement agency, provided an apartment for the five of them – Sally, Josef, Bronya, Saba and Saba's son – and they began to rebuild their life. Harry was conscripted into the Polish Army, joining the Allied effort to defeat the Nazis. Joseph and Bronya opened a grocery store. Though Sally was distraught about the murder of her family and the devastation of the war, she refused to wallow in sadness and depression. At eighteen years old, having experienced the worst of humanity, she desperately wanted to seek out the good she believed still existed in the world.

Several months later, a family moved into their apartment building. The Bedzow family – Charles, his mother, brother, sister and brother-in-law – occupied the ground-floor apartment, several floors below the Golcmans.

Charles Bedzow was born in 1924 in Lida, Poland, and grew up in a traditional Jewish home with his parents, two sisters and a brother. As was the case throughout eastern Europe, conditions for the Jews progressively deteriorated throughout the 1930s and into the 1940s. Charles's father became ill and, because Jews didn't have access to medication or medical care, he died in early 1941. On 22 June 1941, after the Nazis invaded Russia, the soldiers moved into Lida and forced all of the Jews into the overcrowded ghetto where sickness and starvation were rampant.

While in the ghetto, Charles received a message from a close family friend, Tuvia Bielski. He encouraged Charles to escape from the ghetto with his family and join him in the nearby forest, where he and his brothers had established a partisan group later known as the Bielski Brigade. Their escape was complicated and fraught with danger, but Charles, his mother, two sisters and brother made it to the Bielski camp. Charles, just seventeen years old, quickly became a prolific operative for the partisan group, searching for supplies, sabotaging Nazi activities and ambushing Nazi forces. The other Bedzow family members also had roles in the Bielski Brigade, foraging for food, cooking and cleaning. One of Charles's sisters, Sonia, participated in the armed resistance, but was ultimately captured during a mission and murdered in Treblinka.

The remaining family survived the war and moved into the apartment in Lodz during the winter of 1945. A month after they moved into the apartment, Charles's mother asked him to go upstairs to the Golcmans' apartment to borrow dishes for Shabbat dinner. Charles, always willing to help his mother, walked upstairs and knocked on the door, as instructed. Sally opened the door and Charles struck up a conversation with the lovely eighteen-year-old girl in the doorway, all thoughts of the dishes forgotten in an instant. Charles was struck by Sally's beauty and kindness, and he enjoyed their easy conversation. They didn't talk about the war or other difficult topics, preferring instead to focus on the future and their dreams of emigrating to Israel.

The following day, on Saturday morning, Charles returned to Sally's apartment to spend the day with the Golcman family. As the hours passed, Charles, reluctant to leave, suggested they go to a movie together later that evening. Sally, however, already had a date planned and politely refused Charles's offer. But Charles was not easily discouraged. He stayed in their apartment until Sally's date arrived, at which point Sally broke her date and spent the evening with Charles.

Sally and Charles became inseparable. They shared their experiences during the war and spoke of the loved ones they had lost. They discussed their hopes and ambitions for the future and what they wanted out of life. They also shared the dream of moving to Palestine. The more time they spent together, the closer they became. From the day they met, they settled into an easy, comfortable relationship, becoming close friends and confidants. Charles was handsome, charming, well-dressed and well-mannered. Sally felt comfortable around him and valued his friendship. But at the time, neither Sally nor Charles viewed their relationship as one of romance or passion. They were two young people who could understand and trust each other, which formed the basis for their deepening bond.

In an effort to help survivors emigrate to Palestine, a Jewish organization, Bericha, chartered a boat to take two hundred people there. Charles, his mother, brother, sister, and brother-in-law would be going, and Sally was desperate to join them. But they had to pay their own way and Sally could not afford the ticket. She discussed her plans with her brother Josef, hoping he would pay for her ticket. Josef disapproved of his young, unmarried sister travelling alone with a man she barely knew and two hundred strangers.

Sally was determined to go. Living in an already crowded apartment with Josef and Bronya, who were now expecting a baby, Sally wanted to create a new life for herself. Not only was Sally's physical accommodation becoming uncomfortable, but the anti-Semitism around her contributed greatly to her feelings of discomfort and her desire for something new. Even more compelling was her fear that if Charles made the trip without her she would never see him again. She couldn't let that happen and pleaded for Josef's help. Seeing the determination in her eyes, he relented and gave her money for the ticket to what she hoped would be her new life in Palestine. The next day, Sally joined Charles, with the Bedzow family and the others, and they began their journey.

Sally attached herself to Charles's family, recreating the sense of family she had lost. She was a beautiful girl who attracted the attention of many men. But dating or romance was never on Sally's mind. Instead, she was enjoying the friendship she had with Charles and wasn't looking for anything more. Charles was always respectful. He never made advances, touched or kissed her. She liked his intelligence, his adventurous spirit and his optimism, which was especially important to her in the years after the end of the war and in the wake of immense despair, grief and mourning. Sally and Charles shared a love of music and art and the desire to experience all of the beauty the world had to offer, which drew them closer every day.

After six months of travelling by boat, train and bus, from country to country, port to port, they arrived in Italy in late 1945. By this time, only young, strong people who could fight for Israel's independence were granted entry into Palestine. Though Charles and Sally were eligible, his mother was too old and his brother too young to be granted entry, and Charles refused to leave his family behind. The United Nations Relief and Rehabilitation Administration (UNRRA) established a home for the group in Torino, in the northern part of Italy, where they received food, shelter, and professional training. Sally was trained as a dressmaker, taking design classes in the morning and sewing classes in the afternoon. Charles, having become fluent in Italian, began working as a middleman for businesses, successfully making connections between buyers and sellers, supporting his family through his deal-making.

Charles's mother observed the bond that had formed between Charles and Sally and could see that they cared deeply for each other. She and Sally had grown close during their travels, as well; and Sally already felt like part of the family. Knowing the two were well-suited to each other, she suggested they get married.

To Sally and Charles, this suggestion made sense and they realised the depth of their feelings for each other. Charles loved Sally and wanted to marry her, but he had a single condition that was non-negotiable: Charles's mother would live with the couple for as long as she wanted. Without hesitation, Sally agreed, respecting Charles's dedication to his mother. She wanted only to marry this man who understood her and made her feel safe, loved and protected. He was strong and determined, and she knew he would always take care of her. Theirs wasn't a whirlwind romance of attraction and passion, but a deeper, more substantive relationship built over time.

On 8 March 1946, in front of 2,500 people housed at the UNRRA facility, Charles and Sally were married. With a *Chuppah*, marriage papers, and a Rabbi from Torino, their wedding was celebrated with two pails of wine and music playing on loudspeakers. Sally wore a white silk dress that she embroidered herself – and which all brides married in the camp thereafter wore to take their vows. As a newly married couple, they began a daily ritual that would continue for many years: every morning, they would embrace, tell each other, 'I love you' and sing the 'Partisan Song'. This served as a reminder of all they had overcome and the strength of their enduring love.

Seventeen months later, on 15 August 1948, the couple had a daughter, Frances. Then, in March 1949, they left Italy for Montreal, Canada, which had opened its doors to refugees for humanitarian reasons as well as to facilitate the growth of its workforce during the post-war boom. Charles's mother travelled with them, moved into their home, and lived with their growing family. Two years after they arrived in Montreal, Sally discovered that her brothers had emigrated from Europe and were living in the United States. In 1951, Sally gave birth to their son, Michael. In 1956, their daughter Esther was born.

When they arrived in Montreal, Charles began working as a door-to-door salesman, then opened a series of stores before entering the real estate development business. Charles's intelligence and aggressive style served him well as he worked long hours away from home, seven days a week, to build his real estate firm. Sally, who stayed home and raised their three children, was the softer parent, often indulging the children more than Charles would have liked. But this division of roles worked well for them, and Sally mastered the art of selective disclosure, keeping peace in the home.

Charles's mother lived with them until her death in 1995, at ninety-three years old. The adjustment to three generations of living under the same roof was not easy, but Sally attributes her ability to rise above it to advice she received from an elderly friend when she first settled in Montreal:

> What's the nicest thing in flowers? It is a rose! You look at the rose and it's beautiful, until you come to the rose. You prick your fingers. This is life. Do the prickles mean much? No! It is about the rose. You love each other; you will overcome. And remember, he loves you and also, he loves his mother. Don't pester him to make a choice!

And she never did. Sally ascribes the success of their marriage to their shared dedication to family, community and mutual respect. Throughout their seventy years of marriage, they have made it their priority to embrace the good in their lives – their children, grandchildren and great-grandchildren, and their friendships and successes.

Despite the atrocities they witnessed and the hardships and losses they suffered, Sally and Charles rebelled against the evil forces that sought to destroy them. Together, after the war, they resisted feelings of hopelessness and sadness to create a life full of love and adventure, success and philanthropy, resilience and optimism.

Video interviews with Mindelle and Ira Pierce conducted at the home of the Bedzows, in Miami Beach, Florida in the winter of 2016.

3

ISADORA AND
JOSHUA SZERENY

Isadora Rosen was born in Romania in 1928. When she was five and her brother Yisrael was two, her father died of cancer and her mother moved their family into their grandmother's house. There, they lived in close quarters with their grandmother, two aunts and three uncles. Times were difficult and the family struggled to make ends meet. In 1932, hoping for a better life, the family moved to the city of Bucharest, Romania, hoping for more opportunities to work and earn a better living. Though their financial situation improved incrementally, the climate for the Jews deteriorated steadily and in 1941 the family moved to Balti (pronounced Belz) in Bessarabia, now partially in Moldova and Ukraine, to escape the growing anti-Semitism.

When Balti fell under Nazi control later that year, the Jews were either murdered on the spot or sent on forced marches. Isadora and her family were among those sent to march for months through the brutal winter, with little food and wearing only rags. They arrived at Obodovka in Transnistria (then part of the Soviet Union) to wait out the remainder of winter in a ghetto. The thirteen-year-old Isadora and ten-year-old Yisrael witnessed their mother, an aunt and an uncle die slowly in excruciating pain: their mother from gangrene, the result of frostbite from the march, and their uncle and aunt from typhus and dysentery. By the spring of 1942, 90 per cent of the deportees that had been marched to Obodovka had died of disease, exposure or starvation. By the autumn of 1942, after their surviving uncles had escaped and their aunt was arrested, Isadora and Yisrael were the only members of her family that remained in Obadovka, to suffer the brutality of yet another harsh and violent winter in the ghetto. At the end of February 1944, when Russian forces liberated Transnistria, Romania was forced to readmit those who had survived.

After more than two years in the Obodovka ghetto, Isadora and Yisrael returned to Romania alone – without parents, aunts, or uncles, and with no one else to turn to for help. Children were placed in orphanages, but Isadora was too old to qualify for placement. Desperate, Isadora lied about her age and she and Yisrael were placed together in a Bucharest orphanage. They searched for any of their extended family that may have survived, but despite the loss of her close family and the horrors she and Yisrael had endured, their relatives refused to take them in. Isadora and Yisrael remained in the orphanage, grateful, at least, that they had each other. Because the anti-Semitic government wanted to rid Romania of any surviving Jews, the country partnered with a Zionist organisation to send Jews to Palestine. When Isadora and Yisrael were offered spots on a ship heading to Palestine by way of Turkey, they accepted.

On 3 December 1944, Isadora and Yisrael, along with a thousand other refugees, climbed aboard the *Toros*. They descended into the cargo area below deck, which reeked of grief, anxiety and desperation. They squeezed down the crowded aisle between bunks, looking for a place to rest. A kind middle-aged man gestured towards an open bunk. They climbed onto the bunk, Yisrael on the inside, Isadora on the outside, and fell asleep. Isadora woke to the touch of a strange man. She first felt a hand on her shoulder, then it began to slide down the outline of her body. She turned to see the man who had ushered them into the open bunk. Distraught, she leapt off the bunk, ran from the cargo area, and climbed up onto the deck. She found a quiet spot near the back of the ship, where she felt safer, though no less frightened. Sitting out on the open deck, cold, scared and alone, with no one to look out for her, heading towards an uncertain future in an unknown land, she began to sob. As she cried, overwhelmed by pain, loss and fear, a crew member approached and asked if he could help her. His name was Joshua.

Joshua Szereny was born in 1922 in Uzhgorod, Czechslovakia, to a secular but intensely Zionist Jewish family. The Szereny family had lived a good, prosperous life. That all changed in 1938, when the Hungarians returned to reclaim the territory lost in the aftermath of the First World War. In the years that followed, anti-Semitic laws were passed, Jewish businesses were stolen, Jewish students were expelled from universities, and the Hungarian citizenship of many Jews was revoked. Jews were imprisoned, harassed and marginalised. The Szerenys situation steadily deteriorated.

In September 1943, Joshua was drafted into the Hungarian army's Jewish slave labour camp, a vicious mechanism for the persecution of Hungarian Jews. He was ordered to report for duty at Puspokladany, one hundred miles south of Uzhgorod. When he arrived, he was given an army cap, a yellow armband and an ID marked with a ZS, or Jew (from the Hungarian word, 'Zsido'). Despite horrendous living conditions, backbreaking work, meagre food and inadequate shoes and clothing, he was one of the lucky ones, spared the gross atrocities so many others in slave labour were forced to endure. In January 1944, he ingeniously forged a pass for military leave and spent a week with his family. He returned to his unit at the end of the week, unaware that he would never see them again.

During the spring and summer of 1944, the defeat of the Nazi Army was imminent. As the end of the war loomed, the deportation and systematic murder of Hungarian Jews accelerated. In late September, as the Nazis forced Joshua's unit to walk for days to Auschwitz, Joshua and several other prisoners saw an opportunity to escape and fled into the mountains. Those who did not escape the march were killed in Auschwitz. Joshua and his comrades hid in the mountains; ultimately, they survived owing to the kindness of strangers and good luck.

Eventually, Joshua made it to Bucharest and in late November of 1944 he found out about a ship of immigrants that would be sailing soon for Istanbul, the first leg of their journey to Palestine. Joshua was asked to join the crew and manage all passenger-related issues.

He jumped at the chance to be useful and hoped that he would reunite with his family in Palestine. A few days later, he boarded the *Toros* at the Romanian port of Constanta. The *Toros* was a rescue ship chartered to ferry survivors to Turkey on their way to Palestine. To ensure safe passage to Istanbul, the trip was masked as a Red Cross-sanctioned aid mission, complete with bandaged passengers, a quarantine flag and a counterfeit Red Cross flag.

That first evening, after a full day of managing a thousand passengers on a ship meant to hold 600, Joshua was exhausted. He set out to check the ship one last time before going to bed. During this last sweep of the deck, he came upon a woman in tears – terrified, cold and alone – sitting outside on the ship's deck. It was Isadora.

'What are you doing up here?' he asked in Yiddish. When it was clear she did not understand him, he tried asking her in Czech, German, Hebrew and English. Still, she did not understand. Joshua decided to find someone who could translate and discovered what had happened below deck. He invited Isadora to spend the night in the cabin that housed the ship's crew. But after seeing the cabin filled with men, she opted to spend the night outside on the deck. Joshua collected some blankets to keep her warm during the night and stayed beside her until the morning.

The next morning, the translator returned to tell Isadora that he had to handle ship business, but he would come back to check on her. The translator asked Isadora, 'Do you love him?' Isadora laughed. 'I don't even know him!' The translator then asked, 'Do you have any feelings for him?' When she said she did, the woman posed the same question to Joshua. When he also answered yes, she shattered the teacup she had been holding and shouted 'Mazel Tov! You're engaged!' No one took this crazy engagement pronouncement seriously, and Joshua and Isadora parted ways.

Isadora and Joshua saw each other in passing on the ship during the next two days of their journey, but Joshua was busy managing the passengers. And even if he wasn't, they couldn't have spoken anyway, as they didn't speak the same language. When the ship docked in Turkey, the passengers disembarked and boarded a train to Palestine. During the controlled chaos of the ship-to-train transfer, Isadora lost track of her brother and climbed into the train alone. As she peeked into compartments looking for Yisrael, she came upon Joshua, who persuaded her to come sit with him; together they would find her brother.

When they found Yisrael on the train, he joined them in the compartment. A rabbi seated across from Isadora and Joshua offered to marry them, perhaps seeing these two young people (Joshua was twenty-two and Isadora twenty) and knowing the horrors they had survived and all they had lost. Isadora thought this was crazy! Joshua, however, was open to the idea. Though they knew almost nothing about each other, what they did know was powerful. From the little Joshua knew of Isadora, he concluded that she was brave to risk a night on the deck, instead of below deck where she felt vulnerable. She had the courage to travel to a new country and an uncertain future, into a world of strangers.

Isadora had seen Joshua working on the ship and knew he was a smart and able leader. She also knew that he was a kind and compassionate man from the way he helped her that first night on the ship. He was selfless and caring, foregoing a warm bed in the crew's cabin to stay with her, a stranger, on the deck in the cold night air.

Suddenly, surprising even herself, Isadora agreed to the rabbi's offer to marry them. Yisrael thought she was crazy! He questioned her.

'How can you marry a complete stranger? What do you know about him? He could be crazy! You don't even speak any of the same languages!'

Despite the fact that her brother, the only person she had left, thought she had lost her mind, marrying Joshua suddenly seemed like a good option. She did not want to live alone, and he seemed like a nice man. With nothing left to lose, Isadora and Joshua were married on the train as throngs of strangers looked on, witnessing the ultimate victory of survival and hope.

The couple moved to Israel, participated in Israel's war for independence, had two children, and embraced a life of freedom and opportunity. It would have been understandable if, having seen the absolute worst of humanity, they had succumbed to anger, despair and hopelessness. Instead, they chose hope, optimism and love – or at least the possibility of love. They chose to move forward and create new meaning in their lives. They believed that out of the horrors of the Holocaust, they could create something beautiful and meaningful. And they did.

Throughout their sixty-year marriage, they found love and joy, and weathered life's hardships together. They watched their family expand, as their children gave them grandchildren, and their grandchildren gave them great-grandchildren. Their life after the war is a testament to the resilience of the human spirit and the capacity to find meaning in even the worst of times.

Interviews with Michael Benanov, grandson of Joshua and Isadora Szereny, conducted by Mindelle Pierce at the 92nd Street 'Y' and at the Marriott Marquis in New York City, December 2015.

4

MAX AND TOBY BERGER

By the time Max Berger was seventeen, he became the head of his family in Chorzele, Poland, a small village approximately 2 kilometres from the German border. He was born on 1 August 1921. In 1938, a year after Max's father died, his older brother left home for school, and the burden of providing for the family fell on Max, the second of six children.

By that time, anti-Semitism was spreading swiftly throughout eastern Europe. In mid-1939, with the unprecedented build-up of Nazi tanks, trucks and soldiers at the German-Polish border, Max realised an invasion of Poland was imminent and urged his mother to leave Chorzele with his four other siblings.

In the last week of August in 1939, Max packed the family's belongings, leaving behind most of their valuables. He loaded them into a horse and buggy and sent them to be with his family in Warsaw. Several days later, as the Nazis began their invasion of Poland, Max left Chorzele, travelling on foot to reunite with his family. From Warsaw, Max and his family travelled through Poland and across the Russian border.

When the Nazi army invaded Poland, the lives of thousands of Jews were thrown into turmoil. Among them were Toby Kohn and her family. Toby was born on 15 March 1924 in Goworowa, Poland, approximately 55 kilometres from Warsaw.

When the Nazi forces entered Goworowa, most of the Jews were rounded up and packed into the main synagogue. Though two of Toby's brothers, Chaim and Mendel, escaped into the nearby forest, Toby's two sisters, Etta and Shaina, were forced into the overcrowded building. When the synagogue could not hold another body, the doors were locked, trapping the Jews inside. Desperate to break free, Etta and Shaina kicked out some boards in the rear wall of the synagogue and ran, escaping into the forest. They swam across the Orzyc River, hid in the forest, and eventually crossed the Russian border to Bialystok. Shortly after their escape, the synagogue, filled with people, was set ablaze by the Nazis with the help of some of the local Polish townspeople.

Toby stayed with her parents and younger brother until the Nazis took the men of the town into the plaza of the city for public execution. Toby, distraught and desperate, fell to her knees before a Nazi soldier and begged him to spare her father, Nissan, as she wiped the mud from his shoes. Taking pity on the girl, he sent two soldiers to retrieve Nissan and returned him to his family. Immediately, the family escaped to Bialystok and reunited with Toby's other siblings.

Once across the border, Polish families were asked to renounce their Polish citizenship and become Russian citizens. Approximately 100,000 Jews who refused to forfeit their Polish citizenship, among them the Kohns and the Bergers, were sent to Siberian labour camps. There, they were held as prisoners, waiting in long lines for rations of food and receiving little of that, and no medical care.

In June 1941, when Germany attacked Russia in Operation Barbarossa, the Polish prisoners were released. With their newfound freedom, they faced new problems. Where should they go? They knew what was happening in Nazi-occupied Poland – restrictive laws against the Jews, brutality, the mass executions – and they recognised that there was no safe place for Jews in Europe.

Eager to escape the extreme cold and incessant fighting, separately, both Max's and Toby's families relocated to Kazakhstan in the autumn of 1941. In 1943, in Kyrgyzstan, Max befriended a young Russian man named Sasha. Sasha's mother was a resourceful, gutsy woman who worked for a high-level Russian government official and through her connections she wrangled posts for the two men as Russian army sergeants. Both Max and

Sasha were put in charge of remote outposts for the Russian Army troops, stocking and distributing supplies, food and clothing.

In mid-1945 Max and Sasha were selling off their 'surplus' Russian supplies illegally, at a flea market in Kyrgyzstan. One day, an elderly man met Sasha at the flea market and haggled with him over a pair of shoes the man wished to buy. When the exchange between Sasha and the man became heated, the man pointed to Max – with his blond hair, fair skin and blue eyes – who also was trading shoes, and told Sasha he would rather buy from a 'goy', a non-Jew. Max heard this and began to laugh.

When the elderly man realised that Max understood Yiddish, he knew he had to be Jewish, despite his non-Jewish features. The old man, Nissan Kohn, introduced himself to Max and invited him to a *Shabbos* dinner with his family. When Max arrived, Nissan introduced him to his daughter, Toby.

Max was instantly smitten with her black hair, high cheekbones and piercing dark eyes. Max knew, without question, that he wanted to be with Toby. In his official Russian Army uniform, Max was incredibly handsome and had a great sense of authority, maturity and self-confidence about him. Toby was not used to meeting young Jewish men who were so accomplished and self-assured. Max proceeded to court her and provide her family with needed food and clothing. The connection between Toby and Max was undeniable.

Meanwhile, Toby's brothers, Chaim and Mendel, had joined the Russian Army and were serving as non-combatants in a remote Russian military outpost near China. Confiding in Max, Toby's mother admitted she was worried about her sons. Max promised he would bring them home.

Max continued his military duties and travelled on a circuit to transport food and supplies to the outposts of the Russian army. After making some initial stops, Max finally arrived at the designated outpost where Toby's brothers were stationed. When he got off the train and began to look for the young men, he came across a soldier walking through the snow. Max, in full Russian army sergeant uniform, stopped the soldier and asked if he could direct him to Chaim and Mendel Kohn. The soldier acknowledged that he was Chaim, though he was terrified to think of the trouble he and his brother must be in to cause this Russian sergeant to come looking for them. Max shocked Chaim by proclaiming his love for his sister, Toby, and promised to bring home Chaim and his brother, Mendel. Max was true to his word. Later, when he put them on a train back to their family, he gave the young men new identities to insulate them from punishment for deserting their posts.

Max and Toby were married in a small Jewish wedding ceremony in Kyrgyzstan in February 1946. Later, Max, Toby and their families travelled to the American Zone in Germany and settled there.

Max and four other friends became wealthy black marketeers in the American zone. They were selling cigarettes, perfume, chocolate, liquor and other luxury items stolen by US Army servicemen in the German zone. With their wartime experience, including the knowledge of how easily everything could be taken from them, Max and Toby, on behalf of the partners, were appointed by the group to hide the money earned. They did so by stuffing the money beneath their bedroom mattress and Max slept with a gun by his side.

The couple lived a nice life in Berlin. They first stayed in a displaced persons camp, and then in a comfortable apartment with a housekeeper. When Max wasn't selling his goods, he smuggled displaced persons into Germany's American zone. Working with the existing underground movement, Max drove over the border into Poland to rescue Jews who wanted to leave and come to the American zone. He was determined to rescue Jews, undeterred even by Toby's pregnancy. In 1946, Max was captured by the Russian border guards and sent to jail for four months. While he was in prison, Toby gave birth to their son, Faibol, alone.

In 1948, while walking with the housekeeper, Faibol was hit by a car and killed. Heartbroken and devastated, Max and Toby had no choice but to give their dead child up to people from the Jewish underground, unknown to them personally, to bury in a Jewish cemetery in the Russian zone in East Germany. That was the only Jewish cemetery available to them at the time. Because Max was unable to cross the checkpoint between East and West Berlin, he could not attend the funeral or say *Kaddish* (the prayer for the dead) at his own son's grave.

Shortly after Faibol's tragic death, Max and Toby moved to the displaced persons camp in Fahrenwald, outside Munich. In June 1949, eleven months later, Toby gave birth to a daughter, Anita. Hoping to start a new life and move on from the death of their son, Max and Toby emigrated to America. When they arrived in New York City, Max worked at several jobs to provide for his family. In 1951 the couple welcomed a son, Morris, and another son, David, in 1955. The family ultimately settled in Coney Island and then moved to Sheepshead Bay in Brooklyn, NY, where Max became a butcher and renovated homes for low-income families. Committed to raising children with strong Jewish identities, they sent their children to a yeshiva, a religious Jewish school, in Coney Island.

In 1973, as Morris and his fiancée, Cindy, reviewed the guest list for their wedding, Morris noticed a name he didn't recognise: Berok Osdoba. He also noticed that his uncle Mendel and aunt Rivka were missing from the list. His mother explained the story of Max's rescue of her brother, who kept the name Berok Osdoba, the 'new' name Max gave him many years ago. Though Chaim changed his name back to Kohn, Mendel kept the name Berok Osdoba until his death.

On 27 June 1976, members of the Popular Front for the Liberation of Palestine hijacked an Air France plane, which took off from Tel Aviv, Israel, carrying 248 passengers. The hijackers forced the plane to land in Entebbe, Uganda, and separated the Israelis and Jews from the non-Israeli, non-Jewish passengers, who were flown out of Entebbe during the next two days. The hijackers held hostage twelve crew members and niniety-four passengers, all Israeli or Jewish, until 4 July 1976, when the Israeli Defense Force rescued the Jewish hostages.

Max watched the events unfold on television with his son Morris. Upon learning the rescue operation was a success, Max, who infrequently showed emotion, sobbed uncontrollably. Though grateful and relieved that the rescue operation had been a success, Max was reminded of the loss of the millions of Jews in the Holocaust for whom there was no rescue. Max explained to his son his belief that if Israel had existed in 1939, the Jews of Europe might have had a safe haven and an Israel Defense Force that may have been able to protect them. This experience instilled in Morris a lifelong commitment to Zionism.

Max and Toby's wartime experience shaped their commitment to the next generation of Jews and to the State of Israel. Max became deeply involved in Jewish causes, especially 'Friends of the Israel Defense Forces' (FIDF). In August 2017, Morris Berger travelled to Germany to find and visit the grave of his older brother, Faibol. This was the first time the grave had been visited by a Berger family member.

November 2016 interview with Morris Berger, son of Max and Toby Berger, by Mindelle and Ira Pierce.

5

MURRAY AND FRUMA BERGER

Fruma and Murray's relationship had an auspicious beginning. By the time they met, deep in the woods in 1942 in what is today Belarus, they had each endured years of terror at the hands of the Nazis. Defying incredible odds, each escaped the Novogrudek ghetto and found refuge in the forest as part of the Jewish resistance movement, where they formed a bond and helped each other survive two of the most difficult years of their lives – a testament to the power of love, hope and resilience.

Frances 'Fruma' Gulkowich was born in Lublin, Poland, in 1918. When she was young, she moved with her parents, three sisters and brother, Ben-Zion, to Korelitz, a town of 1,500 Jews. The long-simmering anti-Semitism began to escalate in the 1930s and, despite their desire to leave Poland, they were trapped by Nazi laws that prohibited Jews from travelling.

With the Nazi invasion of Korelitz on 22 June 1941, the situation worsened. Jews were evicted from their homes, their valuables confiscated. They were required to wear yellow patches and forced to clean the streets, work in factories and perform other tasks as slave labourers. Within weeks of the Nazi takeover, the SS began their murderous rampage by killing 105 Jewish men. The terror continued as the local Polish police began searching Jewish homes for valuables. One day, the Polish police arrived at Fruma's home to find her mother had stayed home from work with a toothache. Accusing her of faking the toothache and failing to report for work, they beat her savagely. Unable to recover from her injuries, she died within a few weeks.

Fruma's brother, Ben-Zion, and his wife, Judy, knew that it was only a matter of time before they, too, would see their home searched, their valuables taken and their lives threatened. In an effort to preserve the gold that had belonged to Judy's family, the couple pulled up floorboards in their home and hid the gold beneath them.

In May of 1942, the residents of Korelitz were assembled in the town centre and forced to walk to the Novogrudek ghetto, surrounded by heavily armed SS guards. Jews from surrounding areas were also being confined there. Living conditions were appalling. They slept in barns, had little food and water, and they lived in fear of beatings, torture and death. During her time in the ghetto, Fruma was beaten, arrested and jailed.

On 6 August 1942, as Fruma and Judy approached the ghetto gate to report for work, the ghetto erupted in chaos. People ran in all directions, not knowing where to go. Word spread that the ghetto was surrounded by Nazi SS. There was no place to hide. The SS corralled the Jews, sending some to the right for continued forced labour, others to the left for imminent death. Some were shot and killed on the spot.

The prisoners sent to the right were marched back into the ghetto for the night. By the time Fruma entered the barn, she saw only her father, singularly focused on his prayers. Her sisters already had found places to hide in the barn. Fruma and her father locked eyes in a silent goodbye just as Judy grabbed Fruma and, together, they searched for a hiding place. Fruma never saw her father or her sisters again.

With few options, they decided to hide in the outhouse. They submerged themselves in the cesspool full of human excrement, joining two other women who had the same idea. Each woman retreated to a separate corner of the cesspool and waited all night in terror.

The next morning, from deep in the cesspool, the women listened to repeated bursts of gunfire. But none of the women moved from their hiding place. When Nazi soldiers approached with their dogs, searching for any remaining Jews, the women submerged themselves. The Nazis fired into the cesspool, killing one woman and grazing Fruma, and then left. The three surviving women remained hidden in the filth, hoping they would survive.

Fruma later learned that, as the women hid in the cesspool, the Nazis rounded up the Jews in the centre of the ghetto. All of the children, including Judy's daughter and Fruma's niece, were loaded into buses, which had been turned into mobile gas chambers. The others were taken to Litovka, ordered to remove their clothing, and systematically forced to walk a thin plank that stretched over a ditch. When the line of prisoners filled the plank, the Germans unloaded their machine guns into them, the bullet-ridden corpses falling into the mass grave below. This process was repeated until all the Jews had been killed. The bursts of gunfire they had heard as they hid was the execution of 4,000 Jews, among them Fruma's father and sisters.

Six days later, the surviving Jews – those who had been selected to live and those who had been on work detail outside of the ghetto on the day of the liquidation – were brought back to the ghetto from the military barracks. When one of the men who had returned entered the outhouse, he was shocked to find the three women still hiding in the cesspool. Fruma asked the man to tell Ben-Zion, assuming he had survived, that his sister and his wife were alive and in hiding. The next day, after bribing a guard, Ben-Zion snuck into the outhouse and carried the women back to the ghetto. It had become clear that escape would be their only chance to survive.

Murray Berger, the youngest of seven children, was born in 1912 in Wseilub, Poland, a small Jewish community with approximately 100 Jewish families. They lived a good life before the war when Jewish life flourished there, with many synagogues, Jewish groups and active Jewish organisations. With the start of the war, life for Polish Jews changed dramatically. First, the Soviets occupied Wseilub, closing Jewish schools and businesses, terrorizing and arresting Jews. Shortly thereafter, the Nazis invaded the town, inflicting relentless abuse and suffering upon the Jews, who were mercilessly beaten, starved, humiliated and murdered.

On 25 December 1940, watching as Nazi soldiers approached his home, Murray jumped out of a back window and ran until he reached a field, hoping to find a place to hide. He soon realised that the Nazis had set up roadblocks using soldiers and tanks, killing any Jews they found. With few options and no time to plan, Murray set off for Novogrudek, another Nazi-occupied Polish town, hoping to connect with extended family there. He dragged himself for miles through fields and back alleys, avoiding detection.

He took to the forest to look for other survivors who might be in hiding, but he found no one. Desperate for food, warmth and a place to rest, he knocked on the door of a house in the woods. Though the Gentile owner easily could have reported him to the Nazis, he instead gave Murray food, a place to rest and information about what was taking place. Murray left this house and went deeper into the woods, coming upon another farmhouse. He tempted fate again by knocking on the door. This owner also showed him immense kindness, giving him food and a place to stay for the night in return for work. Murray continued to wander in the forest alone for over a year, suffering from cold and hunger. As he hid in the woods surrounding Novogrudek, Nazi activities in the town dictated a change in plans.

On Friday, 5 December 1941, the Nazis began to liquidate the Novogrudek ghetto. Jewish labourers had been forced to dig large pits outside of the city. The city of Novogrudek was surrounded by the SS on all sides, rendering any escape attempt futile. Stories of mass executions were not new, and Murray understood what was about to happen. He made the decision to escape from the area, thinking, 'If death has to come, let the bullet come from behind.'

The next day, Murray hid in the nearby forest, listening to the percussion of machine guns as Nazi bullets ended the lives of 4,000 Jews from the ghetto. He learned from peasant farmers in the area that many of the Jews of Wseilub who had survived the ghetto attack had been caught in the woods and were either captured or shot on sight. Murray spent another winter roaming the woods, cold and hungry, afraid and alone. He pulled off his yellow star to avoid being identified as a Jew, though, by this time, he thought he might be the only Jew left. Murray continued to wander the woods, encountering many kind Gentiles who helped him along the way, giving him food, shelter and information. He never remained long in any one place, to avoid placing his hosts in greater danger than they already had assumed by helping him.

Murray learned from a kind farmer that some Jews still remained in the Novogrudek ghetto. With nowhere else to go, he headed to Novogrudek and snuck into the ghetto, mixing into the ranks of a group of Jewish men on their way back after a day of forced labour. Once there, he reconnected with his fifteen-year-old nephew, exchanging stories and piecing together what had become of their families. Then, one day, his nephew was sent off to work and never returned.

Some time later, a group of men, including Murray, was taken outside of the ghetto walls for a work assignment. This group of labourers included Jews from the surrounding areas, from whom Murray learned that Nazi trucks carrying groups of Lithuanians, Ukrainians and Estonians had come to Wseilub to terrorize and slaughter its residents. Their victims included Murray's sister and brother-in-law and their two young sons. Such attacks had become common throughout Nazi-occupied Poland and, after hearing this, Murray knew he could not return to the ghetto.

Murray turned to his friend and suggested they escape. Quickly, they jumped a fence and ran through the fields until they collapsed, spending the night outside in a forest. Eventually, they came upon a non-Jewish man who gave them food and told them that several hundred Jews still remained in the ghetto under heavy guard.

Three days later, Murray and his friend hid in a mill where the Nazis brought slave labourers to work on a daily basis. They mixed in among the prisoners and re-entered the ghetto, which had become significantly smaller. Murray believed its liquidation was imminent and he decided to escape once again. Several other prisoners asked to escape with him, relying on his familiarity with the surrounding area.

Soon thereafter, Tuvia Bielski, one of the war's most famous Jewish resistance fighters – upon whom the movie *Defiance* is based – smuggled a letter into the ghetto, encouraging Jews to escape into the woods and join his Jewish partisan group. In August 1942, when a ghetto guard was not watching, Murray and seven other men broke a hole in the fence and ran for the forest to join the partisans. Shortly thereafter, a second group, including Ben-Zion, escaped and joined them. Ben-Zion returned to the ghetto a few weeks later to rescue Fruma, Judy and thirty other Jews. They walked throughout the night, joining what later became known as the Bielski Brigade, a powerful force of Jewish resistance against the Nazis.

It was here, deep in the forest during the brutal cold of winter, that Fruma and Murray first met and felt an immediate attraction. Through the intensity of their partisan experience and the extended amount of time they spent together, they forged a deep bond and fell deeply in love. Eventually, they shared an underground dugout, bestowing upon themselves the status of a married couple, as was the custom among the partisans. Both were fighters in the Brigade.

Fruma was the first of the women to carry a rifle. She and Murray gave each other the will to persevere through the hardships and dangers, hoping for a chance to create a life together.

Though outmatched in numbers, weapons and resources, the fighters in the Bielski Brigade were determined to undermine the Nazi war effort. They became expert saboteurs, cutting communication lines and blowing up bridges, train tracks and train cars. They also fought alongside Soviet detachments and rescued other Jews. By the end of the war, the Bielski group had grown to 1,200 men and women.

After the Bielski partisans exited the woods on 13 August 1944, Fruma, Murray, Ben-Zion, Judy and Ellie (Murray's brother) returned to Novogrudek to search for family, but none had survived.

Hoping to recover their hidden gold, they returned to Ben-Zion and Judy's home in Korelitz. They arrived to find a Christian family living there, denying the couple had ever lived there. Determined to reclaim what was theirs, they fought their way into the house. They pulled up the floorboards, retrieved the gold and fled, knowing that throughout Europe, many Jews had been murdered by local townspeople while attempting to reclaim their property.

With heavy hearts, they decided to move to Palestine. Thinking it would be easier to make the trip from a port city, they travelled through Europe and ultimately arrived in Italy. They travelled using money from the sale of some of the recovered gold and with the help of *Bricha*, a Jewish underground organisation that helped Jewish Holocaust survivors escape from Europe after the war.

Each border crossing was treacherous. Patrols searched survivors and confiscated items of value with false promises that they would be returned. Women were instructed to jump up and down to dislodge valuables that might be hidden in body cavities. At one border crossing, Judy bit her gums to make them bleed, then disguised the gold as an ice pack for her 'toothache'. Only then was she allowed to cross the border without being searched, with the gold in hand.

When they arrived in Rome, Ben-Zion used some of the gold they had saved to have signet rings made for himself, Judy, Murray, Fruma and Ellie, as well as wedding bands for Fruma and Murray. Murray and Fruma were married in a synagogue in Rome on 14 February 1947. While in Italy, they met an American reporter who offered to help them find relatives in the United States. With his help, they located Murray's older brother, Harry, who had moved to the US before Murray was born. Harry brought Murray, Ellie and Fruma to the US in the same year. Ben-Zion, Judy and their son Albert, who had been born in Rome, followed them a year later.

Fruma and Murray began their new life together in New York, as did many of the partisans who had fought and survived together. Struggling to build a new life for themselves in the United States, they learned English. Murray worked different jobs, eventually becoming a printer for the Yiddish-language newspaper *The Forward*. Their two sons, Albert and Ralph, were named after their grandparents who had perished at the hands of the Nazis. The couple were open with their children about their experiences during the war and remained determined to educate others about the Holocaust and the Jewish partisan resistance efforts during the war. With little extended family, the other former partisans who lived nearby became their extended family, forever bound to those with whom they had lived, fought and survived.

Murray's rings are now in the possession of his sons, who wear them on the high holidays. Fruma's wedding band was given to her granddaughter just before her wedding, and Murray's wedding band is being saved for his grandson.

From a love affair that began in the woods under the most difficult of circumstances came a beautiful and loving forty-seven-year marriage, a loving family, a lifelong commitment to honour the Jewish lives that had been taken, and a passion for ensuring that the world will never forget the Jewish heroes who fought back.

A video interview with Ralph Berger conducted by Mindelle and Ira Pierce.

6

DANIEL AND
LUCYNA BERKOWICZ

Does a lover's wartime promise have any worth at all? Even if it does, how long can it endure? Let's see.

Seventy miles from Warsaw was a small town (*shtetl*) called Wolanow. Before the Second World War, communal ties between Jews and Gentiles in Wolanow were relatively warm. Not only did they exchange goods and services routinely, but often they were invited to and attended each other's wedding celebrations. Such good interfaith relations were much better than those typical in large Polish cities.

Well-established in Wolanow, the Berkowicz family had owned productive farmland, cows and a horse, and they sold their surplus produce and milk to the townspeople. Szimon Berkowicz was known as an honest, fair businessman. Szimon's wife, Ruchel, was known for being exceptionally sweet and generous. Ruchel would overfill the containers of milk for her customers, Jew and Gentile alike, with no expectations for her kindness. Knowing her maiden name, Malach, Jewish Wolanowers called her Ruchel-Angel; and her Gentile neighbours agreed.

In 1910, Szimon and Ruchel welcomed their newborn son, Daniel, fourth in their family. They would eventually have seven sons and a daughter. Although they were observant Jews, Szimon and Ruchel Berkowicz allowed their first son, Pinya, and later, Daniel, to enlist in the Polish military. In the Ulany, the elite

Polish cavalry into which Jews were seldom accepted, Daniel was proud to be promoted to corporal. Like his brothers, Daniel was a staunch *revisionist*, a right-wing Zionist inspired by the Russian Jewish Revisionist Zionist leader Ze'ev Jabotinsky, scoffing at leftist '*chalutzim*' (pioneers) and their socialist, anti-religious ideals.

On 1 September 1939, Nazi and Russian armies invaded Poland from the west and east, dividing Poland in half. By 5 September, the Wehrmacht had occupied western Poland, including Wolanow. In that short five-day interval, insufficient even to mobilize all Polish army reserves, many young unmarried Jewish men, including Daniel, quickly fled to the east, away from the Nazi beasts. Many Jews perished trying to cross into Russian-occupied Poland; but those who made it there found safety. One of those who reached Lvov in eastern Poland was twenty-nine-year-old Daniel Berkowicz.

In the large metropolis of Lvov, Daniel rented a room from a Jewish widow, Yetta Wiesman. After Yetta's husband Chaim succumbed to a stroke in 1935, she had to take in boarders to supplement her meagre income as a seamstress. Her hazel-eyed twenty-five-year-old daughter, Chaya Sara, had returned to help and live with her.

Chaya Sara was born in Lvov on 12 March 1914, one of three daughters and three sons in the observant Jewish Wiesman family. Bright and curious, little Chaya Sara soon asked her parents for religious education, although it was quite unusual for girls to get such tutoring. When it became apparent to her tutor that he couldn't handle her challenging questions, he discouraged her parents from allowing Chaya Sara to continue her education; and thus, she abandoned this path to pursue knowledge elsewhere. She attended the new public school and she spoke fluent, unaccented Polish. In the freedom of the secular world, she used her Polish name, Klara Sabina; only when at home with her family did she use her Jewish name.

Eventually, Klara Sabina became attracted to socialism. In the light of the evils of the former Soviet Union and other Communist dictatorships, the question arises: why were Clara Sabina and millions of other Jews at that time drawn to socialist ideals?

Simply stated, some of the premises of Marxist humanism did not contradict Jewish concepts. She, and many other Jews, valued 'tzedek', justice, and equality and despaired at not being treated fairly in Polish society. Socialism promised freedom from religious prejudice, more equitable distribution of wealth and an end to extreme nationalism – a seductive mix to oppressed Jews.

Certainly, with Soviet occupation of Lvov in 1939, a world of opportunity opened for Klara Sabina. She entered the university where she studied history and geography. The Russians trusted her to guide the commissars' wives around the city and she was even invited to one of the Russians' soirees. She danced there with Nikita Khrushchev.

Upon meeting Klara Sabina, a sophisticated city girl, Daniel was impressed with her intelligence and good looks. In turn, she was attracted by the military bearing and vitality of this curly-haired 'country boy' with piercing black eyes.

From 1939 to 1941, Lvov was relatively safe for Jews. Daniel and Klara Sabina studied and worked. He was learning Russian while employed as a locksmith and metalworker; she was employed in a department store while studying at the university. They walked together and discussed politics and religion. Despite great differences in their political beliefs, their love blossomed. They danced native polkas and exotic tangos, and listened to popular songs together, especially Klara's favorite Yiddish tango, 'Liebe', a song describing true love and the agony of soulmates who are separated:

Wie azoy gut zu zein in einem, Neshumeleh du bist mein kroin...

How good it is for us to be together
Dearest soul, you are my crown,
If I have you, I need no one other,
Says my heart—and knows it well.
Dear soulmate of mine, without you I cannot be,
Lacking you, my life has no more reason
It is so bad for me, I cannot carry on
My heart succumbs in longing and in pain...

On the night of 29 June 1941, Klara Sabina dreamed of her father. All was quiet in her dream, but as she rose from her bed, silently he pushed her back, as if warning her to stay at home. Awakening the next morning, Klara Sabina remembered that dream; and although she went to work in the city, she carried her full set of identification papers in a departure from her usual routine. That day, Germany broke its pact with Russia, beginning the blitzkrieg with tanks, planes and artillery, including the invasion of Lvov. Overnight, the safe haven of Lvov became fraught with danger.

The Nazis began murdering tens of thousands of Jews near Lvov. By 8 November 1941 they had established the Lvov ghetto. The ghetto quickly became overcrowded. With the establishment of curfews and strict food rationing, young Jews who could work still presumed initially that they would survive. They could not fathom the ultimate evil that would befall the ghetto; why would the Nazis murder a useful workforce, even if they were Jews? As conditions worsened rapidly, however, Daniel and Klara Sabina knew they would soon have to leave the ghetto. By then, it was impossible to escape to the Russian side of the border. The Soviets had withdrawn from Lvov, and crossing an active battle zone was treacherous.

After conversing with Jewish Russian soldiers, Klara Sabina had already been disabused of the belief in the 'Workers' Paradise' of the USSR. Meanwhile, Daniel's brother, Yankel, contacted them, reporting less severe conditions in the *shtetl* of Wolanow. There, the Wehrmacht, not the SS, ran a work camp – not a death camp. For the almost two years since the Nazi occupation, no massacres of Jews had occurred in Wolanow.

In the Lvov ghetto, their escape plan began taking shape. They were deeply in love, and Daniel decided that he would return to his hometown only with Klara Sabina. After many discussions with her mother, Yetta, Daniel had permission to take her back to his hometown. However, Yetta implored him to promise solemnly that he would protect Klara Sabina, and to never abandon her. Daniel declared that he would fulfil that promise.

Yankel had success with smuggling Jews back to Wolanow from Lvov. Near Wolanow, a shoe factory was trucking cowhides from the east. The hides were used for shoe soles. A truck would transport the large, stiff hides, frequently at night. These hides could be piled up in the rear of the truck in such a way that a large space remained hidden within the pile. There, on each trip, up to five Jews lay concealed.

Before attempting such an escape, Daniel needed a practice run alone with the truck driver, to know where he and Klara Sabina would be 'loaded' into the pile of hides. It was simple to enter the cab of the truck, but placing Jews within the pile and rearranging the hides took time and required absolute secrecy. During the night-time test, Daniel and the driver came upon an unexpected checkpoint up ahead. Daniel knew that if he was caught after curfew with the Gentile, not only would his own life be lost but the brave driver and this entire scheme of Jewish escape could be at risk. Better, he thought, was to leave the truck unnoticed before the checkpoint; then, if caught, Daniel would be just a lone Jewish curfew-violator.

Daniel was arrested by Ukrainian police that night, and manhandled while being transported to the precinct jailhouse, where he was tortured. Later, he recounted:

> The Ukrainians beat me, but I just grunted, refusing to give
> them the satisfaction of screaming in pain. They became upset;
> and maybe they needed the German supervisor to hear me, to
> know they were doing their jobs. So, they started ripping hair
> from my head. Then, I screamed, and they were satisfied.

The Polish trucker told Klara Sabina that Daniel was caught. She knew once the Ukrainians transferred their prisoner to the SS for his offence, his life was forfeited. She decided to try to save him. She knew Daniel was liked as a worker by his German Wehrmacht foreman. She hoped that the foreman would get Daniel released for his curfew violation. Risking her own life, she entered Wehrmacht headquarters where she found the lieutenant who was Daniel's foreman. She asked him if he would arrange for Daniel's release from jail – and he did!

Soon after, Daniel and Klara Sabina left Lvov along with three other Jews and travelled to Wolanow, hiding under hides in the truck. There, they were met by Daniel's brothers and father.

(His mother Ruchel had already died.) Daniel's father, Szimon, liked Daniel's 'girlfriend', though she was 'modern' and not a 'traditional Jewish country girl'. Nonetheless, his position was clear. It was unacceptable for them to remain an unmarried couple.

They readily agreed to wed, and in the Wolanow ghetto on 17 March 1942, Szimon married his son to Klara Sabina in a proper religious marriage under a *Chuppa Kadisha*, a traditional Jewish canopy. Klara was welcomed into the Berkowicz family with love, respect and honour.

Sanitary conditions worsened in the Wolanow ghetto. Typhus was rampant. The youngest Berkowicz brother, Moshe, died of it. His older brother, Yankel, likewise stricken, lying in Klara Sabina's arms, asked her, 'Where is my brother?' Klara lied, saying, 'He is still sick, but recovering in the clinic.' Reading her face, Yankel whispered, 'He is dead, and I too shall die.' He died in her arms.

Wolanow ghetto and the adjacent work-camps were closed by August 1942, and the Jews therein were transported to various closed camps, with ever harsher restrictions and random executions. In July 1942, Daniel and Klara Sabina were sent to the Starachowice work camp in Nazi-occupied southern Poland. Despite the camp's official designation as a factory workers' camp, it was known as a place where prisoners suffered flagrant, depraved abuse. In Starachowice, Klara was raped by a group of German and Polish collaborators and left with lifelong emotional scars.

Still young and deeply in love, Klara Sabina and Daniel were able to meet after work in Majowka, a factory that was one of three slave labour camps in Starachowice. Daniel was determined to save his wife, just as she had saved him in Lvov. He knew that, in addition to her 'crime' of being a Jew, her history of socialist ties, if known, and her speaking out against any further abuse, could prompt her immediate murder.

To save Klara's life, Daniel planned to use her remaining leftist connections, coupled with his own metalworking experience, even at the risk of his own life. Secretly, late at night in the gun shop where he worked, Daniel carefully sawed off the gun barrel of a shotgun, creating a concealable weapon. Along with several stolen cartridges, he hid the gun in the leg of his loose trousers. Although prisoners were searched, Daniel depended upon the fact that some guards were reluctant to pat down the crotch area of a dirty prisoner. Later, he remembered, 'Not only would they kill me if I was found, but as well, I risked the life of Benjamin, my brother.' Such was Daniel's desperation to keep his promise to save his wife.

They bribed a guard with the gun and shells. The guard let Klara Sabina 'go missing' from her work in the fields surrounding the camp. Her leftist connections outside gave her money and false identification papers. Daniel's theft remained undiscovered; but he and his brothers, Benjamin, Pinchus and Michael, were all eventually transported to Auschwitz-Birkenau.

Free at last, Klara Sabina walked cross-country, soon passing through Daniel's birthplace. Tired and hungry, she knocked on the door of a farmhouse at random and was welcomed in by the Gentile farmer. She asked if she could purchase a glass of milk. Accustomed to the anonymity of city life, Klara Sabina was shocked to be recognised in the village of Wolanow. The farmer peered at her closely and said, 'You are the "Berkowichova", aren't you?' Not only did he know she was a Jew, but also, he knew whose wife she was. The farmer went on to say, 'Finish this milk; I do not want your money. I am leaving this room. When I return, you must be gone. But be careful! My neighbour is friendly with the Nazis, and he will betray you, gladly.'

Thus, the kindness of Ruchel, the mother-in-law she never met, known for dispensing extra milk, was returned to her daughter-in-law, Klara Sabina Berkowicz – with milk. It was given to her at great risk by a Gentile whose name we do not know. She remembered this kind gift her whole life.

Slipping out of Wolanow, Klara Sabina entered another city and posed as a Christian widow, using a Polish first name, Lucyna. She had attended Polish grammar school and university, and so she spoke Polish without a trace of a Jewish accent. 'Lucyna' got official German identification papers as a foreign worker and became a maid for a German family for the rest of the war. In 1945, near the end of the war and as the Russians advanced toward victory, Lucyna's German employers prepared to escape to Bavaria to avoid capture and implored her to accompany them. Lucyna declared, 'No. I am a Jew. I am returning to Poland to find my family.' Lucyna had judged the character of that German family correctly; they let her go and did not betray her.

Returning to Poland, Lucyna witnessed the extent of the Nazi mass-murder of Jews. Their communities were annihilated and Lucyna was devastated. Although she no longer had any illusions as to socialist help for Jews, nevertheless, with her leftist connections, Lucyna was appointed to the post of City Commissioner in Krakow, Poland.

In those post-war days, carbon-copied sheets circulated listing names of survivors, wherever they were in Europe. In her office, Lucyna searched feverishly for her husband's name. Finally, one day, she saw the names Daniel and Benjamin Berkowicz, listed as together in Buchenwald: the names of her husband and his brother!

Lucyna asked for a two-week furlough from her government job. Long disillusioned with Communism, she had no intention of returning. Together with two of Daniel's female cousins and his aunt Julie, she led the way to Buchenwald, again using her connections in Communist-occupied eastern Europe.

Daniel and Benjamin had suffered horribly in Auschwitz-Birkenau. They survived that nightmare plus the death march towards Mauthausen. Shortly before the march, Daniel had saved his brother's life. It occurred when the Nazis knew that Auschwitz would be lost to the Allies. They forced prisoners to bury corpses of their brethren in large mass graves, covering the dead with lime. That made everything slippery and Benjamin slipped into the pit. Risking his life, Daniel stepped in and was able to grab Benjamin and physically yank him out of the mass grave. All the while, other prisoners threw more corpses in, under the watchful eyes of the Nazi soldiers; anyone remaining in the mass grave was buried.

This, Daniel later said, was the most dangerous thing he had done in the camps. Nearing the end of the death march to Mauthausen, the Wehrmacht officer escorting the emaciated, dying prisoners, including Daniel and Benjamin, was met by a mobile SS soldier on a motorcycle. The SS man handed the officer a satchel of explosives and told him to march the prisoners into a nearby cave and blow up the entrance, entombing them.

Daniel said later, 'We would have gone. We could barely walk, let alone run.' The Wehrmacht officer watched the SS motorcycle leave. When he was gone, he said to the prisoners, '*Mach dass du weckkomst*!' – 'Get lost!' Exhausted and worried about his own survival, the officer ignored the SS officer's order.

When Lucyna and the others met Daniel and Benjamin near Buchenwald, Daniel pleaded to return to Poland to seek out their relatives. Lucyna ordered him to stay. It was dangerous for Jews to return. It was rumoured some Poles continued to murder Jews who came back to reclaim their homes that had been confiscated during the war. In any case, everyone was dead, she said. Daniel obeyed. They never saw Poland again.

Daniel and Lucyna Berkowicz emigrated to the US in 1947 while expecting their first child. Their daughter was born three months after they landed in New York City. Daniel and Lucyna started a business in New York. Later, through the Hebrew Immigrant Aid Society (HIAS), they obtained a mortgage for a farm in southern New Jersey, where Jewish families had been migrating since Baron DeHirsch had established communities for those fleeing Russian pogroms of the 1880s. Near Vineland, NJ, they bought a homestead and started their own chicken farm, as did many other Jewish farmers from eastern Europe. Their son was born there.

It was a long while before they spoke of their memories of Poland. But in time, Daniel and Lucyna told their children of their youthful love and of how they saved each other's lives. They sang songs to them from when they first met. They told them their wartime trials, just as they are quoted here; and they remained devoted to each other for sixty-two years, until Daniel's death.

At Daniel's funeral, Lucyna cried out, 'You promised you would never leave me.' She joined him only a few months later. Etched on their gravestone is a variant of their favourite Yiddish tango, 'It is so good for me to be with you.'

Many details of their experiences, both during and after the war, are lost. But truth remains; Daniel kept his promise to his mother-in-law to keep his wife safe.

Their daughter and son, Ruth and John, are named after Ruchel, Yetta, Shimon and Yankel, their grandchildren after their brothers and an aunt, and their great-grandchild after Daniel. These names of loved ones should remain a blessing, for the love story that Daniel and Lucyna lived also reflected the loves of their families. The promise and its love endure, perhaps forever.

That answers our question: a lover's wartime promise does have worth that endures!

Interviews with Ruth Pengas and John Berkowicz in their homes in New York City and Margate, NJ, in 2016–17 by Mindelle and Ira Pierce.

7

HERMAN SHINE AND MAX DRIMMER

Herman Shine and Max Drimmer were born in Berlin into traditional Jewish families, Max in 1921 and Herman in 1922. They travelled in different circles of friends, and thus their paths seldom crossed in their younger days. But in 1939, the trajectories of their lives were forever altered when they were deported to Sachsenhausen, a concentration camp 35 kilometres north of Berlin in Nazi Germany. During the next five years, they bonded as they struggled to survive.

On 13 September 1939, the Nazis grabbed eighteen-year-old Max off the streets of Berlin along with 2,500 other Jewish men, including Leo Brenner, a childhood friend. They were corralled in a schoolyard and told they were being taken to a work camp. Exchanging tearful goodbyes with his mother, Max was loaded onto one of the trains with the others and shipped to Sachsenhausen. Along the way, the men were beaten, shot, starved and deprived of basic human dignities. They arrived at Sachsenhausen weak and disoriented. Of the 2,500 men taken from Berlin, 1,700 survived to enter the camp.

On 20 September, one week after the first wave of transports, Herman was instructed by his mother to register at police headquarters, as required by Nazi law. When Herman, a seventeen-year-old, arrived at the police station, he was thrown into a truck with several other men and taken to Sachsenhausen.

Conditions in the camp were abominable. Again, the prisoners were whipped, tortured, starved and dehumanised. Herman was ordered to work on a roofing detail. Max was initially assigned to carry bodies of the dying and dead to the hospital. After a short time, he was sent to work in the mines, shovelling coal and greasing cranes. Herman, Max and Max's friend Leo became close during their time together in the camp, relying on each other for the strength to withstand the brutalities that ravaged their bodies and the hopelessness that threatened to destroy their souls.

By October 1942, Max, Herman and Leo were among the 450 or so men who survived Sachsenhausen. They were loaded onto trains bound for Auschwitz-Birkenau in Nazi-occupied Poland. Only 250 men survived that trip, locked up and jammed in cattle cars for five and a half days without water or toilet facilities.

Auschwitz consisted of three main camps at that time: Auschwitz (Auschwitz I), Birkenau (Auschwitz II) and Monowitz (Auschwitz III). While the sub-camps used prisoners mostly for forced labour, probably about 90 per cent of the victims of the Auschwitz complex died in Birkenau, a facility designated exclusively for systematic murder. More than nine out of ten of all deaths there were of Jews.

Immediately upon arrival at Auschwitz, the Nazis greeted them with screams to get out of the box cars quickly. This was followed with the selection process, by which the Nazis determined the fate of each prisoner. The notorious Dr Mengele stood there, signalling prisoners to go left or right. Although the hapless victims did not know what awaited each group, their captors did. One group was sent to the gas chambers; the other was designated for hard labour. Herman and Leo were sent to the right, Max to the left. When no one was watching, Max slipped into Herman's group, determined that whatever his friends' fate would be, it would be his own as well. That move saved Max's life.

Herman, Max and Leo's group was sent to the new Monowitz camp, approximately 5 kilometres east of Auschwitz I, to work themselves to death for IG Farben, the huge chemical product conglomerate. They were forced to build slave barracks and buildings needed to manufacture synthetic rubber for the war effort. Herman volunteered to work as a roofer, as he figured that he would be beyond reach of the cruel Nazi overseers while on the roof. Max handled insulation, pipes and glass work. Leo worked as a structural welder on scaffolding.

Despite the cruelty and hopelessness of his daily life in the camp, Max's girlfriend, Herta, was never far from his thoughts. Meeting in 1938, they used to go to youth parties together and according to Max loved to listen to Louis Armstrong recordings 'laying on the floor'. She was Jewish on her mother's side and lived with her parents in Berlin. In the camps, Herta was his light in a sea of darkness. Once a month, in Sachsenhausen, they were allowed to write letters home. From these letters, Max said, 'Her address was imprinted in my head.' Frequently, Herman joked that he knew Herta just as well as Max did, having listened to him speak of her so often. Max worried about her constantly. He wondered if she was safe and longed for the day they would be reunited. Yet, the brutality of the Nazis made him doubt whether any of them would survive.

In January 1943, Herman and Max were ordered to Gleiwitz, a town near Auschwitz, to construct roofs on the barracks in four satellite camps. While working there on a roof, Herman said that he saw 'three gorgeous girls'. They were teenagers wearing yellow stars on their clothing. Herman became particularly interested in Marianne, one of the girls. Years later, Marianne recalled, laughing, that 'Herman climbed off the roof and he snuck up to my sister, a friend, and me and he asked if we were Jewish'. Herman learned that they lived in Gleiwitz. Because they had one non-Jewish parent, they were known as 'half prisoners', and exempt from deportations. Instead, they were drafted into forced labour and assigned to collect 'leftover food' – inedible scraps (as the prisoners ate everything else) – from their camp twice a week, and from other camps, hospitals and barracks.

Anxiously, Herman waited for the two days a week when the girls came to the camp. Because prisoners and civilians were prohibited from interacting, Marianne and Herman stole private moments to talk, out of sight of the Nazi guards. Herman had become very fond of the beautiful, sweet girl who was his only link to the outside world. She made him feel lighter and more hopeful, and he found himself singing songs on the rooftops when she was around. During one of their conversations, she told him her address, on Niederwall Street, which he committed to memory.

Herman doubted he would survive the war, but he thought Marianne might live on. Wanting to ensure that the world learned of the horrors of the Nazis, Herman told Marianne about life inside the camps and described the Nazis' brutal treatment of the Jews – beatings and torture, the gas chambers and the ovens. Sometimes he would give her a note with specific information about the camp – names, dates, incidents – which she would hide in her sock until she could read them at home. For Marianne, this information answered many questions, like pieces of a puzzle falling into place. Five hundred Jews, including her neighbours and friends, had been deported from her city and were never seen or heard from again. She now understood what had happened to them and why they never returned.

Though Marianne had grown fond of Herman – the nice man with the beautiful voice – her feelings were platonic. The horrible stories he told her of life and death in the camp affected her deeply and she felt overwhelmed with sympathy for him. Then, one day, he was gone, transferred back to Auschwitz.

Herman and Max were ordered into a truck along with a thousand other prisoners and transferred approximately 7 kilometres to Auschwitz II-Birkenau, where the men were again assigned to work in construction. Max's daily work took him outside of the confines of the camp, where he befriended a Polish Christian civilian named Jozef Vrona. He was a member of the Polish International Underground, and offered him cigarettes and bread that, Max noted later, 'was equivalent then to tasting filet mignon'. Jozef warned Max that the SS were planning to execute all prisoners as the Russian army advanced toward Auschwitz, and he offered to help Max escape. Max couldn't fathom escaping without Herman, and Jozef agreed to help both men. He was the 'outside' link.

Leo happened to be foreman of Max and Herman's work group. If people escaped during a work session, the foreman was held responsible, tortured and shot. The idea was for the men to create a plan to save Leo from a certain death when they escaped on his shift.

20 September 1944 was selected as the day of the planned escape, because there was no moon that night. Herman and Max left the camp for work, just as they did every day. As per the plan, Leo called in sick and was taken to the infirmary by an orderly who was a member of the resistance and was aware of the plan. Going to the infirmary was usually one stop shy of the gas chamber, as the SS would make selections from the beds. Every time they came to 'inspect', the orderly would signal to Leo, who would hide in the latrine or be transferred to another ward.

Max became the temporary foreman, so Leo could not be blamed for the escape. Instead of returning to their barracks at the end of the day, Max and Herman ran to the factory warehouse. They put on regular work clothes and they hid in a 6-foot-deep hole, 3 feet by 4 feet, that Jozef dug in the floor for them. He camouflaged it with insulation and other materials from the factory, praying no one would find them.

Herman and Max waited, terrified. If they were discovered, they knew death would be a certainty. When the search for the two men died down, Jozef returned to the warehouse and pulled the men out of their hiding place. The three men crawled through the factory, out the door and to the non-electrified wire fence surrounding the facility. Using wire cutters, Jozef cut a hole in the fence and the men crawled out of the camp to what they hoped would be freedom.

Leo remained in the infirmary for a few days. He was not blamed for the escape, and not caught or selected. He didn't find out until the end of the war what happened to Max and Herman. He was liberated by American forces from a munitions plant in Altenburg, a subcamp of Buchenwald, after a harrowing death march from Auschwitz.

Prior to their escape, Jozef tried to contact a partisan group, including its leader who later became Marshal Tito of Yugoslavia, to inform them that two men escaping from Auschwitz would need their help. But once outside the camp, with no one in sight, Herman and Max realised that help was not coming. The partisans may have thought it was a trap, since Auschwitz escapes were rare. With no other options, the three men walked 18 kilometres to Jozef's family home. Risking their own lives, Jozef and his family hid Herman and Max in a barn on the family property for almost four months. The barn had a second level accessed via a chicken coop that had a trap door above it, and a drop-down ladder.

During this time, Jozef's family took good care of the men and kept them safe. Max desperately wanted to let Herta know he was out of harm's way and to find out if she was safe. With Jozef's help, Max sent a letter to Herta at home in Berlin. She responded immediately, asking whether he still had his pretty curly hair. That was enough for Max to say to Herman, 'This is the girl I am going to marry.' Perhaps he felt beyond the reach of the Nazis, or perhaps his emotional desire to reach out to Herta overpowered his logic and caution. In his letter back to Herta, he explained that he and Herman had escaped from Auschwitz and were hiding in a nearby barn. Herta was overjoyed to have received this letter. She carried it around with her in her purse. One day while she was walking through town, Nazi soldiers stopped her, searched her bag and found Max's letter.

Soon after, seven Nazi SS officers searched Jozef's property for the two escapees with three dogs but did not find them. For many years, Herman and Max wondered why the dogs did not smell them out. Years later, Max asked an officer at the San Francisco Police Department about that. He was told that they would have been found by the dogs had they not been so dirty, having not taken a shower or bath in three months, with mice having bitten at their clothing. That was what masked their 'people' smell.

Realising it was too dangerous to stay, Herman and Max left the barn, hoping to protect the family that had so bravely and selflessly saved their lives. Jozef instructed the men to go to the house of his future father-in-law at the edge of town, where they would be given a safe place to stay for two nights.

Herman and Max needed a new plan. Herman thought of Marianne and remembered the name of her town and street. Desperate for help, and with nowhere else to turn, Herman and Max set off to find her. They went to the train station, hoping luck was on their side. They stepped up to the ticket counter and bought two tickets, hoping for a miracle. The woman at the ticket counter, taking pity on these two dishevelled men who looked like they were running for their lives, gave them two tickets to Gleiwitz. Walking to the train, they spotted SS officers everywhere, checking everybody. Two SS officers approached them, obviously wanting to check their papers, of which they had none. But, as Max put it, 'They were maybe 10-12 ft away. They started walking straight for us, but "that guy up there" got someone to step out between them and us ... They called him over, and we got onboard the train.' Another miracle!

On 5 January 1945, they arrived in Gleiwitz, walked to the centre of town and found Marianne's street. The men were vulnerable, standing on the street, obviously looking like outsiders. They could not risk knocking on an unfriendly door just to be reported to the Nazis. But neither could they stand in the street for very much longer. As the men contemplated their next move, Herman noticed an apartment building with a Jewish star drawn in chalk on the front door.

They took a chance and knocked on the door. A woman opened it and Herman and Max introduced themselves and asked for the Schlesingers. A voice in the back room said to let them in, 'as my office wishes to know why I am not at work today'. The two boys were ushered into the back room, where they found Marianne's mother, Erica, in bed. She did not recognise them from the neighborhood and asked who they were. Herman explained that he knew Marianne from the camp. The woman responded, 'You're the roofer who sings to my daughter so nicely. My daughter told me about you.'

It was by sheer coincidence that Marianne's mother, Erica, happened to be home from work that day. She had worked at a factory for forty years and never missed a day, until that January date when she was home. Furthermore, Marianne had happened to have had her palm read by a mystic, who told her that when she came home that day, that she would meet a young man with whom she would live and 'travel long distances'. With that, Herman and Max told her the story of their imprisonment and escape from Auschwitz. Without hesitation, Marianne's parents hid Herman and Max in their home until Marianne's father could arrange safer accommodation for them.

Marianne and Herman spent the days together and he fell deeply in love with her. He was amazed by her kindness and beauty; also impressed by the courage she and her parents exhibited by hiding them. Marianne was in awe of Herman's strength, tenacity and bravery, which had enabled him and Max to survive more than five years in the camps and risk their escape. She appreciated his sense of humour, wondering how he had managed to retain it through all his suffering. Though she had a boyfriend when she met Herman, he made sure that she ended that relationship quickly, and within three months she had fallen in love with him.

After a short time, Herman and Max became wary of the risk they were imposing on Marianne's family. They knew the family was in danger so long as they hid in the Schlesinger home. Marianne's father contacted an acquaintance, a former millionaire client of his, who was anti-Nazi. It was whispered that he had hidden Jews before. The millionaire agreed and made necessary arrangements to hide Herman and Max. Promising Marianne that they would return for her, the men set off for the villa where they remained hidden safely until the end of January 1945, when the Russians liberated the town. After liberation, the men spoke to a Russian general, who happened to be the youngest Jewish general in the Russian army. Speaking in Yiddish, they told the general their story and were given documents for safe passage to Berlin.

Max and Herman climbed on top of a Russian military train carriage, the only transportation available, and arrived in Berlin in search of their families. They learned that nearly everyone had been murdered. Heartbroken, Max and Herman set out to find Herta, Max's girlfriend. Max went to the home she had lived in before the war, hoping she was still there. He stood outside her window and whistled the secret whistle of the Jewish youth group. Upon hearing it, she almost fell out of her third-floor window, and ran to him immediately, overcome with relief.

After a month, Hermann went back to Gleiwitz to Marianne's home and asked her to join him on his journey back to Berlin. Her parents objected; she was too young and inexperienced. Despite their concerns, she refused to separate from her beloved Herman again. Herman and Marianne moved to Berlin and on 17 February

1946, the couples were married in a double wedding – they thought it was the first Jewish wedding after the war – by a rabbi in City Hall. Herman was acquainted with an American officer who knew of a good band that was playing in a park outside the city. They went together to ask the general to release the band; he did and they played at their wedding. It was a twelve-hour affair, from 8 p.m. to 8 the next morning, with food: a cabbage buffet cooked by both mothers-in-law. The mothers-in-law became close friends, and the two couples became inseparable. The Shines and the Drimmers stayed in Berlin until January 1947, when they emigrated to the United States. Max and Herta arrived in New York in February. In April 1947, Herta and Max travelled to San Francisco to reunite with family members who had found refuge in Shanghai. Six months later, Marianne and Herman followed the Drimmers to San Francisco.

The early years of marriage were difficult for the couples. They struggled to build a new life in a new country, learning the language and looking for jobs. But, as Marianne recalled, 'We pulled ourselves up by our bootstraps.' In 1954, using money he received for reparations, compensation for the horrors inflicted on the Jews during the Holocaust, Herman established a roofing business, which he ran until his retirement in 1980.

In 1989, Max and Herman brought Jozef Vrona to San Francisco for a six-week reunion, which everyone enjoyed. Six months later, Jozef Vrona died in Poland and is counted among the Righteous Among the Gentiles in Yad Vashem, the Holocaust museum in Jerusalem. Leo Brenner found Max and Herman in the US. They remained in touch for the rest of their lives.

Herman and Marianne built a wonderful life together and marvel at the life they lived. Despite the darkest days of the war, their youth, their optimism and love for each other enabled them to embrace the future and look to life after the war. They held onto hope that the future would be better. Herman says, 'It's hard to grasp, to believe sometimes. We are married for seventy-four years, and we live in a beautiful place. I cannot believe it myself."

Years later, Max and Herman returned to Poland to visit Auschwitz, a trip that empowered the men. Despite all that the Nazis had inflicted on them and living through the darkest of times, the Nazis did not break them. They lived and they loved. They overcame the odds, and they did it together.

The couples remained the best of friends and for the rest of their lives resided in the same northern California community. After fifty-two years of marriage, Herta died in 1999, followed by Max in 2013. Herman died on 23 June 2018 at ninety-five at his home in San Mateo, California, and is survived by Marianne. But even though they passed away, Herta, Herman and Max live on in the hearts of their friends and family.

Based on telephone interviews by Ira and Mindelle Pierce, both with Herman and Marianne Shine in January 2016, and with Leo Brenner's son, Dr Ira Brenner, in June 2018.

8

HENNY DURMASHKIN AND SIMON GURKO

Henny Durmashin and Simon Gurko met in 1949, four years after the end of the war, on the USS *Greely* while on their separate ways to the United States. Henny was born in 1921 and came from a distinguished family of musicians and cantors. Simon was born in 1923 in Falenicia, a resort town in the woods not too far from Warsaw. They both suffered terribly during the Holocaust.

They met at a shipboard dance, while Henny was supposedly dating another fellow. She was sitting out the dance because her foot hurt. But when Simon asked her to dance, she joined him on the dance floor because he was 'so cute and irresistible'. They spent the rest of the voyage learning about each other. Once they disembarked in New York, they promised to stay in touch. Simon was headed toward Milwaukee where a cousin sponsored him, and Henny to Brooklyn, where her aunt sponsored her family.

Simon was alone and had no immediate family left. He had two sisters before the war, Necha and Rivka. His father died at fifty, and Simon grew close to Rivka, who also died tragically young. There is no information available about his mother. At age nineteen, when Stalin broke his pact with Hitler, the Soviets sentenced Simon to hard labour in Siberia, and he was trapped there until the Liberation in 1945.

An avowed Zionist and follower of Russian Jewish Revisionist Zionist leader Ze'ev Jabotinsky, Simon joined the *Bricha* in

Germany, an underground Zionist movement that smuggled Jews into Mandate Palestine in defiance of the British. He smuggled many Jews over the border into Switzerland, where they were able to find ways to cross borders into Italy, Spain, France and Portugal, all countries with ports on the Mediterranean Sea. Ships like the *Exodus* left those ports loaded with Holocaust survivors, but too many of them were caught and locked up in fenced camps on the island of Cyprus by the British. Some were sent back to Europe.

Simon wrote to Henny from Milwaukee every day for months expressing his love for her, but Henny wrote back that she wasn't sure she could reciprocate. Her aunt Grace was Henny's confidante, and finally asked her if Simon was a wonderful man, and Henny said, 'Yes.' Grace then asked Henny if she loved Simon, and Henny said, 'Yes.' That is when they decided that Simon should come to New York and they would marry. Simon happily came to New York, and in the months before their wedding took a job as a longshoreman on the New York City docks, not a job for the faint of heart. Later, when he worked for the French Line, he met the famous actress Elizabeth Taylor, who asked him about his life. She was so moved by his story that she sent his children a box full of colouring books to show her appreciation.

Eventually Simon became a successful auto parts distributor. As a family man and husband, he was generous, loving and created opportunities for Henny to enroll in and graduate from college. In 1962, he financed the album *Songs to Remember*, which she recorded with her sister Fanny. Driven by his work ethic, Simon toiled day and night, helping other family members and refugees he met through friends to start their own businesses. His children adored him, and the family was broken-hearted when he died suddenly in 1974, at the age of fifty.

Henny was one of three musically talented children born to Akiva and Sonia Durmashkin. Her brother Wolf and sister Fanny were exceptional performers, too. Wolf was the oldest, Fanny was second in line, and Henny was the youngest. Only the sisters survived the war.

Akiva was born in Mohliv, White Russia. He was a cantor, a composer of cantorial music and teacher who had a great impact on the Jewish community in that region. He became director of the Odessa Symphony Orchestra and developed an excellent reputation.

In 1918, Akiva took his family to Radom, in east-central Poland, and became director of the liturgical choir of the City Synagogue, a choir which became extremely popular. He composed music to the poetry of C. N. Bialik, taught music to youth groups, and conducted bands, orchestras and choirs. He also organised a Zionist labour choir of sixty singers and a Zionist labour orchestra, both of which became important cultural institutions in Radom. A year later, he established yet another orchestra for the Jewish Labour Party, and after just ten weeks that orchestra was being booked for special public appearances.

In 1920, Akiva directed the choir at a memorial for the ninety-five Jews who had been slaughtered in Lemberg, Poland, now Lvov, in western Ukraine. Held in Radom's largest concert hall, he had prepared music for Hebrew and Yiddish texts. The audience was engrossed in the performance when, suddenly, a gunshot fired by an agent provocateur rang out, and panic ensued as people ran for the exits and were hurt in the stampede. Under Durmashkin's strict command, the choir remained on the stage. 'Don't lose your composure! No singer should move from his place! We will continue our program out of utmost respect to the martyrs!' he cried. The choir waited for the police to arrive and impose order, and then continued the program to its conclusion.

Akiva loved Hasidic music and made efforts to preserve it as a Jewish cultural treasure. During the First World War, when the Modzhitzer Rebbe Rabbi Yisroel Taub, a famous singer and composer of Hasidic songs, lived in Radom, he and Akiva became good friends. As a result, Akiva musically transcribed many Modzhitzer melodies the Rebbe sang for him and preserved them. Who could imagine that years later, after 1941, these melodies would float from the Rebbe's little synagogue on Crown Street in Brooklyn and lead to a renaissance of Hasidic music in the post-Holocaust world?

In 1923, two years after Henny was born, Akiva Durmashkin and his family left Radom and moved to Vilna, where Akiva had been asked to become the choirmaster of the Great Synagogue. From

1926 until 1929, Durmashkin worked with Moshe Koussevitsky, the world-famous cantor and tenor. He collaborated with famed Cantor Yossele Rosenblatt, also at the Great Synagogue, and worked with other cantorial greats such as Samuel Katzman and Moses Rontal. Henny remembered their working visits to her home in Vilna.

In July 1938, her father returned to Radom and stayed until after the high holidays (Hebrew year 5699). The following year, he was invited again to Radom and established a choir of twenty-eight boys and six men. They prepared a repertoire of selected liturgical compositions but could not execute the program because the Nazis were on the move.

He stayed in Radom with Cantor Moses Rontal until after the Sukkot holiday, distraught, in tears, thinking only of how he could return to his family in Vilna. Rontal managed to smuggle him out of Poland and back to Vilna (then in Lithuania), paying someone to accompany Durmashkin and endangering his own life in the process.

Akiva had done so much musically, including directing an orchestra for the Czar, directing choirs, teaching music in Jewish and Hebrew schools, and leading an orchestra in a Hebrew college. Understandably, he gave his children a musical education. Wolf, Henny's brother, showed exceptional talent by the time he was five. He gave piano concerts throughout Poland. Akiva had given him his first lessons. He went on to study at the Vilna Conservatory of Music. His genius was so great that the school gave him a full scholarship. When he finished at the conservatory, he continued by studying to become a conductor. He went to Warsaw to study with a Russian professor, Valerian Berdiayev, who also gave him a full scholarship and permitted Wolf to conduct professionally after only one semester.

With the start of the war, Wolf ended his studies and returned to his family in Vilna. He produced, directed and conducted a Hebrew version of the opera *Aida* arranged by his father, and became famous as a conductor in his own right. He conducted the Vilna Symphony Orchestra for sold-out houses. When posters proclaimed Wolf Durmashkin was conducting the Vilna Symphony Orchestra, all the performances sold out. He wore black tie and tails, and was young, handsome, talented and so dignified. When the concerts ended, Henny remembered the audience threw flowers to him. The family would ride home from the concerts in a horse and carriage filled with all the flowers.

Henny was the singer. In a house full of music, where singers and violinists would gather, the street out front would be full of people listening to the music that came out of the Durmashkin house. Even the cat, Tchun, loved the piano; when Henny's sister, Fanny, practised piano, Tchun would jump up on the piano and listen. But when the teacher came to Wolf to accompany him on the violin, the cat would cry out, 'Meow!' She couldn't stand the sound of the violin.

Henny had a great relationship with her father. She was the youngest, and he spent a lot of time with her. Henny remembered that when she was a three-year-old, her father would carry her while composing songs in his head. He would accompany Henny and Fanny to school, sometimes in bitter cold, reciting poetry or singing. Henny loved doing her homework with her friends, and she liked languages, including German, Polish and the language of the school, Hebrew. Eventually, she mastered eight languages.

Henny also loved to be in plays and would participate in variety shows, singing and playing instruments. At six years old, in the summer, she would take walks in the woods. The family would go swimming and listen to orchestras.

Making a living with music was hard, but Wolf helped everyone out. Wolf always told his mother, 'You'll see. One day, I'll get you a beautiful home with all the conveniences in it, and you'll be like a queen.' But the fact that Wolf did not want to be observant aggravated his father.

Henny attended Hebrew high school, where she excelled as a top student and had her eye on a fellow who was with her in a play. Just before the Second World War, Henny studied opera, and her voice teacher, one of the best in Vilna, began training her at fourteen as a coloratura soprano. One day, her teacher asked her to sing 'Ave Maria', something a Jewish girl should not be singing. To avoid trouble, she taught her privately, and in the church where her son was a priest. There were many nuns in the church courtyard who could have hidden her to avoid what was coming;

namely Russian anti-Semitism followed by the Nazi Holocaust. Henny later realised that the older nuns knew her, which made that idea unworkable.

The day her voice teacher determined that Henny was ready to sing on the radio was the day the Russian army arrived in Vilna. It was 21 June 1941, and Vilna was transferred to the Soviet Union. That day, all Jewish activities in Vilna were brought to a stop or went underground. Previously, the city, known as the Jerusalem of the West, was a hub of diverse Jewish activity and became an important Jewish centre. It maintained links with Jewish centres both in Lithuania and around the world, including the communities in Soviet territory and in Poland under Nazi rule. During the previous eight months of Lithuanian rule, 12,000 to 15,000 Jews found refuge from the Nazis in Vilna.

On 6–7 September 1941, Nazis herded 20,000 Jews, including Henny, her parents and siblings, into the Vilna ghetto. The idea was to create a forced work camp, imprisoning the remaining Jews in and around Vilna.

By coincidence, the Nazis sent Henny's family to an apartment in the ghetto to share with one of their best friends, Mira. A total of forty people wound up in this small apartment: the Durmashkins, plus thirty-five other people. Ironically, the Vilna ghetto was known at the Jerusalem of ghettos for its intellectual and cultural programs that enabled many prisoners to forget, for several moments, that they were forced labourers.

Wolf witnessed the unbelievable pain of the inmates, which included the constant fear of deportation to the death camps for the old and young. Wolf believed that the ghetto inmates needed something to enjoy in the time that they had left to live. An old 'legitimate' theatre on Pefinska Street was made available to Wolf. There, he created a symphony orchestra and a hundred-voice Hebrew choir, and he composed new music for them. The ghetto orchestra performed thirty-five chamber and symphonic concerts in the fifteen months of its existence. He assisted in the creation of a school of music for a hundred students and was the founder and director of a Hebrew ghetto choir. Henny sang with them. Interestingly, the leaders in the ghetto underground were against his efforts. They complained that living in the ghetto should be like living in a cemetery, with no music. Henny did not agree.

Akiva was murdered by Nazis and their Lithuanian collaborators during the Ponary Massacre, putting Henny into a deep depression. Between June 1941 and August 1944, they managed to murder 100,000 people near the railway station at Ponary (now Paneriai), a suburb of today's Vilnius, Lithuania.

The music died with the liquidation of the Vilna ghetto on 23–24 September 1943. Shortly thereafter, Wolf was deported to the Klooga concentration camp in Estonia. Henny's mother, Sheine, had been deported to a death camp from the ghetto. The two daughters tried to apply makeup to make her look younger, but it did not work. She was only fifty-three years old. Tragically, one day before liberation, on 18 or 19 September 1944, Wolf was shot at age thirty in the Klooga concentration camp.

Henny and Fanny were shipped to Kaiserwald, a camp on the outskirts of Riga, Latvia, where large German companies used female slaves to produce electrical equipment. Others worked in the camp and in factories, mines and farms outside the camp. From Kaiserwald, they were sent to Dinawerke, Stutthof, Dachau and Landsberg concentration camps.

Henny became involved with an orchestra in Dachau. She was asked by a violinist sitting in the middle of a field to sing, because the Nazis wanted to hear her. There were benches where the Nazis were sitting, waiting to be entertained. Trembling in the cold, Henny had no jacket and was wearing short sleeves. She was terrified. Again, they asked her to sing. Someone gave her a coat and, feeling warmer, she sang along as the violinist played *Aida*. Gradually, they began sending Henny to sing in different camps. She joined with a group of eight musicians who went from barracks to barracks to entertain the forced labourers.

There also were performances for the SS and visitors. For them, they played German marches and popular songs, and were given some extra food rations for their efforts. There were attempts made to put on clandestine performances exclusively for prisoners. After the war, Henny testified that when she sang Yiddish songs, she saw men crying.

From Dachau, the sisters were marched to Landsberg concentration camp in Bavaria. Fanny got a job cleaning the home of a Nazi doctor who treated her kindly. Shortly before the end of the war, guards pulled all the prisoners out of the camp for a death march. On the march, anyone who stopped for any reason was shot. Finally, on 29 April 1945, American tanks met the march. The Nazi guards ran, and the prisoners were liberated.

The Durmashkin sisters, sole survivors of their famous musical family, became part of the Displaced Persons Orchestra at St Otillien. There, a group of Jewish musicians, primarily from Lithuania, established an orchestra in a Benedictine monastery in Germany's Bavarian countryside near the village of Schwabhausen. Originally a Nazi hospital, a convalescence home was set up there for some 420 Jewish prisoners, including Henny and Fanny.

Soon after the war was over, Henny and the orchestra at St Otillien became known in Europe and America for their Yiddish and Hebrew music. Their many fans included Jewish Agency officials David Ben-Gurion and Golda Meir, as well as Leonard Bernstein, whose own works were becoming famous.

Following the creation of the State of Israel in 1948, twenty-nine-year-old Bernstein was visiting Germany on a cultural mission. He asked the Jewish Agency if there was a survivors' orchestra he might contact, which brought him to the St Otillien Orchestra. He performed three concerts with them: one in Munich and one each at Landsberg and Feldafing refugee camps, which had been sub-camps of Dachau. Bernstein accompanied Henny on the piano, but only when she agreed to sing in Hebrew, not Yiddish; Henny's daughter, Rita Lerner, speculated that Bernstein's preference for Hebrew stemmed from his Zionism.

Henny's oldest daughter, Vivian Reisman, in describing how her mother felt about St Otillien, said, 'My mother said it was incredibly moving. For a moment, Leonard Bernstein made them feel they could leave behind the hell they had lived through and soar into the magical world of music they loved so much. He left an indelible mark on her soul as well as an amazing legacy.'

As the world's media was covering the trials of the Nazi perpetrators of their war crimes in Nuremberg, the orchestra's performance at the Nuremberg Opera House received worldwide coverage. To make a point, the orchestra wore their concentration camp uniforms, and displayed their bruises and scars on stage to show the world what the Nazis did to them. Henny became known as 'Little Raiseleh', after a Yiddish song she helped make popular.

During that time, Max Beker, a violinist and assistant manager, fell in love with Fanny. Max was the son of Berel and Pessiah Beker, who, like the Durmashkins, attended Jewish schools and also studied music. After the start of the war, Max had been drafted into the Polish army and soon was taken prisoner. Later, he joined the orchestra and the following year, after Henny and Fanny made plans to immigrate to Israel, Max persuaded them to join him in America.

Henny recorded the album *Songs to Remember* in 1962, and on 11 September 1997, the Museum of Jewish Heritage was dedicated, and Henny Dumashkin Gurko sang the 'Star-Spangled Banner'. Later, Henny donated artifacts to the museum, including posters from the ghetto orchestra concerts and photos of herself with Leonard Bernstein.

In 2007, Sonia Beker, Henny's niece and Fanny's daughter, wrote *Symphony on Fire: The Story of Music and Spiritual Resistance During the Holocaust*, a valuable addition to the expanding library of books on the subject. Henny Durmashkin's daughters, Rita Lerner and Vivian Reisman, with Sonia Beker and others, were instrumental in making the documentary *Creating Harmony: The Displaced Persons' Orchestra at St Ottilien*. The documentary had its world premiere in New York on 10 June 2007 at the Museum of Jewish Heritage.

Based on a video interview in 2017 with Rita Lerner and Vivian Reisman, by Mindelle and Ira Pierce at the Museum of Jewish Heritage – A Living Memorial to the Holocaust.

9

LILLIE BURSTYN AND SIMCHA FOGELMAN

My parents met by chance, after each survived his and her own hell. My mother, known as Lyche as a child in Wyshkow, Poland, later in Israel as Leah, and even later as Lillie in the United States, was the youngest of five children in an Orthodox Jewish family. Her father, Mordechai Burstyn, who was very devout, owned a tannery with ten employees. Her mother, Freyde helped in the business, located on the floor below the family's living quarters. The eldest, Yosel, known as 'the smart one', was involved in the Shomer Hatzair Zionist movement, and aspired to immigrate to Palestine.

When Marshal Jozef Pilsudski (leader of Poland in the early decades of the twentieth century) died in 1935, Jews all over Poland were subjected to a renewed anti-Semitism. My mother was called rude names and classmates shouted to the Jewish children, 'Go to Palestine!' On Tuesday and Friday market days, the local farmers stopped buying leather goods from Mordechai's business. Yosel, who read the papers daily, warned his family that conditions for Polish Jews were precarious because they were adapting and implementing the racial laws Hitler imposed on German Jews. In 1939, my grandmother encouraged Yosel to immigrate to Palestine or to the United States, but the window of opportunity closed with the Nazi invasion of Poland on 1 September 1939.

My mother, who was about to enter seventh grade, instead dodged bombs as they dropped from aircraft – an invention she had never seen before. Her two older brothers, Yosel and Froim, escaped together, but lost each other along the way. At one point, Froim saw a man on a wagon with two horses and engaged him in conversation. The man said he was going to Wyshkow to look for his uncle but did not know how to get there. As it happened, Froyim knew the uncle and promised to show him the way if he would then take the family with him to the east. My mother, her parents and four other siblings got into his wagon with just a few of their possessions, and headed towards the next *shtetl*, one step ahead of the bombs. They rode from one town to another without food and slept along the way. A week later they arrived in Stocheck-Wengrofsky, where the family stayed for three months – hosted for a month by a woman many people did not like.

The Nazis infiltrated the area and kept demanding people's possessions. The fear was that they would kill the Jews, so the Burstyn clan continued their trek in search of safety and crossed the Bug River into Russian-occupied territory to get to Bialystok. When they got there, they found the synagogue packed with people, so that first night they slept on the street. The next day they contacted a relative who found them an apartment to stay in for a few months.

The Nazi troops followed the same route eastward until they, too, reached Bialystok, just as the Burstyns fled to Orsha, a town near Minsk, Belarus. The Burstyns were there from April 1940 until October 1941, when they were forced to cross the border into the Soviet Union for relative safety. The Soviet government suggested that they get Soviet documents, but they chose not to do that, and that later proved to have been a lucky decision. As a result, they were arrested and sent by cattle car to a labour camp in the Ural Mountains for thirteen months. Gershon, the youngest brother, was a woodcutter in the forests. Lyche picked fruit in the local orchards. If you were ever late to work, you were jailed. In springtime, the mosquitos were like a plague.

After thirteen months, the Nazis convinced the Soviets to free the slave labourers. Because the Burstyn family did not have Soviet identification papers, they were still considered refugees and were sent by train to the Asiatic part of Russia. My mother, like others, was close to starving on the month-long journey, and developed frostbite. Along the way they stopped in Stadloff, and Yosel and my grandfather found a restaurant and were given bread and a big pot of *kasha*, which alleviated some of the hunger. When they reached Tashkent, they were not granted permission to stay, so they continued to Kyrgyzstan, and lived in Jalalabad from 1942 until liberation, living next door to an Uzbek family.

My mother and her brother Gershon were recruited to work in the nearby fields after their Uzbek neighbour recommended them. My mother was given a horse and taught to record the number of sheaves of wheat each person produced. Her brother worked in the cotton fields and also made shoes, selling them on the black market. Her other brothers worked as well. My mother told us, 'We were considered rich because of we had what to eat. This made it possible for my mother to run a soup-kitchen for sick and poor people.'

After liberation, Jews in Jalalabad were sent back to Poland, to Szczecin, a border town, where they again experienced anti-Semitism. Szczecin was best known for its information centre, where Jews looked for relatives and left their names for others to find them.

My parents remember catching a glimpse of each other there, but neither of them did anything about that moment of attraction. The Jewish organization *Bricha* helped Jews cross the border into Germany, where they were sent to Goldkop, a displaced persons camp about 12 miles from Kassel.

One day my *abba* (dad), Simcha Fogelman, was riding on a bus with his comrade, and, in a chance encounter, recognised the young girl he had seen in Szceczin. She was sitting on the bus with her brother Gershon, and so he went over and asked if she knew where they could find lodgings. She suggested that they come to Goldkop, which had a few apartment houses. Simcha was an attractive, unassuming man who served in the Polish army before Second World War, then joined the Belorussian partisans. At the end of the war, he served in the military police of the Red Army. My mother, much younger than he, found him quite attractive but kept it to herself.

One of five children, Simcha Fogelman, born in 1913, came from a Jewish religious family from Dokshitz. His father, Berel, immigrated to the United States before Simcha was born in 1907 and remained there until 1912. When he sent a picture to his wife, Wichna, her father, a rabbi, said, 'You can't be Jewish (i.e. religious) in America,' and forbade his daughter to join her husband. Berel returned to Poland and had two more children. A bout of pneumonia killed him in 1924.

My grandmother, a meek woman, was left to care for five children. She could not manage her husband's general store, so she supported herself and children with simple sewing tasks. My dad was sent to Vilna, where other family members could take care of him. At eleven years old, he started working in a relative's bakery and sent his earnings home. He also attended the Slobodka Yeshiva. When the rabbi there noticed Simcha had 'communist' books underneath his Talmud, it became clear he was not destined to become a rabbi.

Simcha's oldest sister immigrated to Palestine in 1930 and paved the way for the others to follow in 1935. My father, who was drafted into the Polish army, could not leave with them. He served until 1 September 1939. The Stalin–Hitler pact of 23 August 1939 divided the area, and the eastern part of Poland was occupied by the Russians while Germany controlled the west. The Bug River was the border between them. The army disbanded and Simcha returned to Vilna, only to face Lithuanian pogroms against the Jews. He fled to a relative's home in Illya, a small town near Vilna, which had a vibrant Jewish life. For the next two years Simcha lived and worked as a baker under the Russian occupation. It ended when Nazi tanks rolled into town on 21 June 1941.

Illya was enveloped in fear and terror as Jews were stripped of all civil rights. Forced to wear the yellow star on their outer clothing, Jews were not allowed to walk on sidewalks or use public transportation. They could not leave Illya and were forbidden to own any businesses or have valuable possessions. Simcha built a wall and dug holes under his house to hide his most valued items, which, when he went back for them, were ruined.

Soon Nazi Gestapo, SS and Belorussian auxiliary police began picking up Jews from their homes, never to be heard from again.

Early on *Purim* morning, March 1942, Simcha had an eerie feeling. He rushed through the streets to the bakery where he worked and watched Jewish men, women and children being dragged out of their houses and brought to the town square. They were told to stand at attention and could not move – not even their heads. They stood for hours until the Nazis deemed that they had enough victims. Simcha climbed into the bakery attic and his co-worker removed the ladder and locked him in. Through cracks in the planks, Simcha watched the Gestapo order all the Jews to undress and dig a huge hole, a mass grave for 1,500. The Jews were then shot and dumped in the grave. The Belorussian Auxiliary Police then sprayed gasoline over the bodies and set them on fire, including those who were still alive.

Simcha was traumatised as he watched his aunts, uncles, cousins and friends killed. That night he left the attic and fled the town. After a few hours he came across some people walking along the roads. They were workers spared by the Nazis for their skills – a shoemaker, a tailor and a druggist. He learned that those who survived the mass murder were incarcerated in the ghetto and fed only 300 grams of bread a day, a starvation diet. In the meantime, the police ransacked Jewish homes looking for loot. They even ripped up walls, floors and ceilings in their hunt for valuables.

In May 1942, in the night, the Gestapo and their collaborators surrounded the ghetto and began shooting Jews. When Simcha saw what was happening, he escaped to a cellar with his friend, Salimyanski, and remained out of sight. At 2 a.m., he and Salimyanski resolved to escape. They crawled out of the ghetto on their bellies. The guards saw them and shot at them continuously as they ran between houses until they finally reached the woods. For the next six months they slept in the fields, rain or shine, on hay or mud. Once a week they knocked on the door of a farmhouse to beg for food. No one let them in. The fugitives were afraid to light a fire for warmth lest they be caught by informants or Nazi collaborators.

Simcha and his comrade heard Belorussian partisans were in the area and realised the only solution for them was to join the group. When they found a small band of partisans and asked to join them, they were suspected of being spies and were asked to give up their coats and boots for a day. They never got them back.

In addition to not wanting Jews in their ranks, the partisans wanted fighters who came with their own ammunition. Because of his training in the Polish army, Simcha knew how to repair machine guns blindfolded, but that was not enough for the Russians. They told him to set up his own Jewish resistance group. The Belorussian partisans challenged my father: 'Did you come to hide under our shoulders? Did you expect us to fight for you? Why do you go like sheep?'

After a few frustrating weeks, Salimyanski approached a family acquaintance, Ivan Safanov, who knew a resistance fighter named Kabilkin. This personal contact and Simcha's ability with firearms finally got Simcha and Salimyanski into the Belorussian partisans. Simcha was eager to take revenge on the Nazis who killed so many innocent Jews. He declared he was willing to sacrifice his life to fight the murderers.

Simcha's first assignment was to blow up a German train packed with soldiers, food and ammunition bound for the Eastern Front between the villages of Ostenovitch and Balachi near Kuranitz, not far from Vilna. The plan took two days to organise. They chose to attack the midnight train, so that they could escape under cover of darkness. Simcha set wires and mines on the train rails, and when the train came closer, he set off the mines. Without sophisticated equipment, he had to pull the detonator and run for his life. The train blew up with everything in it, and Simcha was awarded a Red Star for his heroic actions.

His next mission was to blow up the Nazi police station in Maydel, a town near Vilna. Spies were sent to scout the area. A silenced gun was used to shoot the guard at the entrance, and then twenty more Nazi guards were killed. This was the first time Simcha fought the Nazis face to face. Some partisans remained outside to act as lookouts and covered those who entered the building. Inside, the partisans took ammunition for their men. After the mission, Simcha and the partisans went to the ghetto in Maydel and helped about a hundred Jews escape.

Though freed from their ghetto prison, these Jews now faced another problem. It was impossible to find them shelter. They had to create their own makeshift boltholes in the woods. They sat around fires to keep warm and were wreathed in smoke. To get them food, Simcha knocked on doors and threatened villagers with his gun, demanding provisions. Simcha gave the escapees meat, bread and potatoes that he transported in his small wagon. When he returned to the base, one of the partisans reported to the base leader that Simcha was engaged in illegal activity. My father was immediately arrested and placed under surveillance. A trial was arranged. If he was found guilty, he would be shot. Luckily, a Jewish Russian commissar from Moscow was parachuted into the area and participated in the trial. He suggested looking at Simcha's record, which was exemplary. He also emphasised that killing a valuable member of the group would make no sense, since they were a small group to begin with and needed all able-bodied men. Simcha was found innocent and continued to fight in the resistance.

The next assignment was a surprise attack on the Nazis near Katyn. They and their Ukrainian collaborators were scheduled to cross a critical intersection. The partisans hid until the enemy entered the intersection and ambushed them. They killed a Nazi major along with five soldiers. The rest escaped. Simcha and his comrades ran down the hill to retrieve the ammunition they left behind. Then they ran to the next village to rest. They knocked on doors to get food, but none was to be had. That night, through a window, Simcha saw Nazis soldiers surrounding the houses and warned everyone to start running back to the forest. It was too late.

Forty out of sixty partisans were shot.

The lieutenant was blamed for their deaths because he did not immediately order the men to return to the base. A Jewish partisan was also blamed because he was the first to enter the village. The group was then ordered to return to the village to bury the dead, but it seemed to have disappeared. A ten-year-old boy told them the Nazis had rounded up everyone in the village, poured benzine on them and incinerated them. In Katyn, site of the killings, a statue of a father holding his son stands as a memorial for those who died.

It was 1943 and the Nazis were intent on finding and killing partisans. They sent some 80,000 soldiers to find and eliminate them. By that time, the Russians were attacking the Nazis from the east. By June 1944, Simcha's partisan troops met up with the Red Army near Minsk and were formally recruited. Simcha was assigned as a security guard for a general. Immediately following Liberation, the Red Army sent him to Berlin as a translator. There he bought goods on the black market and, after he was ordered back to the 'Motherland', used them to bribe a guard who looked the other way when he escaped to Poland.

Simcha managed to get to Vilna. From there he went to Lodz, where he connected with Abrasha, a fellow baker and friend from the old days, and together they continued towards Germany, stopping in Szczecin, where he had his first glimpse of his future wife. He and Abrasha made it to Berlin, and from there they went to Munich by bus, passing through Goldkopf before they finally arrived in Kassel.

It was during that bus trip that my *abba* (dad) and *ima* (mum) connected, and she suggested they come to Goldkopf. My mother was one of the fortunate ones who had a mother, father, siblings and extended family who had survived the war, and so was in generally good spirits as she and her siblings sought ways to support them.

The men joined the Burstyn family in Goldkof, and one morning, during breakfast, one of them suggested that Simcha and Abrasha go into the 'peddling' business with them. My mum and Gershon, both of blessed memory, are not around for me to ask whose idea that was. If I were to guess, I would say it was my mother, who was the more assertive and business-oriented of the two, and she wanted to create a connection to Simcha, who was experienced in buying goods.

When my mother heard how he used goods he bought in Berlin to buy his freedom on the German border, she had an idea. Always enterprising, her favourite question was, '*Vus koyfstu und vus farkoyfstu?*' (What are you buying and what are you selling?) Long before they were married, Simcha and Lyche were spending time together, getting to know each other as they took the train to Munich to buy and sell goods like cigarettes, stockings, coffee and, eventually, bakery machinery.

Word got around that pregnant refugees and the elderly would have priority for housing at the D.P. camp in Kassel. My mother, who was not yet engaged or married to my father, stuffed a pillow under her skirt to make herself look pregnant and stood in line with my father to get a house for her family to share with Simcha and Abrasha. She was granted a terraced house on 52 Strasse Mark in Kassel. The kitchen and living room were on the first floor. The second floor had a few bedrooms, and the third floor was the attic where Simcha and Abrasha lived. My grandfather started going back to synagogue regularly and took Simcha along. Although Simcha was very cynical about prayer and about God, he was somewhat knowledgeable about Jewish text and he knew his way around the *Siddur*, the Jewish prayer book.

Simcha was thrilled to be part of a family with a father figure. He and Abrasha got along with everyone in the family, and Simcha truly appreciated having a father figure in Mordechai Burstyn, and really loved him. One day my grandfather said to Simcha, 'I like how you *daven* (pray); why don't you marry my daughter?' Simcha was thirteen years older than Lyche, and was very attracted to her, because she was beautiful inside and out. But he was afraid to engage with her romantically. She was very mature for her age – but she had grown up with three brothers, and never had a romantic relationship, and so her love for him was sisterly. She did not know how to be romantically involved.

The wedding took place in April 1947 in Kassel and was attended by the remnants of the family. My mother wore a flowered dress because buying or making a wedding gown was out of the question. My father had not seen his family since 1935. During the war they assumed he was dead, and they were ecstatic to get the first postcard telling them he was alive.

There was no question that my parents would immigrate to Israel so that my father could reunite with his family. For most Holocaust survivors, Germany was a way station to Israel or America. My grandparents, my aunt and uncle, and my parents opted for Israel. My mother's younger and older brothers chose New York.

The Israeli War of Independence in 1947–49 was a tragic moment for my father's family. Aryeh, his younger brother, was planning to leave his kibbutz to help my father settle in Israel but was killed in the battle for Latrun, a strategic high point in the Ayalon Valley on the way to Jerusalem. I was born in 1949 and given the Hebrew name of Chaviva in his memory. When we arrived in Israel, a year after Aryeh's death, the family was still in mourning.

Arriving in Israel, then in the throes of economic crisis, we were fortunate to have family already settled there who took us into their homes, sparing us the *Ma'abarot*, the refugee camps and tent cities with few services. First, we stayed with Malka and Yehoshua Shiffman, my paternal aunt and uncle. Then we moved in with Bella and Yaacov Tiberg, *abba*'s other sister and brother-in-law. We lived with the Tibergs for many months. There is a Danish saying that when the heart is big, the house is big. The family of three had one room, and we were three in the other room, sharing a kitchen and living room. Yaacov was an administrator at *T'nuva*, the country-wide dairy cooperative. His initiative and know-how enabled us to buy a small house with some land for trees, a garden and a chicken coop.

My father worked in a bakery and my mother managed the house, the chicken coop, and the farming. My mother was pregnant with my sister when her mother died. My sister is named after her maternal grandmother, Gila, a Hebrew version of Freyda – which means happiness. My grandfather died six months later. My *abba* worked nights and slept during the day. I don't remember his night terrors, which woke him up for years. My mother felt she did not suffer as much as he did and was always there for him. When people asked how *she* survived, she often told *his* story. My mother had to learn a new language for the sixth or seventh time but did not complain much. Her biggest disappointment was that she was not gainfully employed. After all, in her teens she supervised workers in the cotton fields in Jalalabad, and in Germany she was a businesswoman.

In 1956 my mother's brother, Gershon, came to Israel to find a bride. In America, he was 'George' and learned women wanted college graduates for husbands. When he went to a dance, he was asked, 'What university did you attend?' George would reply, 'The University of Siberia.'

'What did you major in?'

'Trees.'

Those lines didn't bring him any closer to the altar.

In Israel he was introduced to a woman who as a child lived in his hometown, Wyshkow. Her parents were members of the same synagogue as the Burstyns. George and Rivkah (Ruth) married within the year.

When George saw how his sister was living in a one-room house in a small town in Israel, he was horrified and insisted that she and her family come to America. As a young child, I was not privy to any discussions among my parents about leaving Israel. My father had been reunited with his family, and the thought of leaving them again, particularly his elderly mother, must have been a very painful decision. *Abba* changed his mind about staying in Israel when he discovered his co-workers stealing funds from the bakery cooperative. My father was an honest man, hard-working, and liked by everyone. His favourite saying from the Hebrew Bible was, 'A good name is better than good oil.' So, he decided to leave.

Our plans to leave Israel were considered top secret. I was taking private English lessons, and I had to cover my books with Hebrew newspapers. That was a heavy burden for a ten-year-old. My sister was only seven, and my parents assumed that she could not be trusted to keep a secret. Although our birthdays are far apart, my parents organised a joint birthday party for my sister and me. My father baked and decorated cupcakes for friends in the neighbourhood and for family. It was a farewell party, but no one knew that. It was agonising for my father to tell his sisters that we were leaving Israel. We went to visit my grandmother for the last time in a nursing home without saying goodbye.

I was led to believe that we would be back in Israel after two years. Our journey to New York on a Zim Line ship lasted two weeks. We enjoyed being in the lap of luxury, with sumptuous meals served on white tablecloths. We were surrounded by many other families headed for the *Goldene Medina*, the Golden Land. I, who cannot hold a tune in a bucket, led a group of children in a choir performance on the final night on board. After they were sent to bed, there was a dance party for the adults, when a storm hit, and the rough waves rocked the boat so badly the tables in the dining room tipped over. My parents ran to our cabin to prevent us from falling out of our beds. We learned later that that same night a Nazi ship in the vicinity sank. The next day, the weather was clear, and we passed the Statue of Liberty – a magical moment – and we were greeted with joy on the docks in Manhattan by my mother's relatives.

My aunt and uncle, who then lived in Brownsville, took us in for a few weeks. Within a day or two, my father was working for the baker who sponsored him. I was fascinated to see my male Fogelman cousins binge-watch cowboys and Indians on TV and sporadically watch game shows. We visited relatives I never knew I had; the most significant was my father's aunt Gitta. My grandfather brought her to America in 1907. Her two children, Alfred and Pearl Kazin, were well on their way to becoming literary stars in the New York Jewish intellectual crowd. My father's other Fogelman cousins were Sam, the lawyer, and Jay, the dentist, who helped us out with their professional expertise.

After a few weeks, my father realised he did not like the working conditions in the bakery and visited a friend who owned a bakery in the Bronx. The Jews were leaving Brownsville for better neighbourhoods, and we moved to Borough Park, in Brooklyn. Aunt Gitta would call my dad every day and was worried because he was commuting for too many hours a day. She bemoaned the fact that we had come to America at such a bad economic time. She had been diagnosed with cancer and could not help us in the way she had hoped she could. When we were in Israel, she sent us packages of goodies, which, in those tough years, were a godsend – chocolate, canned goods, sugar, and fabric for clothing. We appreciated her love and care and understood her dilemma completely.

My mother had to learn a new language yet again. She was an outgoing and friendly soul and got to know other Holocaust survivors in the neighbourhood. As it turned out, Polaroid, the camera company, had a factory in Borough Park that manufactured leather cases for their cameras. My mother was introduced to the manager, and she started working there without knowing a word of English. This was not the life she dreamed of in America and at times she regretted the move. No longer a supervisor or businesswoman, she was a worker in a factory, doing what amounted to piecework for a corporation. Nonetheless, having two salaries, albeit meagre ones, enabled my parents to start saving money.

A few years later, my parents were ready to invest money in a business. My father was thinking about buying into a bakery, and almost did so. At the same time, an opportunity from my mother's side of the family presented itself, to go into the knitting business. One day my mother came home and announced that they owned a knitting mill. My dad learned a new trade – as a mechanic on knitting machines – and my mother was now in her element, supervising the production of women's and children's sweaters. In addition to working with jobbers who provided the yarn for knitting sweaters for department stores, my parents started selling sweaters to merchants on the Lower East Side. Together they built a successful business.

As the knitting business declined in the United States in the 1980s, my parents sold their company, Guf Knitting Mills. My mother was eager for me to help them start a business of buying, maybe manufacturing, and selling knitwear from China. But I was entrenched in my graduate studies in social and personality psychology and in filmmaking. I was not about to give up my dreams, and my mother understood because she wouldn't give up her dreams either.

So, my parents came full circle to that day on the bus in Germany, to their chance encounter, which began with 'Vus koyfstu? Vus farkoyfstu?' Every day they would get into my father's car (he drove, my mother never learned how) and go to merchants on the Lower East Side, in Midtown and in the greater New York area to buy and sell knitwear. When they had large orders, Gershon provided the merchandise from his factory and whenever my mother visited his factory, she inspected the merchandise to assess the quality of the workmanship.

For almost twenty years, my parents spent every day working together. My father, who was more formally educated than my mother, often explained politics and history to her. She made sure we were well fed and watered and devotedly took care of him and of Gila and me. She never wanted to relive the hunger she felt during the war and always worried that we didn't eat enough.

Unlike many of their friends, when they retired, my parents were not card-playing types. They enjoyed dancing at parties, taking cruises, travelling to Israel and participating in events organised by Jewish organisations that support Israel. My father learned to cook and helped my mother prepare speciality dishes for the Sabbath and holidays. At other times he read books, newspapers and magazines or watched the news. He listened to Yiddish radio ('WEVD, the station that speaks your language') and did handyman repair jobs around the house. He would visit a blind neighbour and read to him. In later years, my parents spent more time in Florida. My dad had Holocaust-survivor friends with whom he would talk daily, and they would reminisce about the war years.

In Florida, every Saturday, my mom and dad would go to the synagogue in Aventura to listen to the cantor sing. Despite all my father's cynicism about God and ritual, he felt comfortable in a synagogue and enjoyed a good *dvar Torah*, a learned discourse. My grandfather had chosen well for my mother. She had a loving husband who cared deeply for her, whom she had loved at first sight as a brother but grew to love as his wife. Shortly before he was killed in 1998 by a speeding van in Sheepshead Bay, he bought my mother a diamond ring as a symbol of appreciation for her love and devotion. My mum put the ring in the safe because she was never able to wear it. She never stopped loving my father and transferred that undying love to her children and grandchild for the rest of her life. The ring her husband gave her will adorn the finger of her grandchild's beloved when the time comes.

This story was written by Dr Eva Fogelman in conjunction with Mindelle Pierce and Jeanette Friedman.

10

PESKA AND
WOLVIE FRIEDMAN

It was a Passover in the early 1970s, I do not remember the year, when I asked my mum how she met my dad. She was making gefilte fish in the tiny attic Passover kitchen. We were talking about her being one of the hostages on the Kastner transport, a trainload of 1,684 Jews traded for goods and money, along with another 18,000 Jews kept on ice in a camp in Austria instead of being sent to Auschwitz. This is the story she told me. Some of the blanks were filled in by extended family members and friends who survived the war, as well as stories and details she told in her book, *Going Forward*, which I published for her in English and in Yiddish.

During the Holocaust, Peska Rabinowicz was able to escape the Warsaw Ghetto and was smuggled to Munkacs, now in Ukraine. On 30 June 1943, she boarded the Kastner transport that left Budapest for Mandate Palestine via Bergen-Belsen. This was only possible because Wolvie Friedman, and her brother, Rabbi Baruch Yehoshua Yerachmiel Rabinowicz, arranged it all. At the time her brother was the new Admor of Munkacs, successor to the Minchas Elazar, R' Chaim Lazar Spira, his father-in-law, leader of the Munkacser Hasidim, in what was, for the moment, Hungary.

Wolvie's father owned the kosher flour mill in nearby Strabychovo, and was a *gvir*, a big shot, who sat at the right hand of the Minchas Elazar. That's how Wolvie and R' Baruch met and became close friends.

Wolvie, a brilliant scholar and a descendant of an impressive lineage – his grandfather was the Dombrader Rov – was also quite modern. When in yeshiva in Frankfurt, he went to the opera with the Rosh Yeshiva (head of the school) and they would turn the chairs in their box with their backs to the stage because of *kol isha* – the prohibition against watching a woman sing. He received his ordination from the yeshiva in Mir, a place where the students took pride in their Talmudical studies, as well as their personal appearance. They were considered the Dapper Dans of the yeshiva world. He was what they considered in those days 'modern', and in these days 'Yeshivishe'. He loved Yiddish theatre, the opera and the good life. And, as modern as he was, he still was the Admor's best friend – the rabbi's link to the world beyond Hasidism.

Despite his ordination, Wolvie, who spoke seven languages, became a travelling salesman for a candy company. He was a promoter of Agudath Israel, an umbrella organisation of Orthodox Jews, in its formerly inclusive iteration. As the noose tightened around the Jews in Europe before the war, according to the late Rabbi Cheskel Besser, Wolvie was very useful because he smuggled money and information between Jewish communities across central and eastern Europe. He was an ordained, non-practising rabbi who travelled from city to city on his motorcycle.

Peska, the youngest of eleven siblings in a combined family (both parents were married previously), was a true Hasidic princess and descendant of a dynasty that went back to the Grand Rabbi J. J. Rabinowicz, The Holy Jew (1766–1813), and King David way before him. She was very Orthodox and was attending the first Jewish school for girls, Beis Yaakov, on the banks of the river in Krakow.

Peska was born in Siedlce, where her father, R' Nosson David Rabinowicz, the Parcever Rebbe, had his court. After he died from heart failure in 1930 when Peska was barely ten years old, her mother moved the family to Warsaw and established what today would be considered a bed-and-breakfast and catering hall on Gesia Street in Warsaw. Because her siblings had friends everywhere, many of them stayed at the B&B when they came through Warsaw, as did many prominent Orthodox Jews and rabbinic leaders. Most of Peska's siblings had married prominent rabbis and leaders of their own Hasidic sects, or daughters of such distinguished persons. Peska was considered quite a catch. She had what they called *yichus* (distinguished family history), and the matchmakers had her at the top of their lists as highly desirable marriage material, even though money was an issue.

On one of Peska's school breaks, the dark-haired, attractive seventeen-year-old was in the kitchen talking to her mother, Yuta, when a well-dressed twenty-year-old in a cashmere coat with a Persian lamb collar walked in. Peska noticed every detail, from the spotlessness of his coat and hat, to the wire-rimmed eyeglasses, and the jaunty tilt of his hat. In her book, she describes him as 'outgoing, self-sufficient ... [he] had already travelled through many yeshivas ... to gain an eclectic learning background'.

His mother died young, in the influenza epidemic of 1918, and her sister, his stepmother Leah, was but a child herself. Wolvie and his three brothers grew up very independent and secure. He was from Munkacs, like Peska's mum, who considered him a 'prized visitor'. They spent hours talking in the kitchen whenever he was in town.

Break over, Peska headed back to Beis Yaakov in Krakow, and was really surprised to be called down to the office a few weeks later and told that a gentleman had come to call for her, and that it was not appropriate. It was Wolvie bearing a gift of chocolate-covered almonds, her favourite treat, ostensibly sent by her mum. Of course, the headmaster would not allow her to accept the package. Wolvie asked her for dates a few times. She said no. Then he asked R' Baruch for her hand in marriage, and R' Baruch said no. That was because Wolvie was considered too modern to be his little sister's husband.

Then came the Nazi invasion of Poland in September 1939, and the girls in Krakow were sent back to their homes. Peska returned to Warsaw and was confined to the ghetto, established in late 1940. From the start, her mother wanted her to escape, but she refused to leave her mum alone in the ghetto. Peska describes everything in her book, *Going Forward*.

Finally, on a cold spring day in 1941, she followed the directions she had gotten from R' Baruch and Wolvie and was smuggled out of the ghetto in the trunk of a vehicle driven by a Swiss citizen, a Mr Domb. He dropped her off on the first stop of a journey filled with hair-raising and faith-inducing adventures on her way to Slovakia. After her harrowing undercover journey, she stayed with a family whose matriarch told her the Nazis were punishing the Jews because girls like Peska wore nail polish.

In dismay, Peska went out into the yard to brush dried mud off her coat, looked up and saw Wolvie coming up the path.

> It was fantastic, dreamlike, that the very first person I should meet on the free soil of Slovakia was one of the oldest and most frequent faces from our table in Warsaw! A breath of relief rushed through me. If familiar people were alive in the world, perhaps there was still hope. After mountains and fields, the heavy tramping of Nazi boots, the muddy darkness of endless and nameless villages, after being so long a stranger in strange places, I allowed myself to think that perhaps things would turn out all right.

They talked for a bit, and she learned R' Baruch sent him to bring her to Munkacs, where Wolvie was living. When he heard Peska was censured for wearing nail polish, he moved her over to his aunt's house, where she was treated with kindness and generosity. Plans went awry when she missed her train and Wolvie couldn't find her on it as it headed to Budapest. The next day, she caught the first train, and Wolvie met her at the station in Budapest. She had not expected to see him. 'For the second time in two days, I was surprised to see a familiar face where I least expected it, somehow providing me with an anchor in a world that had lost its balance. And for the second time in two days, I regained my footing.'

Of course, he proposed marriage to her three more times, once through a surrogate, his cousin, who took her for a ride in a surrey with a fringe on top. This time, she turned him down not because she didn't want to marry him but because of the war, and because she knew what the Nazis did to Jews. Until the war was over, she refused to marry anyone.

She was also warned not to talk about the realities of what was happening in Nazi-occupied Poland. By then, Peska's siblings and in-laws had been separated or taken to Treblinka, the death camp. Her oldest sister had moved to Palestine after marrying in the early 1930s, as had her brother Lazar. One brother, Leibel, crossed the Bug River into Russian territory and disappeared. A half-brother and his family survived in Romania. One brother who escaped from Treblinka and joined Oneg Shabbes, the Warsaw ghetto fighters, died on the first night of the uprising. She didn't learn that until 1947, when she read it in Hillel Seidman's *Warsaw Diary*. Once in Munkacs, Peska lived with R' Baruch and his family for a year, where she helped her sister-in-law, Frimele, with her little children. Frimele suffered from tuberculosis.

In the meantime, Wolvie's father, convinced that it would not happen in Hungary, told Wolvie he needed to get married and could not moon over Peska forever. Wolvie moved on and married a girl from Szeles, and they had a son. At the same time, Peska was getting offers and turning them down, one after another, though she was 'aging' out of the market.

At R' Baruch's request, Wolvie continued to help Peska. He got her false Hungarian papers in the name of Rochel Landau. When the gendarmes came to deport the family to the border at Kamenetz-Podolsk, and they had taken R' Baruch and his oldest son, Wolvie was the one who found her. It was after the raid, and she was huddled in a locked closet in her brother's house with two of her infant nephews. Because Frimele was so ill, the gendarmes let her stay behind until she had to be moved to the hospital. Peska, who was at her side, realised that she was being hunted and got up to leave. As she ran from the hospital, the gendarmes were walking in to look for her.

Peska hid in a friend's bunker. After a week, fed up with being trapped and learning that her mother had died of typhus in the ghetto, she gave up. Believing she had no recourse, she sneaked out to turn herself in. As she left the house, Wolvie showed up to check on her, as he had promised R' Baruch he would. He asked where she was going, and when she told him, he asked her if she was crazy. She stood there, not knowing what to do, until he hailed a horse and buggy. He put her inside and drove around Munkacs for hours talking about everything and nothing, just to distract her. Then he told the driver to go back to her hiding place and informed her she wasn't going anywhere; she was to stay in hiding.

Peska, too tired to argue, gave in, and whenever the gendarmes came looking she hid in the bunker under the floor. Within months, R' Baruch and his son were rescued, and it was decided that the family would move to Budapest, where R' Baruch had a following, and where it was safer.

Once in a while, Wolvie would show up in Budapest at Stern's or Nissel's restaurants, famous hangouts for refugees, to make sure Peska was alright. His wife and son were with her parents in Szeles in March 1944, and he was planning to stay in Budapest until he heard from her. He figured she would come to Budapest and they would be safer in the city. Peska reminded him of what had happened in Warsaw and told him it was going to happen now, too. She told him, 'You'll see. You have no idea what's going to happen tomorrow, and you should never have any reason to question your conscience about whether you did the right thing or not. You should be with them.' Here she was, talking to the person she considered her guardian angel for so many months, telling *him* what to do. He asked if he should go back. She said yes. And he did.

Years later he told Peska he was glad he listened because he was with them when they were deported to Auschwitz. While he was on his voyage through the inferno, Peska was supposedly on her way to freedom in Mandate Palestine.

In Budapest, R' Baruch wanted to get the family to Eretz Yisrael (Mandate Palestine), but his mother-in-law did not want him to go. One day, Wolvie showed up in Budapest with a message for Peska. The *rebbitzen*, wife of the rebbi, wanted Peska to convince R' Baruch not to leave. Peska told Wolvie she would do everything she could to ensure they left, because she saw what was coming, and that she was going with them. When the Palestine certificates from her sister in Tel Aviv arrived, Peska's certificate was not among them. Not waiting, her brother's family left and Peska was on her own in Budapest. Before leaving, R' Baruch put her in the care of Freudiger and Stern, leaders of the Jewish community, and paid for her passage on the Kastner transport.

When the Nazis occupied Hungary in March 1944, Wolvie's son was eighteen months old. His cousin Fred was hiding as a Gentile and was able to join the Gestapo, where he would gather information about planned deportations and warn potential Nazi victims of the danger. As a Gestapo agent, he could also escort families to safety. Fred warned Wolvie to bring his family to Budapest immediately because there was going to be an *aktion* in Munkacs. Wolvie didn't listen, and by mid-May, the three of them were deported to Auschwitz, where his wife and son were murdered.

On Friday 30 June 1944, Peska boarded the Kastner train, a strange journey that ended in Bergen-Belsen, where some hostages were released after three months, and the rest were released in Switzerland in December 1944.

By that time, Wolvie had gone through Auschwitz and a slew of other camps, including Gross-Rosen, landing in Bergen-Belsen – a filthy, disease-infested hell hole where, he later said, you couldn't put your foot down without stepping on a corpse. But he was alive.

Peska found out about him after she was released in Switzerland. She had introduced her best friend to a Mr Walter, who turned out to be Wolvie's cousin, and the couple married. That's when Peska began to think about her own chances for marriage. By then she was twenty-four and wondering why none of the proposed matches were interesting to her.

So she thought it through – and realised she loved Wolvie Friedman, even though she had turned him down more than once. She thought about how he made her feel safe, and how he turned up in moments of crisis, how it felt natural somehow, that he was her protector. He knew her mother, her family, but she wasn't even sure if he was alive, or whether his wife and son were still alive. That made it off-limits to even think about him, let alone fantasise about a future with him in it.

She was in Switzerland, waiting for her visa to Palestine where she would be reunited with her family, when she met a young man who very much wanted to marry her. Instead of beating around the bush, she told him she had a 'thing' for Wolvie but didn't know if he was alive and what his status was. It turned out the young man had once gone to yeshiva with Wolvie, and though he was disappointed when Peska said no, he decided to find out what happened to his old schoolmate.

Then the almost impossible happened. Peska was on the train, heading for the boat in Italy that would take her to Palestine, when the conductor called out her name. Fearful, she was too terrified to respond. He left, came back, and called for her again. One of her fellow passengers pointed her out. The conductor handed her a telegram from the young man she had rejected. It said Wolvie was alive and running a displaced persons camp in Bregenz, Austria. But she wasn't staying in Europe. She was going to fulfil her dream of going to Eretz Yisrael, to her family.

Once in Tel Aviv, Peska discovered that R' Baruch's wife had died, and that her oldest sister, Devorah, was doing her best, but the children had been farmed out. Peska got the family back together again, and the children began to thrive. By then there were four boys and one little girl. Once the home was stabilised, people began focusing on getting Peska married off. But no one clicked.

At one point, Peska met Chaim Yerucham, Wolvie's first cousin, who told her that he had survived, but his wife and son did not. Every time they would run into each other, he would mention Wolvie, and though she knew he was single, she still felt uncomfortable thinking about him. Yet, he always lingered in her mind. She finally confronted Chaim Yerucham and asked him why he always brought Wolvie into the conversation. 'It's not my business to think about him,' she told him.

'You're wrong. You *should* think about him,' he would answer.

When she said she didn't know anything about him any more, even his address, Chaim Yerucham got the information and gave her the address of the DP camp Wolvie had set up in Bregenz. Still, she held off, deeming it inappropriate.

A few weeks later, when she and Devorah, who knew English, were taking R' Baruch's children for a walk, she dragged them to the post office, because she decided to send Wolvie a telegram, and her sister had to write it. Devorah looked at her as if she had lost her mind, but she sent the telegram to Bregenz. It read: 'Glad to hear you are alive. Perhaps our paths will cross. Peska.' She sent it because she felt she had nothing to lose, and trusted God to figure out if it would work. In the meantime, Devorah was reading her the riot act, telling her that she no longer knew Wolvie. But Peska knew that none of the matches presented were for her. Wolvie's wife had died in 1944, two years earlier, and if something positive could come of it, so much the better. Devorah told her again she was crazy, and Peska said that maybe she *was* crazy, but the deed was done. There was nothing to do but wait. And wait she did. Just when she was about to give up hope of ever hearing from him, a carefully worded letter arrived from Wolvie.

He wrote he was no longer the carefree yeshiva boy he once was, and was no longer a free man in the ordinary sense. Since he had lost his wife and child, it made him a second-rate catch, and he did not want to prevent Peska from getting a better one. He ended by saying that years had gone by 'and the mountains had grown tall between us'. He wondered if they would still understand each other and get along. She thought his cautious response showed some 'barely repressed interest' (her words), writing back that they should not make decisions until they met face to face, and that she could arrange to have R' Baruch get him a visa to Mandate Palestine.

That letter was the first of many exchanged between the two of them. She learned that he was very involved with the *Agudah*; and he was about to leave for a relief conference in the States. He was working with a number of DP camps, and said it would be easier for her to come back to Europe. He wrote that when he came back from New York, he would meet her in Paris. It had been six months since she had sent him that first telegram, when her sister had told her she was 'nuts'. Now Devorah told her to follow her heart. R' Baruch, who relied on her so heavily, was more reluctant to see her go, but saw she had her heart set on his friend, so he hired a nanny (whom he later married) and held his peace.

Wolvie's relatives in Eretz Yisrael were her brother's Hasidim. His stepmother lived there too, and gave Peska her blessing, asking her to be a good wife to him. His uncle, a kind man who lost his wife and seven children to Hitler, was a source of strength to Peska and many others. He, too, gave her his blessing, as she boarded a ship to Cherbourg, heading toward Paris and an unknown future.

By the time Peska got to France, the Bregenz camp was dissolved. Paris was a major transfer point for survivors who were hoping to go either to Israel or to America, and Wolvie and his relief team set up another DP camp in a neglected old estate, Chateau des Boulayes, in Tournan, a small town outside of Paris.

Eventually Wolvie brought most of the refugees to Paris, where they waited for their visas to other countries. It was about that time that he and Peska began their correspondence. And then, in the course of his work, he found her brother, Leibel, who had been missing for more than five years and had been given up for dead. Wolvie's letter said Liebel had been in a Soviet prison all that time and had made his way back to Poland. He left Poland with the help of the Jewish Rescue Committee, and went to Prague, where Wolvie found him. Peska never knew the full extent of Wolvie's rescue activities – very few did – though she realised he was very well connected and had asked his Viennese friend Dr Kolmar to arrange for Liebel to come to Paris.

Peska's ship was supposed to dock in Cherbourg on the eve of *Rosh Hashanah*, 1946, one of the holiest days of the year. She was supposed to arrive long before sunset, but her ship was delayed. Wolvie waited as long as he could, and then headed back to his rooming house to get ready to lead the local congregation in prayer that night and the following day. When the ship docked the following morning, there was no one there to greet Peska and she almost panicked. All Peska had was a scrap of paper with Wolvie's address on it. She couldn't speak the language, and she couldn't shlep her luggage with her, so she left it on board with the purser and tried to find Wolvie by showing everyone she met that scrap of paper, basically finding the place by accident. Later that day, her belongings were brought to her, intact.

She sat in the garden of the little house and waited for Wolvie, asking God to forgive her for not praying in a synagogue on such a holy day, and using her own words to ask for a bright future. Around four o'clock in the afternoon, she heard voices in the hallway, asking if she had shown up. She opened the door, and there they stood, both of them: Wolvie and Leibel. Peska wrote:

All of a sudden, after so many years of distance and toil and sorrow, here was Wolvie, the same familiar face, greeting me once again at a time when I was alone and in strange surroundings, re-invoking the pattern of the past. And here was my brother, alive from the world of the dead. I didn't know who I should be gladder to see! All three of us were speechless. It was a moment of unreality, and yet at the same time so natural. At last, we were together, as we should be.

To Peska, Wolvie seemed the same, and the three sat there, with hope in their hearts for the new year. She and Wolvie took walks, talked, and were comfortable because Leibel was there as a buffer. They soon realised that they were still connected, and that they would be getting married. After the High Holidays, they went to Paris, where in addition to working with the Jewish Rescue Committee Wolvie had started some business ventures. Although Peska was surrounded by his friends and family, she hardly knew them, and Wolvie did all he could to make her comfortable. He paid for anything she and Leibel needed, and even bought fabric so he could have matching coats made for the three of them.

Following a pattern that she would continue for the rest of her life, Peska began cooking cholent, the traditional bean and barley stew, for his myriad friends from every walk of life on a little hot plate (graduating to kitchens in America). She was serving fifteen or sixteen people every *Shabbos*, and discovered it was the secret to their acceptance of her.

Wolvie and Peska had been engaged informally for about a month when his surviving brother, Yerucham, and his wife, Rachu, decided to throw a surprise engagement party for them. When the witnesses signed the betrothal agreement, the *Tanaaim*, Peska realised that the war was finally over, and that she was safe and engaged to the love of her life.

The wedding was planned for the beginning of January in the Pletzel, the Jewish Quarter in Paris, and she very much wanted R' Baruch to officiate. She spent two months trying to prepare for the wedding, but it was hard to find what she needed. One of Wolvie's friends was able to help her find white fabric so she could make her gown, and fashion a crown of white doves that reminded her of the doves on the bride's throne in her mother's catering hall in Warsaw. Peska missed her mother terribly and felt sure she had her blessing, because she knew she had always liked Wolvie – but it was painful to march down the aisle without her.

The wedding day dawned, grey and damp, with a drizzle that would not quit. Peska sat on the bridal chair in her homemade wedding dress, waiting for Wolvie to come and place her veil over her face. She began to tremble. She knew that many brides were afraid of what they were heading into, but she was about to marry a man who had already lost a wife and child. She was essentially an orphan, entering into a relationship that in her Hasidic, straitlaced world, was considered unconventional.

She didn't regret her decision, but she was scared. When R' Baruch came in to give her a blessing, she burst into tears and cried as she had never cried in all the years of the war and after. Peska was accompanied down the aisle by her first cousins, the Bialer Rebbe and his wife. She sensed the presence of her mother as she took each step toward the wedding canopy, set up in the courtyard of an apartment house. Dozens of people crowded the balcony overlooking the ceremony, and many more filled the streets around the venue. It was one of the first Jewish weddings in Paris after the war, and it seems that more than 700 people showed up, including Slovakian officials and others Wolvie met through his relief work. They said they wouldn't miss it for the world.

The wedding reception consisted of potluck from various sources. Homemade herring salad, baked goods, fresh fruit and fish were all on the menu. Devorah's husband had a cousin in Paris who was a winemaker and provided some wine. There were no flowers, no smorgasbord, no music, because there were no musicians in their group. As Peska said, 'There were only hopeful faces and good wishes and sincerity – and on those, we built our union.' Peska was now Mrs Wolvie Friedman, headed to new adventures in a new land, with a new language, tied to the past by tradition and Jewish values. She was nervous, determined and very, very happy.

The Friedmans arrived in New York City, penniless, Peska pregnant with twins. They built a life filled with everything one could expect, including challenges that needed to be met. They did so with fortitude and courage, joy and *naches* (pride) to share with others – building a community, raising children and helping others. Peska and Wolvie were dedicated to each other and the Orthodox Jewish community, where he was a political activist and helped build the *Agudah*, different synagogues and schools and helped Hasidic sects flourish, until he died of cancer in January 1982, one day after their thirty-fifth wedding anniversary.

Although Peska lived for another thirty-three years after Wolvie died, she never remarried and always kept him in her heart and soul.

This story is based on interviews of Jeanette Freedman by Mindelle Pierce. It was written by Jeanette Friedman.

11

NARDUS AND SIPORA GROEN

Sipora Rodrigues-Lopes was born in Amsterdam, the Netherlands, in 1922 into an accomplished family. Her brother was born three years later in 1925. Sipora and her brother were raised in a loving house where education, manners and respect for others were priorities. Sipora led a full life, attending public school, playing piano and tennis, going ice skating and spending time with friends. Because her mother was ill, she learned how to cook for the family.

When Sipora was thirteen and her brother was ten, their mother died, altering the family dynamic dramatically. As Sipora recalled, 'To lose your mother is to lose your father, too.' Her father remained devoted to his children, and never remarried.

Four years later, Sipora's friends introduced her to a nice young man, Hans. Their chemistry was immediate, and their relationship blossomed. One year later, in 1940, Hans proposed marriage to Sipora with a gold ring and the couple began to plan their wedding.

On 10 May 1940, their wedding plans were thrown into disarray by the Nazi takeover of Amsterdam. Soon after the Nazis occupied the city, the implementation of anti-Jewish policies began. The Chief Justice of the Dutch Supreme Court and forty-one university professors, all Jewish, were removed from their positions. All Jewish individuals and businesses were required to register with the government and the Nazis created maps with the locations of all Jews, identified by name, age and marital status. With Amsterdam now under Nazi occupation, anti-Semitism seeped into the fabric of daily life and for the first time Sipora experienced the viciousness of the Nazi regime. Hans and his siblings were taken away immediately by the Nazis to Westerborg, the Netherlands, a camp which served as a transit hub. Soon, they were transferred to Auschwitz, where they were murdered.

Sipora, a nurse then twenty years old, was assigned to work in the Nederlander Isranlitsch Zikenhaus, the Dutch Israeli Hospital. There she met Nardus Groen, also a nurse at the hospital. Nardus was born in Rotterdam, the Netherlands, on 18 December 1919. Nardus' strawberry blond hair, fair skin and blue eyes belied the fact that he was a Jew from an Orthodox family. Despite Nardus' Orthodox upbringing, his Aryan appearance enabled him to pass as a German. Sipora had dark hair, dark eyes and looked very Sephardic Jewish.

Sipora noticed that Nardus always seemed to be nearby and often she felt him staring at her. Though she suspected that he had romantic feelings for her, she did not reciprocate. She held on to the hope that she and Hans one day would find each other and marry, as they had planned. Instead, Sipora and Nardus became good friends. Unbeknownst to Sipora, Nardis worked for the Dutch underground, saving Jews and thwarting Nazi efforts.

On 13 August 1942, the Nazis began rounding up patients for deportation. Sipora was determined to accompany her patients wherever they were being sent. But Nardus knew, through his work with the Dutch underground, that the people taken by the Nazis would be shipped to a concentration camp where they would be beaten, starved, raped and killed. Before the soldiers reached Sipora's ward, Nardus instructed her to leave with him. When she refused, he said, 'I will throw you out the window myself, since you are going to your sure death anyway. Get up and let's get out of here!'

Nardus took control of the situation, assuring Sipora he would take care of her. He instructed Sipora to change out of her uniform and pretend to be a sick patient. Then he placed her on a gurney and loaded her into a truck with the other sick patients who were being transported to a nearby nursing home. Once inside the nursing home, Sipora put her uniform back on and started working in the facility as a nurse once more.

The following month, September 1943, Sipora's father and brother came to say goodbye before they attempted to escape into Switzerland. She found out later that they were caught and sent to Auschwitz.

In October 1943, as the situation worsened, Sipora went into hiding in the home of her father's friend. As random searches of Jewish homes, hospitals and schools increased in frequency, it became clear that Sipora still was in danger. Through his underground connections, Nardus knew of a safe house in Kampen, a town north-east of Amsterdam, where Jews were hiding. Though he believed Sipora would be safe there, he also knew they were risking their lives in making the journey. After obtaining false identity papers, Nardus donned the uniform of a Dutch police officer and headed to the train to travel with his Jewish prisoner. Nardus knew that the success of his plan depended upon their ability to maintain the appearance that Nardus was a cold-hearted Nazi collaborator who was transporting a terrified Jewish woman to a camp. If, somehow, they were discovered, he would use the gun that he found in the uniform to end their lives quickly, on their own terms, rather than allow them to torture Sipora.

They boarded a train and found two empty seats in a car filled with Nazi soldiers, many of them high-ranking officers. Nardus ordered Sipora to sit as he pulled out a cigarette, exuding calm and control. When a Nazi officer asked for their papers, Nardus explained that he was taking the Jew to the next transport; but he planned to have some fun with her first. When the officer expressed an interest in having his own fun with her himself, Nardus drew his gun. After a brief standoff, the other officer backed down and the train ride continued without incident.

When they arrived at the safe house in Kampen, they found twenty-five Jews hiding on the top floor of the house. Something about the situation made Nardus feel uneasy. Following his instincts, they left the house and set out on foot with no plan or destination, only the desire to get as far away from Kampen as possible. In the rush to leave, Sipora left behind a small bag of personal items. Nardus assured her he would return for the bag.

As Sipora became more dependent upon Nardus for her survival, she felt a shift in her feelings for him. His interest in her had been clear from the start, though he treated her always with respect and compassion. But slowly, during their time together, she noticed that following his lead had become as natural to her as breathing. She recognised that the closeness between them filled the sad and lonely space in her life. Though she still thought of Hans, that romance was from a simpler, more innocent life. Her life now was fraught with danger and doubt, and Nardus was a constant in a world of uncertainty.

As they walked to their next location, they spoke about their families and wondered if they would see them ever again. Sipora admitted her feelings for Nardus. She trusted in this man who risked everything to save her, and she felt safe with him. Instead of *needing* to stay with him for her safety, she *wanted* to be with him. After all the time they spent together and the depth of feelings he had developed for Sipora, Nardus was elated. Though he had not expected her to reciprocate his feelings, he was overwhelmed that she felt the closeness and love for him that he felt for her.

Later that evening, Nardus and Sipora came upon a house where they found food and shelter for the night, the first of no fewer than seven safe houses Nardus would find for Sipora. She was given a spare room in the house while Nardus was to sleep in the barn. But after revealing their love for one another, Sipora could not bear to be apart from Nardus, and they made a plan to be together that evening. After the lights in the house went out, Sipora opened her window and Nardus snuck into her room. He never had expected a physical relationship, but now here he was in her bedroom. He knew after this evening that their relationship would be changed forever. They knew that the intimacy they were about to share would connect them for the rest of their lives, though neither knew how long that would be.

The fabric of their lives had changed because of the Nazi occupation. 'Conventional' notions of good and bad, right and wrong, no longer applied. All that mattered was life and death. The night before, it would have been considered wrong to make love to a man who was not her husband. But this night, it felt right.

The next morning, Nardus returned to the safe house in Kampen to retrieve Sipora's bag. As he walked, he began to envision a future with Sipora. He thought of his beloved family, wonderful childhood, *Shabbat* dinners, boyhood adventures. He dreamed of having a family with Sipora. He didn't know what had become of his family, if he would ever see them again, or if he and Sipora would survive to realise a future together.

When he arrived, he learned that all of the Jews they saw in the safe house the night before had been killed in a Nazi ambush, which had been arranged by the owner of the house. Nardus was grateful that his instincts had saved his and Sipora's lives, but he wondered how he would continue to keep Sipora safe.

The man who had put them up the night before had offered to introduce Sipora to the owner of a boat, who needed help with cooking and cleaning. After the safehouse ambush, Nardus encouraged Sipora to work on the boat for the time being, until he could make better arrangements. Meanwhile, Nardus took a job at a local Dutch land reclamation project to be near Sipora and keep her safe. During the weeks that followed, Nardus moved her from the boat to several other safe houses before settling her in the small town of Lemerlerveld, where Sipora connected with a family Nardus knew through his underground connections. The family provided Sipora with room and board in exchange for domestic work. Despite the warmth and compassion of the couple, Sipora could not help but feel anxious, uncertain, and fearful among these kind strangers. The uncertainty and instability of her life made her hesitant to trust them. Soon, her fear gave way to gratitude to this couple for risking their lives for her protection, and for providing her with a comfortable place to live and for being kind and decent. After a few weeks, she began to relax into her new life.

Soon, the couple built an underground dirt room for Sipora in the cellar, hidden from view and connected to their home by a trap door. The couple told her this was necessary for her protection, as well as for their own. Sipora was uncomfortable with this new arrangement, especially during the long, cold winter months. Nardus and Sipora missed each other terribly and struggled to stay positive during their separation. After a few weeks, Nardus was able to visit her; and the intimacy and passion they shared in the privacy of her small earthen room rekindled their spirits and renewed their optimism. Sipora once again allowed herself to imagine their future together.

For the year and a half that followed, Sipora stayed with the family, spending each night locked in her underground room, which felt more like a coffin than a bedroom. Occasionally, she would go ice skating when the canal was frozen, giving her the feeling of normalcy, until that, too, became dangerous. With each excursion out of the house, Sipora risked being captured by the Nazis and their collaborators. After all, she had survived; and with the life she and Nardus were planning, she did not want to take any unnecessary chances.

As the end of the war drew near, Nardus was captured and taken to Camp Erika, where he was forced to endure hard labour in brutal conditions. After many weeks of incarceration and deprivation that left him weak and starving, he was ordered to dig a hole. By this time, Nardus had seen enough to know the hole would become his own grave. He had seen this before.

In a desperate attempt to escape, Nardus waited until the sky became dark, then climbed into the back of a horse-drawn wagon parked nearby. He saw that the back of the wagon was filled with hay, and later he learned that it was left there expressly for his escape by the family who had been keeping Sipora hidden and would be driven by one of their nephews. Nardus was on his way to see Sipora. Soon, however, he was off volunteering again with the resistance forces for the coming end of the occupation.

In April 1945, the Jews of the Netherlands were liberated by the Canadian Army. When the victorious Canadian soldiers marched into Lemerlerveld, Nardus arrived too! He was riding on top of a tank, aiming to reunite with Sipora, his love, and to thank the family who had protected her.

In the five years since the beginning of the war, nearly 75 per cent of the Netherlands' Jews had been systematically murdered. The staggering truth of the horrors that had been inflicted on the Jewish people throughout Europe was devastating. Nardus and Sipora questioned their relationship, wondering if they would be able to create a new life together. Could their love transcend the pain, suffering and loss they had endured?

After liberation, Nardus and Sipora parted ways. Nardus joined the Dutch Marines and was stationed at the US Marine Corps' Camp Lejeune, North Carolina. He was training to become a second lieutenant in the Allied marine 'shock troops' destined for the campaign to end the war with Japan. That never happened, due to Japan's unconditional surrender after the US dropped the atomic bombs.

Sipora found a job as a nurse in a sanitarium in the town of Helendoorn. With few options, she moved back into her old home in Amsterdam, haunted by the memories of her family, friends and community murdered in the Holocaust. The world was so different now, and the enormity of her loss and loneliness was nearly unbearable. Adding to the emotional toll was the physical exhaustion she experienced. She blamed it on summer heat, but her growing belly indicated something else entirely. She was shocked to learn that she was pregnant. Because her mother had died while she was only thirteen, she never was taught about sex and reproduction and she failed to appreciate the clues that were so obvious to others. Now twenty-three and pregnant, Sipora was learning the basic facts of pregnancy and childbirth alone!

Sipora sent a letter to Nardus, letting him know that she was pregnant with his child. Though not shocked, this certainly was not an announcement he was expecting. In November 1945, she gave birth to a baby boy, Marcel, named after her father. Sipora took this as a sign from God that their love and life were starting again; and through motherhood, she gained a new purpose in her life.

A few days after Marcel was born, two men on a motorbike arrived at Sipora's home looking for her. The men introduced themselves to Sipora as Nardus' brother and brother-in-law. They delivered a message from Nardus. Though he was thousands of miles away, he would be in touch. It would have been easy for Nardus to ignore her letter and pretend he did not know about her pregnancy, but the thought never occurred to him. Sipora was touched by the effort of these men to find her, and she was confident that Nardus would play a part in her and Marcel's life.

In January 1946, Nardus returned to see Sipora and his new son, Marcel, for the first time. Before returning to the Marines in the US, Nardus realised that Sipora was weak. In March, thin and feverish, Sipora was diagnosed with the early stages of pleurisy. This led her to a period of loneliness in a sanitarium, while her son was being taken care of elsewhere. With excellent medical care, Sipora was released in September. By that time, Nardus had completed the studies necessary to be appointed a rabbi to head up the Jewish community in the town of Apeldoorn in the Netherlands.

In the mid-1950s, Nardus worked as a psychologist at a Jewish orphanage for Holocaust survivors and then was appointed Chief Rabbi in Surinam, South America, formerly Dutch Guyana, at the oldest congregation in the Western Hemisphere. There, alternately, he led the Sephardic congregation one week and the Ashkenazic congregation the next. Later, in 1952, he served as the Rabbi in Eindhoven in the Netherlands.

Upon completing his assignment in Surinam in 1955 and wishing to move to America with their three sons, Nardus accepted sponsorship for a residency under renowned Professor Dr Jacob Marcus, President of Hebrew Union College in Cincinnati, Ohio. Later he had the opportunity to study with Orthodox Rabbi Eliezer Silver of Agudath, North America and Canada, more in line with his beliefs, and he received an additional rabbinical certification. Sipora gave birth to a daughter, their fourth child, in 1957 and had their fifth and final child, another son, in 1962.

They remained in Cincinnati until 1963 when Nardus accepted a pulpit at the Conservative Beth Israel Synagogue, Lansdale, Pennsylvania. After serving there for a short time as their rabbi, he and Sipora moved to the Atlantic City area for two years, and then back to Europe. He retired in 1986 as the Chief Rabbi for the eastern six provinces of the Netherlands.

After his retirement, Rabbi Groen and his wife Sipora lived in the Netherlands and Delray Beach, Florida, before settling permanently in Florida in 2005. They have twenty-six descendants and counting, from their children, Marcel, Leo, Ruben, Deborah and David. Nardus died in June 2007 and Sipora passed away in July 2017, both in Florida.

This story is based on several interviews with Sipora Groen, conducted by Mindelle Pierce in 2017.

12

DINA AND FRANK KABAK

Dina Kabak lived in Vilna, Poland with her parents, two sisters and grandfather. When the Nazis occupied Poland in 1939, laws were enacted forcing Jews to wear yellow stars on their clothing, register their property and report for forced labour. First, the Nazis arrested Dina's father, quickly followed by the arrest of her grandfather.

Then, in the fall of 1940, the Nazis imprisoned the rest of the family in the Lukiski jail in Vilna. Dina and her older sister were separated from their mother and other sister and tossed into a prison cell with other women. Soon after, the prisoners were instructed to leave their cells and line up for roll call. Dina exited the cell and stood in line with the other prisoners, but her sister refused. Dina worried about her sister, but followed the Nazis' orders, fearing what would happen if she failed to comply. She and the others were loaded on to trucks and taken to the Vilna ghetto, and Dina never saw her sisters or her mother again.

During the summer and autumn of 1941, the Nazis conducted mass executions of Jews, shooting thousands of them at a time and dumping their bodies in large pits in Ponary, Nazi-occupied Poland. It became known as the Ponary Massacre. Seeing what was happening, the superintendent of Dina's apartment in the ghetto warned Dina about the executions and wanted to save her from this fate. This woman handed Dina the birth certificate of her deceased niece and arranged for her nephews to drive Dina to the countryside the next day. With their help, Dina escaped the ghetto and found work in the countryside, where she posed as a non-Jew. For a year or so it appeared Dina had found safety from the Nazis. However, a year later, amid rumours that Dina was Jewish, she boarded a train searching for a new place to live. Once on the train, she realised she had stepped into even greater danger. The Nazis were monitoring the trains, checking papers and searching for Jews. At the next stop, she disembarked from the train near Breslau, Germany, and began to wander along the tracks, frightened, hungry and alone.

Meanwhile, In the autumn of 1942, twenty-two-year-old Frank Kabak was one of forty men working in Breslau, building a bridge over the railroad tracks. Though he was not Jewish, he had been drafted to work for the Nazis as a forced labourer.

On 16 October 1942, Frank and his group were busy working when they heard screams and gunshots. They watched as a Nazi soldier pushed a man into a deep ravine and released a torrent of bullets into it. Miraculously, the man had escaped serious injury, and he jumped out of the hole and ran away when the soldier paused to reload his gun. This incident served as just one of many reminders to Frank of the constant danger that surrounded them. By this time, he had witnessed numerous Nazi atrocities, heard stories of many others, and understood the vicious nature of their rule.

Later that day, as he worked, Dina, looking dishevelled and frightened, walked up to the group of men. In desperation and on sensing something in Frank that led her to believe he might help her, she asked him for something to eat. Regretfully, he told her he had eaten his lunch and had no food to share. Dina, tired and alone, felt that this man was her only chance for survival. She hoped Frank would help her, but she knew that he easily could report her to the Nazis, which would certainly lead to her capture and certain death. Dina took a chance and introduced herself, explained her situation and pleaded for any assistance he could provide. In all the turmoil, she had lost the identification papers that had been her safety net thus far, and now felt completely exposed to the Nazis.

Frank felt compelled to help Dina. He had been tormented by the evil acts of the Nazis and could not turn away from a young, innocent woman who needed his help. He knew that he would do whatever he could to save her, even if it meant risking his own life. He asked her to meet him later that evening. When they met, Frank told Dina his plan, which he thought might be crazy enough to work. With her consent, they put his plan into action.

The next day, Frank told his Nazi boss that he and his girlfriend wanted to get married, but they had a problem: she had lost her identity papers. Frank explained that Dina had been walking toward a bridge when she saw a soldier checking passes. Realising she didn't have her work pass with her, she became frightened and jumped into the water, hoping to cross to the other side and avoid facing the soldier. Unfortunately, she stumbled in the water and dropped her purse, containing her identification. Her purse was carried away by the current before she could get to it, and her identification along with it.

Frank's plan worked and his boss directed Dina to bring two photos, so he could issue a work pass for her. With her new work pass in hand, Frank and Dina went to the courthouse and applied for a marriage licence. Two weeks later, they were married. On their wedding day, they agreed that their marriage was for the explicit purpose of saving Dina's life. After the war, they would go their separate ways.

Dina and Frank maintained the appearance of a married couple and Dina was given a job preparing meals for Frank's crew. In the months that followed, Dina and Frank began to develop feelings for one another. Dina surely was moved by the selflessness and bravery Frank demonstrated as he attempted to save a stranger. Frank recognised the strength in this young woman who, after losing her family, escaping the ghetto, hiding in the country and jumping off a train, never lost faith that she would find a way to survive. Her determination in the face of overwhelming odds amazed him.

Eventually their marriage of convenience gave way to romantic, passionate love, evolving into an authentic married relationship. It is easy to understand how Dina, with her entire family decimated, and Frank, who had been alone for so long in a forced labour brigade, would reach out to each other for comfort, companionship and love.

In early 1943, when Dina became pregnant, the Nazi foreman forced Dina to leave the crew, refusing to be responsible for a pregnant woman. Dina had no choice but to ask Frank's family in Novy Sacz, Poland, for help. Frank was forced to stay with the crew, now headed for Smolensk, Russia.

When they arrived in Smolensk, the Russian front was approaching and the men were instructed to report to the city of Minsk, approximately 190 miles south-west of Smolensk. Frank was consumed with thoughts of Dina, pregnant and far away. He had no idea if she had reached Novy Sacz, if she had connected with his family, or if she was safe. She was due to give birth any day, and he worried for her health and the health of their new baby. In the train station in Minsk, a Nazi soldier struck up a conversation with Frank. When Frank mentioned his pregnant wife was about to give birth in Nazi-occupied Poland, the soldier told him to go home to his family.

Frank wasted no time and immediately travelled to Novy Sacz, where he reunited with Dina and met his son, Elias. Worried that the Nazis would come looking for Frank, they moved frequently, town to town, hoping to go unnoticed.

Frank secretly harboured a deep insecurity about being able to support his new family. Desperate for a way to earn a living, he fell back on one of the few things he knew how to do: he made soaps and sold them in the villages. Frank developed a loyal customer base, which allowed him to barter for food and other necessities. Later, he worked with a farmer, butchering small animals, to increase his earnings.

When the war ended, Frank and Dina decided to leave Poland and in 1947 they moved to Cuba. There they built a new life and welcomed a daughter, Ida, to their family. Frank had taken Dina's last name, Kabak, to honour the family she had lost. Now he wanted to take on their religion as well. Soon after they arrived, Frank met with a rabbi and explained his desire to convert to Judaism. The rabbi, however, refused to convert him, saying, 'No man should change his religion for a woman.'

The couple moved to Miami, Florida, in 1960. It wasn't until 1970, after his son announced he was getting married to a Jewish woman, that Frank finally converted at Temple Israel in Miami. He was given the Hebrew name Efraim.

When Dina passed away in 2011, Frank was heartbroken and wanted to ensure that their story would be passed on to their grandchildren and great-grandchildren. In 2014, Frank wrote a memoir, *The Matchmaker and the Miracle: How We Deceived the Nazis*, outlining his and Dina's experience during the war. He wrote: 'I miss [Dina] very much. She was the first and only woman in my life and my love for her is forever. Dina, wait for me in paradise because you went first.'

On 4 June 2016, at ninety-six years old, Frank joined Dina. He died in his home, surrounded by his children, grandchildren and great-grandchildren. Frank and Dina taught their family, by example, what is most important in life: love, family, kindness, humanity.

Video interview with Mr Kabak in his apartment in Miami Beach, FL, January 2016, conducted by Mindelle and Ira Pierce.

13

CHAIM JOSEPH AND HANKA KEMPNER

My parents' romance unfolded among the rubble of the Third Reich in 1945 like a Hollywood love story.

My mother, Hanka Ciesla, was born in Kielce, Poland in 1925. Eleven years later, the family moved to Soseniewc, where they lived in the years before the outbreak of war. Hanka was the oldest sibling of brother Dudek and younger sister Cesia. My grandfather Leon Ciesla was married to Helenka Piotrkowski. He was a successful entrepreneur who operated a lumber mill, and she was an educated linguist. They lived as assimilated Jews in a large and pleasant house on a lake.

In the autumn of 1939, Soseniewc was among the first Polish cities to be invaded by the Nazi Army. Eighteen months after the invasion, Leon, Helenka and their three young children were forced into two small rooms within the Soseniewc ghetto.

Leon used his business connections to obtain false papers for the entire family, including my mother Hanka. At the last minute, Helenka would not leave her mother because she was too frail to travel. During the Soseniewc liquidation, the Nazis shot Helenka's mother, my great-grandmother, in front of the entire family.

In the chaos of the subsequent days, my mother became separated from her family. Leon had an emergency plan in place in case anything happened to the family. He had arranged for his daughter to receive false identification papers directly from a Catholic friend.

My mother's papers identified her as Helena Matusik. Mata means mother in Polish. Having a maternal-sounding false name brought special comfort to Hanka, who missed her beloved mother. Leon's exit plan worked. My grandfather correctly determined that my mother, possessing goyish (non-Jewish) looks with her blond hair and green eyes and speaking an upper-class Polish dialect, could easily pass as a Polish *shiksa* (slang for a non-Jewish woman).

Accompanied by a hometown friend who also had false papers, the two Jewish girls escaped from the Nazi occupation in Soseniewc by going west – right into the belly of the beast. Though the war raged beside them, they survived by passing as forced Polish labourers, working in a Nazi factory near Stuttgart that produced barrels to hold ammunition. The two Jewish friends kept their identities secret while working in the factory. When she could my mother would throw apples over the fence into a nearby work camp occupied by starving Jewish inmates, at great personal risk.

My mother prayed the war would end soon, so she could be reunited with her family. To give her comfort at night to help fall asleep, Hanka would recall scenes of old Shirley Temple movies she had seen in her youth. As the Allies were attacking German cities, my mother watched the bombs dropping on nearby Stuttgart. She was convinced that her father was leading the attacks on the Nazis and would be rescuing her soon.

Instead, my mother was liberated by American soldiers. She gratefully remembered how kind the soldiers were to her by celebrating her twentieth birthday on 27 July 1945. She also was surprised when their commander, a Major Lewis, asked to see her. He informed my mother that the nearby liberated inmates wanted to thank the young girl who was brave enough to secretly provide them with food.

The soldiers offered my mother transportation to Berlin by having her sit on their tank. She was taken to the offices of the United Nations Relief and Rehabilitation Administration (UNRRA), and was given a place to stay with female soldiers. She started working with other displaced persons who were settling in Berlin. Her ability to speak several languages was very useful.

My mother's primary goal was to find any surviving family members. She asked anyone who was travelling east to carry a letter with her name and that of her parents and siblings carefully written down. One of my mother's dozens of appeal letters was taken by a man who was especially indebted to her, since he had been fed by the 'blonde angel'. The courier landed at the Feldafing Displaced Camp in Bavaria. There he handed the note to one Dudek Ciesla – a young man who had survived Auschwitz. He was my mother's brother. Until then, Dudek had not known if any of his family members were still alive. The messenger told the newly liberated young man that his sister Hanka had survived the war and was assisting Jewish refugees in Berlin.

Overjoyed by the news about his sister, Dudek immediately hitchhiked to Berlin. He and his sister were reunited at the office where she worked. The siblings moved in together and began living in the small quarters that UNRRA had provided to Hanka. My mother was concerned that her brother would seek revenge against Nazis in Berlin.

The sibling reunion also delivered devastating news about their immediate family and the horrors of Auschwitz. Throughout his incarceration, Dudek had stayed alive because his father had taken care of him. His father had volunteered to work on bomb disposal tasks, which allowed him to receive more food, which he then shared with his son. After harsh winters in Auschwitz, the camp was evacuated, and the inmates were sent out on a death march. When Dudek became ill, he was separated from his father. My grandfather likely died during this forced march. Dudek finally landed at Mathausen. On 6 May 1945, Dudek's eighteenth birthday, Americans liberated the camp.

My father's arrival in Berlin had a very different trajectory. Chaim Joseph Kempner was born on 18 December 1908 in Ponevezh, Lithuania. The youngest of ten children born to Hannah Abels Pokempner and Joseph Pokempner. He kidded that his parents 'gave up after he was born', and that he was 'a miscarriage of justice'.

When his parents separated, Chaim joined his father, moving to Kovno. His father worked for the Cunard shipping company which provided passage to America for him and his siblings. Chaim made his way to New York from Cherbourg, France, on 1 July 1927 on a Cunard ocean liner. As did his family members before him, Chaim joined siblings and cousins in Pittsburgh, the locale of 'Litvak' Jews. Not waiting for Ellis Island to pick his immigrant identity, he buried the 'Po' prefix at sea during this first voyage to the United States, shortening his last name to Kempner and calling himself Harold.

He attended the University of Pittsburgh where the young student confessed to 'almost burning the chemistry lab down'. Harold claimed he intended to go to medical school but was prevented from being accepted by the restrictive Jewish quotas. After graduation, Harold made a living during the Depression by teaching Hebrew and Yiddish to young students up and down the East Coast. Decades after his death, we found out that my father had married one of his young students, but the marriage did not last long.

As soon as the Second World War broke out, Harold wanted to fight. He had to wait until he received his citizenship papers to do so, which came through finally on 2 September 1942. Not wasting any time, he enlisted in the US Army in Philadelphia on 22 September, hoping to be sent to Europe. Harold was trained at Fort Riley, Kansas, where he remembered encountering overt anti-Semitism.

His desire to fight the Third Reich was not realised, as he was sent to the Pacific and stationed in New Guinea. He described his time there as 'fighting with his typewriter', and became a war correspondent. My father edited a publication for Jewish servicemen in New Guinea, entitled *The Yiddish Glicken*. He also published a newsletter entitled *Yiddish in a Jiffy*, full of suggestions listing Yiddish words the Jewish soldiers could write in their letters to their *bubbes* (grandmothers).

When the war ended, Harold left the army in the Pacific on 25 November 1945. When officials became aware that he spoke Hebrew, Yiddish, English, Russian, German and Lithuanian, he was sent to Berlin to work for the US military. My father became a captain working as the Public Relations Officer of the Office of the Military Government for Germany. Once in Berlin, Harold continued his journalism. He was the features editor of *The Grooper*.

My father's biggest scoop was achieved in early November 1945 when he crashed Soviet General Marshal G. K. Zhukov's reception and quoted the Russian military leader as saying the Allied occupation of Germany 'could be completed in less than ten years if the Germans are cooperative'. This interview was reported in American newspapers and one account reported that 'Kempner had no invitation to Zhukov's party, at which General Eisenhower was the ranking guest, but after he got inside, he went straight to the point'.

Shocked by the annihilation of eastern European Jewry, my father's stories focused on the miraculous first events happening in the months after liberation. As a Jewish member of the US Armed Forces, he concentrated on the poignant stories of Holocaust survivors celebrating Jewish holidays and being reunited after the war.

His story of one reunion quickly became his favourite. It was of the account of Dudek Ciesla, a young Jewish teenager from Poland and survivor of Auschwitz, being reunited with his sister, Hanka. 'The happy reunion of a brother and sister, after being separated by the Nazis for three years, marked one of the brightest moments of camp life.' Accompanying their photo, my father's story was written using anglicized names: 'Helen and David Ciesla, Polish Jews torn apart by the Nazis, who gassed their parents in the murder mill of Auschwitz.'

David had survived cruel ordeals in many concentration camps, while Helen, who was a slave worker near Stuttgart, was liberated by the Americans.

My mother claimed that Harold was smitten with her at their first meeting and would not leave her alone for even a day. She thought he was very smart. His army uniform of course reminded her of her American liberators. She felt his empathy for her plight, and he was also Jewish and originally from eastern Europe, a common bond. The American correspondent continued to write about my mother, the beautiful Polish and Jewish survivor.

Another story was entitled 'DP Orphans Are Survivors of Persecution'. For this story, he highlighted my mother's work with the young orphans:

> Children at the newly-established UNRRA camp here in
> Berlin get their first lessons in the three R's from UNRRA
> official, Helena Ciesla. These youngsters, orphaned by the
> persecutions of the Nazis, are awaiting transportation to
> permanent homes. They are our precious jewels, said Helena
> Ciesla, UNRRA worker as she led him on a tour.

My father fell in love with the UNRRA employee. My mother
claimed ten other men were also pursuing her, but that my father
prevailed!

Then the American Jewish soldier became part of a romantic
news story in Berlin, when he proclaimed his love for my mother.
The exact length of their courtship is unknown, but appears it was
just a few months. Harold proposed to Hanka and she accepted.
There was a formal invitation to a planned ceremony sent out:
'Your presence is requested at the Wedding of Helena Ciesla
and Harold J. Kempner at 78-79 Unter den Eiden in Berlin on
Saturday, February 23, 1946 at 8 pm with a reception immediately
following.' Living up to the image of a war bride, my mother got
married in an elegant wedding dress cut from an army parachute.
My father was dressed in uniform, as were most of the guests.
Pictures of their wedding were published in *The Grooper*. My
mother had the joy of having one member of her immediate family
attending the wedding. Her brother Dudek witnessed the wedding
and toasted the couple.

As part of the military government, my parents lived in an
impressive house. My father wrote to his brother back in the States
that they found a 'huge house, eight rooms and a gorgeous garden
with a pond full of goldfish'. My father went on to describe how
he picked the house himself and bragged that he 'had two Nazi
families kicked out pronto – which was a *mechaiye*' (a pleasure).
He also proudly wrote to his brother about how his activities
helped Jewish orphans and relatives find homes or relatives in the
States, and also about arranging cultural activities for the survivors
in the DP camps.

On 23 December 1946, ten months to the day after the wedding,
I was born, a US citizen in the US Army hospital in Berlin. A
photograph of me, wrapped up in a blanket, adorned the front

page of *The Berlin Observer*, with the dubious headline of 'Miss 1947, the first American Jewish war baby born in Berlin'.

My father had wanted a Bris (circumcision) in Berlin to show those Germans that Jews had survived. When a female was delivered, he derived great satisfaction in writing a Hebrew name on his child's German birth certificate. My mother, who had found out that her mother died in Auschwitz, gave me my grandmother's name, Helen, as my middle name.

My father left the military to work in Munich for the American Joint Distribution Committee as the public relations director. For two years, we had a very upper-class lifestyle and I had a nanny, very different from those living in Displaced Persons (DP) camps. My parent's life was very busy, entertaining American visitors to the DP camps and relatives who had miraculously survived. Most of them were destined for Israel.

My father was offered a position as a foreign correspondent in eastern Europe. My mother vetoed the offer, as she wanted to go to America, where her brother already had emigrated, to Hartford in June 1946. My mother also rejected my father's wish for us to move to Israel. These differences might have caused an early rift in their relationship. When I was three and a half years old, we left Germany, my mother vowing never to return. We arrived in the US on 22 February 1950 and moved to Detroit, Michigan, where my father's brother and family lived. My orphaned mother decided to take her deceased mother's name, Helen, as her English first name. Dudek Ciesla became David Chase upon arriving on America shores.

When my brother was born on 5 March 1951 he was given a Hebrew name, Jonathan, 'Gift of God', because my mother was told she might not have any more children after my birth. He was given the middle name Leon, in honour of our murdered grandfather.

My father first worked with a Jewish organisation and then he switched to real estate. Our life in the Detroit suburbs was idyllic. A favourite activity was being taken by our father to Little League games. My parents continued to entertain visitors who spoke Polish and Yiddish. We were close to my father's family and celebrated all the Jewish holidays together.

By 1958 the marriage had begun to unravel. When I returned from Girl Scout camp that summer, they were clearly feuding. Divorce proceedings began, and they were acrimonious and painful. My father contested the short time originally allotted for his visitations with us. The drama continued. My mother travelled to Reno, Nevada, to obtain a 'quickie' divorce in 1959.

My father moved to an apartment nearby, so he could live close to us. Later he bought houses nearby to make it easier for our visits on half of the weekend and on Wednesday nights. My father, who had been active in the Jewish War Veterans, often took us to the Jewish Community Center and professional baseball games.

Back in the late 1950s it was an aberration for parents to divorce, and my brother and I felt embarrassed. Friends patted my shoulder saying, 'I am so sorry.' In retrospect, my mother showed a lot of courage asking for a divorce. Maybe she came to the realisation that my father no longer represented the dashing Jewish soldier who had swept her off her feet. The bloom of the post-war fairy tale had faded.

The seventeen-year age gap may indicate that the soldier saviour symbolised her father, who would rescue her. Once in America, the fantasy may have ended, and she fell out of love with the civilian.

My father was able to fulfil his dream and made *Aliyah*, moving to Israel with citizenship in 1973. He never remarried but had girlfriends in both the States and Israel. He went back to being called Chaim. Sadly, after enjoying life for only three years in Israel, he was diagnosed with acute leukemia. Within three weeks, he died in the spring of 1976.

My mother started working and attending college. At Wayne State University she fell in love with her history professor, Milton Covensky, who had been a confirmed bachelor. He was a brilliant orator and much sought-after teacher. She often referred to him as the love of her life.

My mother also fell in love with painting, and she became a successful abstract expressionist artist. Milton was very supportive of her paintings and was a loving stepfather. Painting for my mother was an emotional outlet for the horrors of the war. She signed her works Helen Ciesla Covensky, and wrote in her catalog:

> In my lifetime, I have witnessed a world of extreme change which saw great destruction and rebirth: World War, a terrible Holocaust, the displacement of millions of people, and the loss of my loved ones are part of this experience... Painting for me is an absolute necessity, expressing personal needs, a constant struggle, and a never-ending search to portray the reaffirmation of life.

Mother and Milton moved to the Washington area to be close to their children and grandchildren. The grandchildren had the joy of knowing their grandparents. And it was a blessing to us all.

Story from Aviva Kempner, assisted by her niece Delaney Kempner and Dukek's grandson-in-law Ross Deyer, who contributed to the research and writing of this chapter, for which help Aviva is grateful.

14

CHAIM KLEINBERG AND NECHAMA BAUM

Chaim Kleinberg was born in Wierzbnik, Poland, in 1926, the youngest of ten children. Nechama Baum was born in the same town in 1929 and lived with her parents, five brothers and two sisters. They both had pleasant childhoods, living in a sleepy, peaceful town that consisted of Jews from many different walks of life. They even had a *Beis Yaakov*, a pioneering Jewish school for women. Nancy spent carefree summers at her grandparents' farm, and Chaim spent time in the forest with his friends, singing Zionist songs.

When Chaim was an infant, his oldest brother died. Two years later, after being refused visas to the United States, the family travelled to Warsaw on their way to Canada. In Warsaw, Chaim's father failed the strict immigration health examination because he was underweight. His mother refused to travel ahead with Chaim and his eight siblings and wait for her husband to follow. Instead, she sent the older children to Canada and returned to Wierzbnik with her husband and younger children.

As Europe's depression worsened and Jews were blamed for everyone's problems, their idyllic lives in Poland changed radically. By 1933, 3,920 Jews lived in the town of 8,000 people and the neighbours were aggressive towards them. Chaim grew up surrounded by hate and anti-Semitism. With the Nazi occupation of Poland in 1939, and the imposition of rules and restrictions on

Jews, their lives were turned upside down. In 1939, the town was merged with one nearby and became Wierzbnik-Starachowice. (Since 1952, the town has been called Starachowice.)

Immediately, the Nazis appointed a *Judenrat*, a committee of Jewish elders to control the Jewish community and carry out their orders. One of them was to deliver Jews to labour camps and nearby steel factories. Every day, for most of 1940, 500 Jews were instructed to line up in a certain area early in the morning, where they were counted and then marched to the factories.

In 1941, along with all the other Jews, the Baums and Kleinbergs were confined to the Wierzbnik ghetto and forced to wear armbands marked with Jewish stars. They had lost their freedom. The Jews were brought to the town square, where the able-bodied were selected for work. The vulnerable among them – the elderly, the children, the sick and the handicapped – were placed in cattle cars and taken to death camps: Treblinka, Majdanek and Auschwitz.

The Baums and Kleinbergs and some of their neighbours were healthy enough to work in the factories and thought they would be exempt from the selections. But they were not exempt from suffering. Chaim remembered overcrowding, hunger, sickness and humiliation, with children crying for food and adults getting on each other's nerves. They thought it was awful; it was going to get much worse.

The liquidation of the Wierzbnik ghetto began on 27 October 1942, when the entire Jewish population was rounded up, a selection was made, and most of the Jews were sent to die in Treblinka. The day began to the sound of bull horns, shootings, barking dogs and yelling, as Jews were directed to go to the town square without luggage. At the square, Howard suddenly was pushed to one side and noticed his family was on the other side, crowded with sick people and children. It was the last time he ever saw his parents.

Chaim, Nechama and her aunt Toby were among 1,600 strong young people sent to work in a Nazi ammunition factory in Starachowice. Chaim remembered, 'We were given barracks to live in, so we went to have a look. We saw no bunks, no blankets, no cushions, no nothing – just a V-shaped platform, so we lay down and cried!'

The next morning, Chaim was put to work on an assembly line in the Hermann Göring Works in Starachowice, hard labour for twelve hours a day. The prisoners were lined up at 6 a.m. for breakfast, a small portion of bread and a little water. They were marched back to the barrack for a bowl of soup. Nechama worked in the factory kitchen, peeling potatoes from 8 a.m. until 11 p.m. every day.

November was bitter cold. If they were lucky, Chaim remembered, 'We would find a cement bag or something to cover and protect ourselves from the cold. We worked and slept in the same clothes. With December came a typhus outbreak that took a great toll on us, as there was no medication.'

In May 1943, Nechama and her aunt Toby were among a group of prisoners loaded onto a crowded cattle car with little air and no food or water. When they arrived in Auschwitz, Nancy was tattooed with the number A14015.

By this time, the Russians were on the offensive and the Nazis were facing retreat and defeat. They began shipping their prisoners to various locations, looking for places to discard them. All through 1943 until mid-1944, Chaim heard rumours about Russians advancing toward Nazi-occupied Poland, thinking he would be liberated soon because his work camp was just 100 miles from the border. But that was not to be. In July 1944, his camp was closed, and he was transported from Starachowice to Auschwitz. Chaim recalled:

We were packed into wagons like sardines. We arrived to breathe the stench of burning flesh and Germans screaming at us to get out of the boxcars. After a real shower, people were screaming and yelling out of fear. Suddenly, instead of gas, water poured out and we were marched to an area where a girl with a dirty needle was tattooing numbers on our arms; mine was A19186.

Chaim was selected for work. Those not assigned to work were killed. By this time, the prisoners were aware of the gas chambers and Chaim explained, 'We died 1001 times each day, knowing what awaited us.'

In August 1944, the Nazis moved a group of prisoners including Chaim to Katowice to work at the Laurahutte metallurgical plant. They were kept there until December 1944, when the Russians surrounded the city. From there, Chaim and the other prisoners were transported in cattle cars through Czechoslovakia, Austria, Vienna and the Alps, arriving at Mauthausen on 30 July 1944.

Five months later, on 1 January 1945, the Nazis moved the prisoners to Hanover, Germany, to a large ammunition factory. From there, they were forced to walk 60 miles through the freezing and unforgiving winter cold to Bergen-Belsen in early April 1945. By then Howard was sick, weak, emaciated and without hope.

In early January 1945, after six months in Auschwitz, followed by many months of transports to various locations, Nechama and her aunt were forced to join a death march. They and the other prisoners, sick, weak, and starving, were forced to walk for days in the bitter cold with no food, water, or rest. Those who lagged behind were shot. Days later, hungry, freezing, and terrified, the group arrived at Bergen-Belsen.

When Bergen-Belsen was liberated by British soldiers on 15 April 1945, Nechama, her aunt and two friends who had survived the camps together found a room with a small stove, an indoor washroom and two bunk beds. They claimed the room for themselves and set out to search for survivors on the men's side of the camp. Nancy hoped to find her father and brothers.

Chaim had been at Bergen-Belsen for only two weeks when the camp was liberated but had accepted his fate: he was going to die there. He looked around the camp and saw piles of corpses in every direction, all of them victims of violence, disease and starvation. The living seemed more dead than alive. He had been sick and weak for so long. His body was ravaged by typhus and hunger, and his spirit was destroyed by despair and resignation. Only eighteen, he waited for death to set him free. 'I will lie down and meet my maker,' he thought. 'There was nowhere to lie down, because there were so many corpses, so I moved them,' and he lay on the ground between two bodies and waited to die.

Two days after liberation, on 17 April, Nechama and the other women walked past piles of corpses that extended as far as they could see. They were astounded by the nightmarish scene. Death was everywhere. Despite the gruesome landscape before her, a young man on the ground caught Nechama's eye. He appeared near death. She recognised him as her brother's friend, and suddenly was seized by the desire to save this man, who was barely clinging to life.

She was only sixteen years old, but Nechama possessed wisdom and experience far beyond her years. The war had robbed her of her youth and naivete but had not stripped her of her determination, optimism and kindness, which sustained her through the war. Nechama was determined to help this young man. Chaim remembered, 'I don't know how long it took … but suddenly … I heard the young girl saying, "I think this fellow is still alive. We should save him!"'

The other women tried to discourage her from wasting her energy on a man who had no hope of survival. Aunt Toby admonished her, 'There's nothing you can do for him. Surely, he will die soon. What do you think you are you going to do with him?'

But Nechama refused to listen. 'He's not dead yet. If we leave him, he will be dead for sure. I think we should save him.'

Chaim heard the voices, as if from far away, but was too weak to open his eyes or respond. But he never forgot what he heard that day, the voice of a young woman arguing with an older woman. 'Before I opened my eyes, I heard only her voice. I knew I would never forget her voice. After seeing her, I knew I would never forget her face.'

Nechama, unable to understand her aunt's reluctance to help, ignored her. She was going to try to save this young man with or without help. She persisted and they acquiesced, helping Nechama carry Chaim back to their room. He was sick, dehydrated, weak and unable to keep any food down. Nechama realised that her aunt was right. He was more dead than alive. But she refused to give up, motivated by the thought that if she tried to save him, maybe somebody would do the same for her family. Chaim doesn't remember how he got to the bunk. 'All of a sudden, I heard and later, I saw a young girl tending to me…'

After the first week, Chaim grew a bit stronger, and was able to speak. He asked to see a doctor, but Nechama had no access to medical care. Though the Nazis fled the camp and had been liberated, the war was not over, and Allied and British medics had yet to arrive. Nechama continued to care for Chaim as best she could. She would leave the room periodically to search for food and return to feed him.

Chaim knew if he did not get medical care, he would die. He decided to try to find someone to get him to a hospital. The three weeks Nechama spent caring for him gave him the strength to crawl out of the room alone. He lay down in the middle of the road, hoping someone would pick him up. After a few minutes a British military vehicle came along and took him to a hospital.

Six months later, he was released, healthy and strong. He returned to Bergen-Belsen, which was turned into a displaced persons camp. It also served as a hub for survivors searching for loved ones. He went back to look for the girl who saved his life. He would never forget the kindness of this wonderful stranger, and he was determined to find her.

In the meantime, after Chaim crawled out of her room to get help, Nechama was shocked to discover he had disappeared. She remembered, 'Just like that, one day he was gone, and he never came back. They stole my baby!' During the months that followed, Nechama wondered about the fate of the young man she had tried to save, hoping he had survived – but felt it was unlikely. She focused on moving forward and getting on with living.

Despite her desire to go to Israel, Nechama could not bear to leave Toby, the only other surviving member of her family. They stayed in Poland for a brief time before going to Buffalo, New York, by way of Ellis Island, in June 1947. They were part of a transport of orphaned children from Germany. While waiting several weeks for the transport in Germany, she met a nice young man who asked her to marry him, just as she was about to board the ship. She knew that this was no time to get married, given the turmoil and family losses she had just experienced. A few weeks after she arrived, she was taken in by a childless couple in Toronto.

In late 1945 in Bergen-Belsen, Chaim was sitting with friends who realised they had no place to go. He said, 'I heard Canada selected refugees, ten Jews and forty Gentiles, to be wards of the government. Everything was a miracle. I got selected.'

Toronto's Jewish community was deeply connected and close-knit, and news of survivors coming to the city spread quickly. Chaim, now known as Howard, arrived in Toronto on 3 May 1946. It appeared that the whole Jewish community was at the train station to greet him. The same thing happened in Montreal, at the previous stop. There, he was reunited with his four older siblings who had left Poland before the war. They were the only family he had left. His parents and five other siblings were murdered by the Germans and their collaborators.

Toward the end of June, Howard heard that perhaps the girl who saved him had arrived. He never forgot her, despite being sick, starved, weak and semi-conscious while she cared for him in Bergen-Belsen. He prayed she was the Nechama who saved his life; the one he looked for in Bergen-Belsen immediately after his release from the hospital. Excited by this possibility, Howard bought flowers, found her address, came to her cousin's house with his two sisters, and knocked on her door. A beautiful young blond woman opened the door and Howard could barely contain his excitement. 'Remember me?' he asked.

Her eyes grew wide. She remembered. 'It's you!'

Howard gave her the flowers; and in those days, he noted, 'She didn't kiss!' Orthodox girls and boys didn't kiss until marriage. Howard looked at her hands and exclaimed, 'These are the hands that saved my life.'

He didn't feel he could marry her yet because 'I had no language, no trade, nothing to offer. But she was very beautiful; still is, and I did fall in love.' A love affair for a lifetime.

Nechama, by then known as Nancy, wasn't ready to marry, either. 'I was not ready. I felt guilty I survived, the only one from my family!' She needed the time to grieve for the family members confirmed lost to the murderous Nazis. Nancy and Howard knew they were in love with each other, and three years later, after Howard found work and saved enough money to support a family, they were married. The wedding was attended by 300 people and Nancy was walked down the aisle by the family who took her in, while Howard was escorted by one of his brothers.

Throughout the war, Nechama and Chaim had led parallel lives, struggling through separation from their loved ones, inspections, selections, starvation, pain, sickness and the constant threat of death. When their lives intersected in Bergen-Belsen, Nechama's heroic efforts to save a stranger changed her life in ways that were unimaginable. Later, when their lives converged in Toronto, where Howard became a successful businessman. They appeared on the CBS show *Live! With Regis and Kelly* as one of the 'World's Greatest Love Stories'. They created a beautiful family of their own, with four children, eleven grandchildren, and two great-grandchildren, building a world of love, meaning and a lasting legacy for their family. Howard passed away on 9 December 2020 at ninety-four.

From video interviews with Nancy and Howard Kleinberg, January 2015, conducted by Mindelle and Ira Pierce, supplemented by the Shoah interview of Nancy Kleinberg.

15

JUDITH AND GUS LEIBER

Judith and Gus, the Leibers, had a seventy-two-year romance that began in Budapest in the aftermath of the Holocaust. It ended on 28 April 2018, when they both passed away. They left for the Garden of Eden within hours of each other, buried together to continue their loving partnership on the journey through eternity, artisan and artist living and leaving in perfect harmony. She was the artisan; he was the artist. They shared a common passion for art, fashion, living and loving.

For more than half a century, Judith Peto Leiber created extraordinary handbags and accessories for celebrities ranging from Elizabeth Taylor to Queen Elizabeth II, from Barbara Bush to Barbara Walters.

Her first love and husband, Gus Leiber, was an artist whose etchings and lithographs grace the halls of America's finest museums, including New York's Metropolitan Museum and Museum of Modern Art.

She was tall. He was not. She was a Hungarian Holocaust survivor; he was an American liberator. She was the showroom; he was the back office. Her preoccupation was her work; his was art for art's sake.

Together the Leibers created a niche in the fashion firmament. And they managed to do it without destroying their very special, loving relationship. Snippets of their story have been told before in newspapers, in magazines and even in the Congressional Record which, in the early 1990s, described Judith's life as 'the story of America'. It's a romantic Second World War film script, an old-fashioned love story with some very modern twists.

Bernice Steinbaum, a New York gallery owner who knew the couple well, said:

> It's difficult enough in a typical marriage to resolve conflicts in the struggles of power, security, independence, public success and personal admiration. The marriage of two artists requires the loosening of ego boundaries. Artists work in isolation, they are often asocial, obsessed and don't display the attributes of ideal mates. The Leibers were different.

Others also saw the tenderness and genuine affection they shared, and how they were always supportive of each other.

Judith Peto was born in Budapest, where her father, Emil, owned a successful jewellery business. His travels took him to Milan, Paris and London, and when he came home he brought with him beautiful handbags for Judith to add to her collection. He taught Judith and her sister, Eva, to gain an appreciation for the world's best arts and fashion. Judith's mother, Helen, was a homemaker.

Allies of the Nazis, the Hungarian government imposed anti-Jewish policies restricting Jewish enrolment in institutions of higher learning. As anti-Jewish sentiment grew, Judith couldn't continue her education in Hungary.

In the summer of 1939, shortly before the outbreak of war, Judith was a bright, ambitious eighteen-year-old student studying chemistry at King's College in Cambridge, England, where her parents had sent her to be safe in case of conflict. Though Judith's family was quite well off, they could not afford to let her remain in England for the entire summer and brought her home. By then, her father's side of the family had been part of the Austro-Hungarian empire's flourishing Jewish middle class for generations. Around the turn of the nineteenth century, one of her great-grandfathers had worked as a baker in Hungary's Trans-Danubia, and proof of this pedigree saved the family from deportation to Nazi-occupied Poland in the early 1940s.

Her mother's side of the family emigrated from Slovakia to Vienna in the early 1900s. They owned and operated a successful ladies' hat factory and lived right across the street from a synagogue. On her mother's wedding day, a red carpet ran from the family's home to the synagogue's front door. (The synagogue was destroyed on *Kristallnacht*.)

When the war began, her family held a meeting and decided, rather naively, according to Judith, to stick together through whatever happened. 'We didn't think things through,' she explained. 'We should have known what was coming, because some of our relatives had already suffered in Austria. In fact, my father turned down a chance to take us to Australia. That,' she noted remorsefully, 'was a mistake.'

Because university was not an option (she wanted to study chemistry, so she could create a top line of cosmetics) she said, 'I knew I had to learn a trade in order to survive. And, because I shared my mother's love of handbags, I decided to become a handbag maker.'

Childhood memories of her family's hat factory probably influenced her decision as well: 'The model-maker there used to create little hats for all my dolls ... it's also where I learned to sew.'

As the first woman ever to apply to the Hungarian Handbag Guild, Judith was a pioneer in a field that always had been regarded as 'fit only for weaklings and cripples'.

Judith apprenticed with the prestigious Pessl handbag company, sweeping floors and making glue. She quickly moved up the ranks, learning every aspect of bag-making, from creating patterns to working with raw materials and taking ideas from concept to final product. During her four years at Pessl, she learned every step in the manufacture. In three years, less than half the normal time, Judith advanced from apprentice to master handbag-maker. Judith would later quip, 'Hitler put me in the handbag business.'

By the time you're a master, you've been through all the stages of making a handbag, from sewing to cutting to skiving the leather [thinning the leather at its edges to make it more malleable], to framing and adding hand-tacks, even cleaning and polishing it. Because you learn the trade from the bottom up, you have the basis for a whole business.

While Judith was perfecting her craft and attempting to survive, the Nazi war-machine was marching across Europe, and trains carrying human cargo were rolling towards Treblinka and Auschwitz. But, during 1942–43, Hungarian Jews lived in relative safety compared to other European Jews. There were no mass deportations until after Germany invaded the country in 1944, when over 400,000 Jews were taken from the Hungarian countryside to Auschwitz and other death camps and murdered in record time. The Jews of Budapest, although spared from the mass deportations, also faced increasing harassment and death.

The situation went from bad to worse in the autumn of '44, when the Nazi puppet Iron Cross party seized control of Budapest. By that time, the Soviet army was in eastern Hungary, advancing several miles each day toward the Hungarian capital. Although the Nazis knew the end was near, they continued with their mission to exterminate all of Hungary's Jews. As the Russians encircled Budapest and as Americans carpet-bombed the region, ghettos were established, and Jews were executed in the city or sent westward on forced marches that very few survived. As the violence escalated, the Nazis killed three of Judith's uncles for leaving their homes without yellow stars affixed to their clothing, dumping their bodies into the Danube. Soon after, they grabbed Judith's father and sent him into forced labour to dig anti-tank trenches in a labour camp.

As the fighting intensified, the Iron Cross and the Nazis were unable to fulfil their mission to murder all the Jews of Budapest for a number of reasons: their administration was falling apart because of the fighting; Raoul Wallenberg, the Swedish diplomat who saved more than 50,000 Jews, was on the scene; and Adolf Eichmann and Heinrich Himmler were attempting to strike deals with the Allies, exchanging Jews for much-needed supplies. In these types of situations, little miracles, little coincidences, often meant the difference between life and death.

For Judith and her sister Eva, that little coincidence was being assigned to mend Nazi uniform trousers at the Jewish Community House, which, for a time, was deemed vital to the war effort. So, even as Jewish women were being herded into the local soccer stadium, the Peto daughters were spared.

To have any real hope of surviving in Budapest, however, the family needed *schutzpassen,* papers issued by the Swedish, Swiss and Spanish legations that often guaranteed the bearers' safety. A girlfriend's Jewish uncle working in the Swiss legation issued Judith's father a legitimate pass to get him out of the labour camp. Much later, when he was ninety-five years old and living in Budapest, the Leibers, who dislike travelling, flew to Vienna to help him celebrate his niece's seventieth birthday.

'I don't like going back to Budapest or Vienna,' Judith said when she was interviewed in the mid-1990s. 'Once, I was sitting with Gus in a cafe behind the Sacher Hotel in Vienna and men marched by in their *lederhosen*, looking just like the troops did 50 years ago. It left a bad taste in my mouth.'

She continued telling the story of her father's *schutzpass*:

My mother hired a messenger to bring my father back to Budapest because they were starting to empty the Jewish houses, and we needed to find a place to live. My sister and I had forged *schutzpassen* that we managed to obtain from a girlfriend. But we were worried because they were so obviously fake. There was an American family living in the Swiss House with us. And when the 16-year-old son examined my father's legitimate pass, he said, 'You know, this was typed on an Olympia typewriter. I'm going to ask around the building for an Olympia typewriter and type in "and family".' And that is exactly what he did – which is the reason that I am sitting here today. Otherwise, my sister and I would have been deported. By December 1944, the Germans were beginning to remove Jews from the protected legation houses and place them in the ghetto. So, when the Russians liberated us, we were happy to see them. The first rank of soldiers looked absolutely fabulous in their fur-lined coats ... until they began looting and raping and God knows what else.

The family returned to their apartment building, holing up in the basement for warmth and water until the street-to-street fighting shifted across the city, to the other side of the Danube. 'I was impatient,' Judith recalled. 'I couldn't wait to leave the apartment because I wanted to register for emigration, so I dragged my father to the American legation, five or six blocks away – and was hit by a bullet fired from the other side of the river.'

She pulled up her sleeve to show the scar on her left forearm. 'This is where it went in, and this is where it came out,' she said pointing. 'My jacket was full of shrapnel, and I was bleeding. My mother took me to the only hospital in the city, where an anti-Semitic doctor told me that I would never be able to use my hand again. But I sought out Dr Molnar, a friend of my father's, who was operating a makeshift hospital out of a cellar. He removed the shrapnel and sent me home.' She recovered the use of her hand quickly.

(In 1991, that old hospital became a new Jewish school. And, unbeknownst to Judith, Laszlo Tauber, an old childhood friend she had long ago given up for dead, financed this mini-Renaissance of Jewish culture that blossomed in the heart of Budapest. Tauber became a real-estate magnate in Virginia. Fifty-three years after the war separated them, they were reunited in New York; and Judith discovered that Tauber's wife – not realizing Judith Leiber was Judy Peto – was an avid collector of her evening bags.)

Gus Leiber was born in Brooklyn in 1921. The second of six children, his parents were hard-working, devout and Yiddish-speaking. They moved to Titusville, Pennsylvania, when Gus was three. He was a quiet boy with a paper round, was enthusiastic about school and loved to draw. Although he was a high-school valedictorian, he didn't attend university, choosing instead to remain in Titusville with his family.

First, he worked in a candy store and then as an apprentice printer at the local newspaper until Uncle Sam drafted him into the US Army in 1942. Because he kept pigeons as a hobby (and did all his life), he was assigned to the Signal Corps. 'Out I went, into the big world,' he said with a smile.

He was stationed in Algiers, where, in addition to his duties, he began haunting the local opera and movie houses. He was next assigned to Italy. During his nine months there, he absorbed more culture and adventure. Then he was assigned to a special detachment that kept track of the Russians as they won battle after battle against the Nazis. Eventually, Gus was stationed in Budapest.

Judith had a friend whose family was looking to rent out a room in their apartment for some much-needed income. Because Judith spoke perfect English, her friend enlisted her to communicate with American soldiers. The women approached an American soldier to ask if he wanted to rent a room. It was Gus, and it was his second day in town. But he wasn't interested in a room. He was, however, very interested in Judith.

She was the girl of his dreams. Their eyes locked. He said it was love at first sight. 'It was love at first sight for me, too,' Judith said. 'I noticed him immediately, but I didn't pick up people in the street. My friend did all the dirty work, and I reaped all the benefits.'

Gus was determined to find out more about Judith. He found out where she lived and the two began spending time together. On their first date, they went to the Hungarian State Opera. They couple realised they shared a love of music and the arts and attended concerts and the opera as often as they could. Knowing that Judith's family was struggling to get back on their feet, Gus began to bring food to her family.

The pair quickly became inseparable. They would spend hours roaming through what was left of Budapest's museums. The artists whose work they explored followed the European trends – the Nabis, the Impressionists, the Expressionists.

As their love continued to grow, Judith went on making beautiful handbags. Two US State Department secretaries she knew acted as her sales agents. Judith was soon creating handbags for the women in the American legation and getting paid in American dollars.

Meanwhile, Gus had some free time on his hands, so Judith took him to the Royal Academy:

I passed the entrance exam. There was a specific size piece of paper. They asked me to draw a nude male. I was sure that they would never have rejected an American soldier, it was not good politics. I was not very good; I only had cursory training in high school in a very rural sort of art class.

I allegedly passed the examination, but none of the instructors spoke English. The windows were broken. The other students were very interested in me, but I keenly felt my lack of ability. One of the students, a young man who was clearly a talented Jewish artist, was Peter Foldes... He took interest in me and became my mentor. He spoke excellent English and began to instruct me.

For the rest of the year, he was tutored by Peter Foldes, whose work was 'basically realistic, but free and beautifully drawn', Gus said. 'I sent a number of my drawings home,' Gus recalled. 'Among them were some nudes, which my mother burned. My parents, you understand, were not sophisticated people, and I didn't think much about what my mother had done because the drawings weren't all that great. For me, that time of my life was a lark.'

No wonder: Gus had dollars in his pocket and could afford German art supplies, a box at the opera, large numbers of books – and he was madly in love.

Judith and Gus wanted to marry but despite their daughter's obvious happiness with Gus, her parents were not pleased with the relationship. They had big dreams for their daughter and did not want her to limit her opportunities with a man of little means whom she barely knew. They were disappointed that he wasn't taller and more interesting. Gus knew they thought Judith was marrying beneath her; that Judith was too good for him.

At twenty-four years old, after dropping out of college, surviving the Nazi occupation and starting a small business selling her handbags, Judith wasn't about to let her parents dictate to her. She took charge of her future, determined to start a life with Gus. When they realised the depth of the couple's love and Judith's determination to follow through with the marriage, her parents warmed to Gus and Judith's mother planned the couple's wedding in Budapest. They married in February 1946. Judith didn't like the Rabbi and opted for a civil wedding. Unafraid to buck convention and staying true to herself, she wore a brown silk dress with a lace collar and Gus wore his military dress uniform.

Gus said, 'I was faced with the situation where, either I would have to re-enlist in the army, as I was a draftee, or to go home and get discharged. Because many American GIs had married European girls, the American army set up a system of boats to bring the GIs back to the States with their wives.'

Gus and Judith boarded *The Thomas Barry*, a Bermuda runner ship, in Bremerhaven, Germany, and landed in the Brooklyn Navy Yard. Judith brought nothing with her except her green toolbox and her design skills, her imagination and her determination to make a new life with Gus. She was twenty-six years old.

Gus remembered, 'It wasn't as romantic as you might expect. The men and women were separated – except for the officers – and Judith was sick during all 11 days of the voyage.'

The Leibers settled in a rooming house in the Bronx, which was more affordable than Manhattan. In their spare time, they assisted their immigrant friends by sending parcels to their surviving families in Hungary. Later, through these friends, they found a small apartment in Brooklyn.

It was difficult to convince the bosses in the American textile industry that a woman could design and create handbags. At that time, women were seamstresses, period. They could sew, but they surely couldn't design patterns, make samples, work with tools – that was for men only. Determined to get a job doing what she loved, she went to the Pocketbook Makers Union and got a job at a factory that mass-produced handbags. Meanwhile, through the GI Bill, Gus enrolled in college and received a monthly stipend. The couple supported each other, encouraging and pushing each other to follow their artistic passions, though they did not collaborate creatively together.

'I immediately went to work making handbags,' says Judith. 'Much of the industry was schlock. But I worked for 14 years for Nettie Rosenstein, well-known for designing the day-to-night "little black dress" – and owner of one of the finest handbag companies in America – until it moved to Italy.'

Judith broke through in 1953 with the creation of her iconic crystal-rhinestone pink beaded purse for the Nettie Rosenstein brand. Mrs Mamie Eisenhower carried it to the 1953 inaugural ball, wearing a 'Renoir pink' gown designed by Nettie Rosenstein and commissioned by Neiman Marcus. Judith continued in the industry until she was fired from a company going through tough times. That was in 1963, and Gus decided it was time for Judith Leiber and Company to be born.

'We scraped together $5,000 from our personal savings and from our relatives,' Judith continued, 'and rented a tiny loft that my I. Magnin buyer described as manufacturing in the bedroom and selling in the living room. I had four workers and did everything relating to the creation of the handbags. Gus worked on the invoicing and shipping ... it was really a family business.' They worked together for almost seventy-two years. What was their secret?

'I don't know,' admitted Judith. 'Maybe it's because we love each other. Maybe it's because we have a similar mindset. We do very well together, I must say.'

It is 1993, and Gus is seated at an oak table in his studio on East 31st Street, a few blocks away from his other life. (In mid-afternoon he would switch gears, and visit Judith's showroom on West 33rd Street, to assist in tying up loose ends and winding down the day; then they would travel home together.) That day, he was working on an abstract canvas sitting on coffee cans and propped up against a wall. The place was immaculate, and he wore a baker's apron over Bermuda shorts and a T-shirt. His omnipresent baseball cap was pulled low over his forehead, and his glasses sparkled in the sunlight. Behind them, his blue eyes twinkled with suppressed amusement.

He was surrounded by thousands of prints and hundreds of paintings. It seemed that Gus had done for fashion shows and models what Degas has done for ballet and ballerinas. His post-impressionistic paintings are bright, large and often witty comments on the fashion industry. A Matisse, a gift from a friend, occupied a place of honour.

From 1947 until 1951, Gus attended the Art Students' League in New York, studying graphics with Will Barnet and other contemporary artists. 'The place was really jumping with lots of GIs,' he said. 'I was doing etchings, lithography and graphics.' Then, while his wife worked for other companies, Gus hung paintings at the Whitney Museum of American Art, studied and taught art courses and became a prize-winning lithographer. Many of his works are now owned by America's finest museums, including the Metropolitan, MOMA, the National Gallery, the

Whitney and the Philadelphia Museum. Dozens of other museums and private collectors have also made acquisitions.

Gus was always supportive, and even a little bemused by his wife's huge success. 'She dragged me to all the shows,' he said, smiling. How did he learn that sometimes a man had to cook for his wife? 'I saw she couldn't handle it anymore,' he replies. 'She had too much work. So, I started doing the cooking and I enjoyed it.' Why did Gus help out at home? What made Gus so different from many other men his age? '*Parnosa*,' he cracked. 'You know *parnosa* [Yiddish for livelihood]? And the fact that we try not to take each other for granted.'

At that point, Gus grew thoughtful and uncomfortable talking about private matters, about himself. But he was part of Judith. An extremely important part.

Gus reached the stage where he could afford to enjoy art for art's sake. He had a complete print shop at his disposal and experimented with sculpture and bas-relief. His paintings are massive fields of bright colours on huge canvases. Their scenes depict blowsy, elegant women with wise faces in a smoky microcosm of 'fancy' events. His models hover in perpetual twilight between the fabulous and the painful; the result is often bitingly witty.

But Gus's garden in the Hamptons was his lasting work of art. It was also his passion. The Leibers bought their sprawling country home out on Long Island's South Fork back in 1956 and transformed it into their own intimate haven. More than two acres of farmland was turned into formal and magical gardens. For years, the couple hunted flea markets for finds with which to garnish the garden. According to Judith, 'You never can tell where you'll find inspiration.'

'It isn't Versailles, of course,' noted Bemadine Morris, senior fashion writer for *The New York Times* way back when, 'but it has its long, uninterrupted vistas, its unpredictable classic sculpture at the end of a path (the sculptures are mostly by Gus), pieces of pottery that serve as planters or simply as objects.'

Judith Leiber and Company occupied two floors of a building located in the shadow of the Empire State Building. You entered through a large reception area. The rugs and walls were a rich toffee-beige. They acted as backdrop to Judith's extraordinary handbags and Gus's paintings. This was their fourth loft and at the time they were interviewed, thirty years after they began, they employed 180 workers. She designed five collections a year, which meant about one hundred different bags.

'When you run a business, you find that you have to be a little bit of everything – a psychologist, even a mother hen. Some of my help insists on calling me "Mama". I have to worry if someone comes in with their nose out of joint – because their car was stolen, or they had a fight with a spouse – because everything affects the work.'

Since each bag is made individually, by hand, the work had to be of the highest quality. Each one was a work of art and craftsmanship. Even the tiny change purses placed in the finished bags are made by hand. Workers in the atelier worked on old straight-stitching Singer sewing machines and did remarkable things with golden leather. The linings were minuscule and delicate. It was very quiet, as craftspeople concentrated on applying tiny rhinestones one-by-one to create the trademarks of Judith's menagerie of '*minaudière*'.

Just a few of her commercial clients were Neiman Marcus, Bloomingdale's, Saks Fifth Avenue, I. Magnin and Bergdorf Goodman. She won all the coveted fashion awards, the dress designers adored her, and she even designed a line of jewelry for Harry Winston. The Leiber showroom, brightly lit and lined with massive antique French armoires, glittered with thousands of rhinestones applied to hundreds of bags. The leather goods were on racks and bags were visible behind the latticed doors. Judith would spread her arms and present her menagerie: the puppies and the kittens, the piggies and the tigers. Even the leathers sparkled. These little numbers stole the spotlight, so the outfits worn with them had to be very simple, because the Leiber handbag was, and still is, '*la chose*'.

In Judith's office, a very elegant escritoire and sideboard were covered with ashtrays brimming with beads and baubles. The office walls were lined with photographs of Judith Leiber fans, including Queen Elizabeth II. Bette Midler, always a *kibbitzer*, wants to know, 'What could the Queen possibly carry in her handbag?'

Judith Leiber had the answer: 'A lipstick, a hundred-pound note and a handkerchief – with them a woman can go anywhere!'

Other celebs who owned her works of art included Elizabeth Taylor, Diana Ross, Nancy Reagan, Mary Tyler Moore and Beverly Sills – diva and friend – who has a large collection on display at her home. And, of course, there was the late Barbara Bush. When she visited the factory with her entourage, she was thrilled by the 'doggie bag' Judith made for her, modelled after her pet pooch, the famous Millie. 'Mrs. Bush was wonderful to my staff,' Judith remembered. 'She had her picture taken with everyone, and then sent us autographed photos. She was really very nice.'

Other proud Judith Leiber owners are Claudette Colbert, Barbara Walters and Marlo Thomas. Two of her handbags, carried by two first ladies at their husbands' inaugurations, are on display at the Smithsonian Institution. Even Raisa Gorbachev owned a Judith Leiber, courtesy of Barbara Bush. 'I never dreamed I would be hobnobbing with first ladies,' she said. 'I'm just delighted to have survived. It wasn't easy at first, but when you are young, you can take a lot.'

The Leibers never will forget their past. Perhaps that is why they shared such a strong sense of commitment to the State of Israel. Despite all they went through, they are Jewish to the core. Judith constantly donated 'minaudière' and other bags to the organisers of many charitable events. As an item at an auction, or as a door prize at a luncheon, her handbags were an excellent way for organisations to raise funds. In a single year, Judith was honoured by Stern College for Women, by ORT and by the American Academy of Achievement – where even Robert Gates, then head of the CIA, was impressed by her.

For the Fall 94 season, *Harper's Bazaar* featured a two-page Judith Leiber spread with a posse of sparkly piglets nestled on cottony clouds. In *Vogue*, each bag, whether pavé, metal, leather or a combination of media, made its own statement. Alas, her handbags do not come cheap, often costing more than the owner's outfit and the money carried inside them. The ever-practical Judith said, 'I've always believed that a handbag should be soft and cuddly, dainty and graceful. It should make a woman feel happy and lady-like. What I am doing now, I couldn't have done while I was working for someone else. When you work for others, you have to realise their dreams. What you see now is a result of my past, what I've developed. And none of it would be possible without Gus.'

The Leibers sold their business in 1993 for a reported $16–18 million to the British company Time Products, and Judith stayed on as the designer until 1997. Her handbags were often on view in museums, but when Andy Warhol said her bags were works of art, Judith disagreed. 'Truthfully, I don't consider them art,' she said. 'I'm an artisan.'

In 2005, Gus opened a museum of his own design to display Judith's works, the Leiber Collection Museum in East Hampton, New York, adjacent to their residence. Their goal for the museum was to buy back and house an example of every one of her more than 3,500 pocketbook creations.

While Gus painted, Judith was on the hunt, looking for her bags. All told, there were about 3,500 handbags, purses and accessories, and Judith wanted a copy of each to put on display. They included penguins, polar bears, the Clintons' black-and-white cat, Socks, a watermelon slice, peppermint candy, sunflowers and stalks of asparagus, many glittering with thousands of Swarovski crystals and shaped from metals, Lucite, seashells, textiles and leathers, landscapes and the New York City skyline. Ann Stewart, the manager of the Leiber Collection, said Judith managed to recover 1,700 pieces, 'including many purchased over eBay or acquired from collectors as donations'.

In May 2018, the collection reopened with an era-defining exhibition, 'A Marriage of True Minds Remembered', displaying about 380 rarely seen bags. There were also four new paintings by Gus on view for the first time. The show contained one of the few known Leiber-to-Leiber pairings, 'The Much Admired', in which Gus' oil portrait of two fashionable night owls inspired his wife's corresponding handbag.

Jeffrey Sussman, the couple's biographer and spokesman, said Gus, who had congestive heart failure, told his wife on Friday night, 27 April, 'Sweetie, it's time for both of us to go.'

Patti Kenner, surrogate daughter and close neighbors of the Liebers, received an urgent call from their in-house caregiver that

Above: Joseph and Rebecca Bau.

Above right: Sally and Charles Bedzow.

Right: Isadora and Joshua Szereny.

Below right: Max and Toby Berger.

Murray and Fruma Berger.

Daniel and Lucyna Berkowicz.

Herman Shine and Max Drimmer
and their wives.

Right: Henny Durmashkin and Simon Gurko.

Below right: Lillie Burstyn and Simcha Fogelman.

Bottom right: Peska and Wolvie Friedman.

Below: Nardus and Sipora Groen.

Frank Kabak
with Mindelle
Pierce.

Chaim Joseph
and Hanka
Kempner.

Chaim Kleinberg
and Nechama
Baum.

Judith and Gus Leiber.

Victor and Regina Lewis.

Henry and Lydia Lilienheim.

Manya Hartmayer and Ernst Breuer.

Jacob and Reisel Najman.

Ernest and Sara Paul.

Rabbi Salomon Rodrigues Pereira.

Above left: Jack and Ina
Soep Pollack.

Above right: Rosi and Fritz
Schleiermacher.

Right: Sala and Sidney
Garncarz.

Above: Lunia and Leo Weiss.
Left: Rose Weisz and Joska Cseh.
Below left: Millie and Jack Werber.

she could not awaken Gus. Patti rushed over to find that he had passed. A few hours later, Judith had a heart attack and died. It was a Saturday afternoon, and they were buried, together forever, on the following Monday.

Artisan and artist. Judith and Gus. The Leibers. Together they fashioned the stuff of dreams, to delight ladies on enchanted evenings. They both said they were 'enormously blessed'. So were the rest of us, thanks to their talent.

Interviews of Gus and Judith Leiber in March 2017 in Springs, a hamlet in East Hampton, NY over dinner hosted by Patti Kenner, in her home, by Mindelle and Ira Pierce.

16

VICTOR AND REGINA LEWIS

This story is about the lives of Victor Leserkiewicz (Lewis) and Regina Steiner Lewis. It begins during their teenage courtship in Kraków, continues with their coming together and being pulled apart several times during the Holocaust, and reveals how they built very happy and fulfilling lives in America.

Regina Steiner was a petite, refined and socially confident private school (*gymnasium*)-educated girl living the good life in the Jewish cultural, social and political centre of Kraków, Poland, called Kazimierz. Regina's father, Israel, was a well-known and respected government labour representative and owner of a fur and fine-clothing store. Regina's mother, Ida, worked in the store with her husband. They had a full-time, live-in maid at home whom the entire family loved and respected.

Victor's family lived on the other side of the Vistula River in an anti-Semitic section of Kraków, called Podgórze. Knowing how and when to fight and defend oneself against racism was essential for Jews there. Victor adapted to his harsh reality by learning self-defence skills early in life. As a young teen, he was not afraid to be the only Jewish member of a local gymnastics club. But at the age of fifteen he began playing sports in the predominantly Jewish Kazimierz section of Kraków where Regina lived. There, he joined the Maccabi Soccer Club, eventually becoming team captain.

Owing to financial difficulties at home during the depression, Victor was sent to live with a wealthy uncle in Bierzów, Poland. He resented being sent away and saved enough money from allowances to buy a one-way train ticket back to Kraków. Once back home, he was forced to abandon his career dreams to become a pharmacist and dropped out of school to help support his family in his father's textile business.

One day in 1935, Regina embarked on a train in Kraków for a weekend getaway. Victor, a handsome young teenager riding his bike around the train station, caught Regina's eye. They later were introduced by a friend. The attraction between them was immediate. From that moment on, Victor and Regina became an item, spending much time together at Jewish youth organisations, Zionist dances and with groups of friends. Victor often recounted how they used to ride around Kraków on his bicycle, with Regina on the handlebars. Regina would say, 'We had a beautiful social life together in the Jewish youth organisations. We danced the tango, fox-trot, waltzes.' The couple fell deeply in love. Regina expected that they would be married within a few years.

With her solid stenography and typing skills as a graduate from commercial school, Regina began working as a secretary for the Furrier Commission in Kraków. She worked in the same office as her father.

On 31 August 1939, their lives changed radically and immediately. The Nazi army invaded Poland just two days before Regina's twentieth birthday. Regina's father was soon forced to surrender the keys to his furrier store. The Steiner family then spent most of their time at home, avoiding the violence against Jews that was frequently taking place in the streets.

Victor also was twenty years old during the invasion. At this immortal age, he believed he could outwit the Nazis as food became scarce. He used his contacts and business acumen to establish a black market for cigarettes, milk, butter, bread, potatoes, whiskey and anything else he could find. When Regina's father asked Victor to sell the Steiner family's paintings and jewellery for badly needed cash and food, Victor obliged and succeeded. Afterwards, Regina's father told her, 'If you and Victor survive this war, I will know that you will be in good hands because he is taking care of all of us.'

The Nazis established a Kraków ghetto in Podgórze in March 1941. Along with thousands of other Jews, Victor and Regina were forced into the ghetto with their families. Regina's immediate family and relatives were crammed into a small, two-room apartment. Nevertheless, when her father learned that Victor had nowhere to live at the time, he insisted that Victor move in with them. Victor did that until he was able to secure a living space for his own family.

Jews with working papers had a better chance to survive the ghetto than those who were idle. Victor's survival mentality prompted him to persuade a Nazi officer to prepare working papers that identified him as an auto mechanic. Victor knew nothing about automobiles, but he knew that auto mechanics were permitted to leave the confines of the ghetto. This was critical for continuing his black-market business and for continuing to support his and Regina's families.

Suddenly, in June 1942, the Nazis rounded up 7,000 Jews in the Kraków ghetto for a 'work transport', and many Jews were mercilessly murdered and beaten. Victor's and Regina's families were not captured during this roundup. Observing the extreme violence that had taken place, Victor doubted strongly that the roundup was to transport Jews to work. As a precautionary measure, he decided to steal a hacksaw from his auto shop and insert it in his boot – not knowing if or when he would need it.

Four months later, on 28 October 1942, the Nazis loaded 6,000 more Jews from the Kraków ghetto onto cattle cars. Again, many people were killed and beaten during this second roundup. This time, however, Victor, his parents, sister, brother and Regina's mother and sisters were among those caught in the roundup. They were all forced into the cattle cars. The train doors closed, packing the prisoners in so tightly they could barely move or breathe. Victor was aghast at the horrible conditions inside the car. He realised that this was his opportunity to use his hacksaw to cut out the bars on the small window at the top of the train and escape.

Victor pleaded with his family to escape. His father felt too weak to jump, his mother wouldn't leave her husband, and his sister didn't want to leave her parents. Brother Leon was willing to escape. The idea of separating from his family caused Victor much anguish that remained with him throughout his life. But he and his brother felt compelled to jump out of the window and escape.

The brothers made a plan to meet up after they jumped. Victor cut out two half-inch thick steel window bars and, trying to calm dissent from those who objected to his sawing, encouraged everyone to jump after him. After a heart-wrenching goodbye to his family, Victor climbed up to the window and leapt from the train. A few minutes later, Leon followed, and then another young man also jumped out the window. Unfortunately, the brothers were not able to meet on the ground because Victor hit his head as he landed on the tracks and lay unconscious for some time. The train continued on to Bełżec, an extermination camp in Nazi-occupied eastern Poland. Nazi documents indicate that everyone on board was murdered.

After regaining consciousness, Victor found himself alone and trying to figure out how to survive amidst Nazi troops invading nearby towns. Victor decided his best chance to survive was to go back to the Kraków ghetto that he knew so well. He snuck back into the ghetto and was reunited with Regina and her father. Fortunately, Leon survived the train jump and also returned to the ghetto. The brothers had to figure out ways to survive the horrible situation that they were all in. Victor thought he could survive by working hard. He volunteered to build barracks at Płaszów, located just outside of Kraków. He didn't know at the time that Płaszów was to become a deadly slave labour camp.

On 13 March 1943, the remaining Jews in the Kraków ghetto were separated by the Nazis into two large groups: those who were fit to work and those who were not. Some two thousand Jews deemed unfit for work were murdered on the streets and in their homes.

Fortunately, Regina and her father were among those selected for work. They marched to Płaszów where they were reunited with Victor. But life was very dangerous in Płaszów. Amon Göeth, a notoriously brutal Nazi officer, was in charge of the camp. Under his direction, Jews were starved, beaten, shot at and murdered on a daily basis. Many welcomed their death as an escape from the horrors of their lives. According to Victor, Göeth's inhumanity was depicted accurately in the movie *Schindler's List*.

Despite restrictions preventing men and women from interacting in Płaszów, Victor was able to visit Regina in the women's barracks nearly every day. He knew several Jewish policemen that let him into the women's area. 'I really took chances,' Victor said. 'We spent a half hour, an hour together regularly.' These brief moments gave the couple hope for survival and strength to endure another day.

On 6 August 1944, Regina was forced onto a transport to Auschwitz. She was devastated by her separation from Victor and her father. But her thoughts were soon consumed by how to survive in the camp. Upon her arrival, she was met by Dr Josef Mengele, the infamous Nazi who determined the fate of all incoming prisoners. Mengele directed Regina to go to the line designated for those who would work. Her best friend was given a towel and sent to the showers. Regina heard rumours that the showers were deadly gas chambers. She never saw her best friend again.

Life at Auschwitz was dehumanizing. The Nazis shaved, stripped, tattooed and degraded their prisoners. Death was a constant companion and the determination of who lived and who died was arbitrary.

During roll call one day, a friend insisted that Regina run back to her barracks with them to hide. Regina was not a risk taker and defying Nazi orders was not in her character. But once her friends ran from the lineup, Regina ran after them. It turned out that a Nazi guard at the lineup liked one of the girls and enabled all of them to escape safely. But back in the barracks, a terrified Regina hid and hoped that Nazi hunting dogs, that often were sent there, would not find her. The dogs were not dispatched, and the girls survived. After the war, Regina learned that those who remained on the lineup were transported onto ships that were 'blown to pieces'. One of Regina's aunts and several of her cousins were among the casualties.

Life for Victor at Płaszów became increasingly harsh. Each day was a struggle for survival. He was double-crossed one day by a Nazi SS officer who reported him for illegally selling cigarettes, while giving Victor the cigarettes and forcing him to sell them. Victor was whipped mercilessly and left for dead. Weak and debilitated, he dragged himself out of a wheelbarrow that was pushed by Jewish workers. They were headed toward a pile of dead bodies waiting to be burned. He was fortunate to receive quick medical attention from Jewish nurses.

All alone in Płaszów at this point, Victor responded to a job posting for an electrician. He was ecstatic to be selected for the job, given that he had little knowledge of electrical work. What he didn't know was that he would be transferred to Oskar Schindler's 'real' work camp at Brünnlitz, Czechoslovakia, and that he was placed on what was to become known as Schindler's List.

Victor arrived at Schindler's ammunition factory on 15 October 1944. He noticed that the prisoners at Schindler's factory were treated humanely, given food and clothing and spared the violence prevalent in the other Nazi camps. Victor would say often that his arrival at Schindler's factory at that point in the war is what saved his life.

Victor had a close call when he caused an electrical blackout at the factory. He ran to Schindler's private residence and pleaded for his life. Schindler helped him by telling Victor's supervisor that he wanted Victor to be transferred to Schindler's residence and to a flour mill to do odd jobs. Victor spent his remaining time at the camp working for Oskar Schindler. He joined the underground toward the end of the war and took up arms. But the underground did not need to liberate the camp. It was liberated eventually by the Russian army.

Victor later learned that his second cousin Mietec Pemper was responsible for compiling the names on Schindler's List. Victor never found out whether Pemper put him on the list intentionally to save his life, or whether his placement was just pure luck.

As the Nazis retreated from Russia's army, Regina was transported from Auschwitz to concentration camps in Oederan, Germany, and then to Theresienstadt, Czechoslovakia, where she was liberated.

After liberation, Victor learned that his brother, Leon, was ill with typhus and malnutrition at Theresienstadt. Victor left Brünnlitz to look for his brother. When he arrived, he asked an acquaintance to bring him to Leon. The man told Victor that Leon was very ill and said, 'Before I take you to your brother, I'm going to take you to someone I'm sure you'd like to see.'

Just a few minutes earlier, Regina had been talking to a group of survivor friends in her barrack. 'I know that my parents are not alive. I know my sisters are not either. But at least Victor should be alive. Knowing that he jumped off the train, I have a feeling that he should be alive,' she said.

The acquaintance brought Victor to Regina's barracks. Regina looked up and saw Victor standing by the doorway. They stared at each other, frozen for a moment, disbelieving that they were together again. Regina jumped up and wrapped her arms around Victor. She recalled, 'It was like he was sent from God. It was like I was calling him to me!'

Despite his joy and relief at seeing his long-lost girlfriend, Victor could not revel for long in their reunion. His focus was on his brother. When he arrived at Leon's bed, he realised immediately that he had to get him to Kraków for professional medical treatment as soon as possible. He decided to take Leon on a train to Kraków that same day.

Victor asked Regina to meet him in Kraków in a few days. To prove his love and his desire to be with her, he asked her to hand him her suitcase and come to Kraków within a week, where her belongings would be waiting for her. But Regina was confused. She loved Victor and wanted to be with him. But, if he loved her and wanted to have a future with her, she wondered how he could leave her behind so quickly.

At a hospital in Kraków, Victor was told that the medicine Leon needed was unavailable but that he could get good medical treatment in the American Zone in Austria. Not wanting to leave Kraków without Regina, Victor wrote to Regina several times to come to Kraków as soon as possible. Regina did not want to travel with Victor without a marriage commitment. After discussing the situation with her aunt and others, Regina decided to board a train to Kraków with a few friends and determine whether Victor was committed to her.

Regina arrived in Kraków on 1 July 1945. The following day, she and Victor were married by Rabbi Menashe Lewartow. Two Steiner cousins and two friends were witnesses. Others were brought in from the street to make a minion (a prayer quorum). Victor placed a wire-thin gold ring on Regina's finger – a ring she wore for decades. The ceremony lasted just twenty minutes. 'It was a very poor wedding, nothing to talk about,' Regina often said. 'But it was meaningful.'

The day after the wedding, Victor, Regina, Leon and several friends departed for Austria. The group crossed the border into Austria and settled in a gorgeous alpine village hotel in Bad Ischl that was transformed into a displaced persons (DP) camp. After four months of medical care at a local hospital, Leon was released and settled in the DP camp. Regina often said that Bad Ischl was a perfect environment to recover, emotionally and physically, from the scars of the Holocaust. The couple reconnected with old friends and found new ones. They had their civil wedding there in 1946.

Victor became Chief of Police at the DP camp. He also co-captained its soccer team in the newly formed Macabbi league. On 26 July 1947, Regina gave birth to Ida, whom she named after her mother. Looking to settle permanently in Palestine, the family was advised by Victor and Leon's sister, Lola, who lived there, that a war for independence was imminent. Lola suggested they immigrate to America instead. The family followed Lola's advice and applied for immigration to the US.

After four years as displaced persons in Austria, the US Army transport ship *General Sturgis* brought Victor, Regina and Ida to New York City on 25 October 1949. Leon arrived just a few weeks earlier. Eventually, the brothers changed their last names to the same name as that of the US relative who sponsored their immigration, Bill Lewis.

Life as an immigrant family in the US was difficult. Unfamiliar with the English language and the American way of life, it took time before the Lewis family felt settled in their new country. Three years after they arrived, their son, Alvin, was born. Five years later, the family of four moved to Kew Gardens Hills in Queens, New York, joining a large community of Jewish Holocaust survivors. By 1965, the area had become the seedbed for what would become the extraordinarily successful New Cracow Friendship Society, a social and charitable Holocaust survivor organisation which grew to some 375 families. Victor, a founder of the society, became a life-long board member and active committee chairman who spearheaded many important initiatives. Regina worked closely by his side on membership, communications and other committees. Through their work, they supported Jewish charitable organisations in Kraków and Israel, including Israeli bond investment drives.

That same year, Victor flew to Germany to testify against SS Lieutenant Colonel Martin Fellenz, the commander in charge of the 28 October 1942 Kraków ghetto deportations that killed many members of his family, as well as thousands of others. Fellenz was tried twice and served a prison sentence for his crimes.

Victor became a tool and die machinist in the US. Eventually, he built a tool and die manufacturing business with his brother and later founded his own business, VR Precision Inc. The letter 'V' stood for Victor; the 'R' was for Regina. Regina was delighted to help her husband, working diligently in customer service, bookkeeping and occasionally operating a lathe machine at the shop.

In 1995, Victor and Regina celebrated their fiftieth anniversary with a party for more than 100 of their close friends and family. The couple spoke about how they were determined to get past the obstacles of being Holocaust survivors and find the happiness they had hoped for, which they surely did.

Regina and Victor travelled to Poland several times with their children and granddaughter. These trips gave the family a deeper understanding of their pre-war lives and their Holocaust experiences, and enabled the family to pay their respects to their relatives who perished there.

In her testimony, Regina said, 'We were happy that we met after the war, that we joined each other and that we have a very happy life.' In his published autobiography, Victor wrote, 'I am thankful to my dearest wife, Regina, who fell in love with me before the war, remained in love with me during the war and married me after the war.'

Victor passed away in 2009 at the age of ninety. Regina, now ninety-eight years old, lives in her Kew Gardens Hills home with her daughter, Ida. Her son, Alvin, and his family live just a few miles away.

There is an extraordinary footnote to this story.

In 1994, a Kraków ghetto and Schindler survivor living in Haifa, Israel, Dr Alexander Allerhand, finished reading the Victor Lewis chapter of Elinor Brecher's book *Schindler's Legacy*. Alexander realised that finally he could locate the two men he had been trying to find for fifty-two years. Alexander phoned Victor and introduced himself. He then asked, 'Are you one of the two brothers who cut off the bars from the cattle car during the October 28 transport from the Kraków ghetto to Bełżec, and then jumped out of the train?' When Victor said yes, Alexander explained that he was a fourteen-year-old boy with his mother in that same cattle car. Alexander's mother ordered him to jump out of the train after the brothers to save his life, and then save the lives of his sisters, who were hidden by Gentiles. Alexander expressed immense gratitude to Victor for saving his life. When the war ended, Alexander, his sisters and their father immigrated to Israel. Their mother, who remained behind on the transport, was never seen again.

Victor and Regina's testimonies were videotaped by their son Alvin Lewis in 1985, by the USC Shoah Foundation in the 1990s, and by their granddaughter Jennifer in 2005. Alvin also conducted videotaped interviews of Victor's sister, Lola Kleinberger in 1986 and of Alexander Allerhand's escape from the 28 October 1942 transport to Bełżec, in 2007. Regina and her daughter, Ida Lewis, recounted the couple's experiences on videotape to Mindelle and Ira Pierce, 2014–2016.

17

HENRY AND
LYDIA LILIENHEIM

Lydia Turkus and Henry Lilienheim were married by flickering candlelight on 12 November 1939. They had been introduced by friends in Warsaw before the war, and quickly began planning their future together. They envisioned a joyous celebration dining and dancing with family and friends. Instead, the couple married huddled in a cramped apartment within the confines of Nazi-occupied Warsaw, surrounded only by eight immediate family members and their rabbi. Henry was thirty-one, she was twenty-three.

At the conclusion of the ceremony, the family entered into a difficult and emotional discussion. Henry and Lydia pleaded with their parents to escape Warsaw with them, but they feared the trip would be too strenuous, and they refused to leave. After much heart-wrenching deliberation, it was decided that Henry's brother would stay with their parents. The newly married couple, along with Henry's sister, Edwarda, her husband, Szymon, and their seven-year-old daughter, Misia, would escape to the Russian-occupied part of Poland. If they made it to the Russian zone, they would return for the rest of the family.

The next day, they said their difficult goodbyes and left. After sneaking past several Nazi guard posts outside of Warsaw, they travelled to Lida, a Polish town just 10 miles from the Lithuanian border. There they hired a guide to take them across the border, paying him one-third of his fee in advance. Although they waited for a cloudy evening to provide some cover for their journey, without the luxury of time they were forced to take their chances under a bright night sky.

One evening, surrounded by ice and snow, they started on their trek. Edwarda carried Misia on her back across the snow-covered fields while Szymon carried their two backpacks containing their meagre belongings. Henry carried a backpack in which he had stashed two hollowed-out loaves of bread filled with rolls of gold coins. Several times throughout the freezing night, they were instructed to lie down in the snow to escape detection. After trudging through a heavily wooded area, they reached a field about a hundred yards long, separating them from the cover of the next grove. After scanning the field for signs of danger, the guide instructed the group to run as fast as possible across the field. They ran quickly, one behind the other, breathless with fear, exertion, and hope. With only a few steps to go, they heard a booming 'Halt!' pierce the night.

Henry looked back to see a Russian soldier appear behind him, as if from nowhere. Henry, fearing what the Russian soldier would do if he found the hidden money, shoved his backpack under a bush. Just then, two other soldiers appeared and retrieved the backpack from the snow. The group was ordered into a truck and taken to a military guardhouse where Lydia and Henry were separated from the others. Henry was then taken into a room for interrogation, seated before a Russian officer with a menacing grin. The officer was playing with the stacks of coins from Henry's bag.

'So, we have caught a capitalist. We can use men like you for hard labour.'

Henry and Lydia were loaded onto a truck, driven back to Lida and forced into a two-storey stucco building where they were separated again. After weeks of imprisonment, Henry was notified by a Russian soldier that he and his pregnant wife would be released the following day, since they didn't have the facilities to manage a pregnancy. This came as a shock to Henry, who had no idea Lydia was pregnant. The next day, when they were released, Lydia privately admitted to Henry that she had tricked the officers into thinking she was pregnant, hoping they would let the couple go.

Henry and Lydia learned through the grapevine that Edwarda, Szymon and Misia had made it safely to Vilna, Lithuania. The next evening, with clouds obscuring the moon and stars, they set off again to cross the border. After a night walking through the cold and snow, they arrived in Lithuania and boarded a train to Vilna, where they joined Edwarda, Szymon and Misia.

But what had originally seemed to be a successful escape from Nazi-occupied Warsaw actually had turned into a cruel twist of fate.

The Nazis seized Vilna shortly thereafter, on 24 June 1941. Henry, Lydia, Edwarda and Misia were trapped. Tragically, Szymon had been grabbed off the street and taken to a labour camp. He did not survive. The remaining four of them were now residents of the Vilna ghetto, sharing one room with a friend of Henry's, a Mr Feferberg, with his wife and two others.

Mr Feferberg had been a well-known and wealthy watch importer in Warsaw before the war. When he travelled to Vilna, he had brought with him a suitcase containing his most expensive watches, which he planned to use to bribe his way to Venezuela where he had family. Because of their close friendship, Feferberg intended to bring Henry and his family along.

While interned in the Vilna ghetto, Lydia and Henry were assigned to work in the German military hospital in Antokol, a suburb of Vilna, Lithuania. Each day they were transported to and from the hospital by truck. One evening after work, in October 1941, Lydia and Henry boarded the truck back to the ghetto. As Henry was boarding the rear of the truck, it suddenly lurched into reverse, crushing Henry's leg between the vehicle and a brick wall. When the truck returned to the ghetto, Henry was rushed into the operating room of the hospital. An aged surgeon performed an operation to straighten and stabilise Henry's broken leg, but it was not successful.

Unwilling to accept this as the final outcome, Lydia took matters into her own hands and decided that two outstanding surgeons would perform a second operation. The first was a surgeon in the ghetto hospital. The second was a highly regarded, non-Jewish specialist from Vilno University. Determined that Henry would receive the best possible care, Lydia removed her yellow star and ventured beyond the confines of the ghetto, risking her life to persuade the latter to risk his life, in turn, to operate on Henry. The surgeon agreed. Lydia bribed a Nazi guard to let the surgeon into the ghetto, and the surgeons successfully repaired Henry's injured leg, though his months-long recovery was slow and painful.

While Henry was healing, Mr Feferberg visited and told him that he had a chance to escape and could not wait any longer. Henry was bitterly disappointed to miss the opportunity to free his family from the horrors of the Vilna ghetto. Two weeks later, Henry learned that the officer Mr Feferberg had bribed was actually an informant and had revealed his escape plan to the authorities. Mr Feferberg and his wife were shot.

In the spring of 1943, while still in the Vilna ghetto, Henry and Lydia heard about the Warsaw ghetto uprising and the Jews' last desperate attempt to resist the Nazis. Those who were not killed in the ghetto were sent to the death camps, most to Treblinka, an extermination camp in Nazi-occupied Poland. Henry believed with certainty that his mother, father and brother were dead. Memories of his family haunted him, and he became filled with rage and despair. A few months later, on 23 September 1943, the Vilna ghetto was liquidated, its prisoners sent to Vaivara, a concentration camp in Estonia. As they walked out of the ghetto, flanked by Ukrainian and German guards, Henry was besieged by guilt and helplessness. Looking at his sister, young niece and wife, his inability to protect them weighed heavily upon him. Suddenly, Henry was shoved to the right with the other men, not knowing what would happen to Lydia, as she was pushed through a gate to the left along with the other women and girls.

Henry soon was shipped to Vaivara, where he met a woman from Vilna who explained the selection process on the women's side. Young, strong, healthy women were assembled into one group; older women, disabled women, children and women who refused to separate from their children were sent to die in Treblinka or Auschwitz. Lydia had been placed in the first group and had been sent to Kaiserwald, a labour camp in Riga, Latvia. Knowing his dear sister would never have left her daughter's side, he realised with heartbreaking clarity that Edwarda and Misia were dead.

Henry was moved to another camp, where he met a Dutch labourer on his way to Holland by way of Riga. Henry gave him a letter for Lydia, hoping it would find its way to her. The Nazis continued to move Henry and his fellow labourers from camp to camp, but the already overcrowded camps couldn't accommodate more prisoners. At every stop, Henry asked for news about Lydia. Eventually, in Stutthoff concentration camp in Germany, he met a woman who told him that Lydia had received his letter. She informed him that the Kaiserwald camp, where Lydia was a prisoner, was being evacuated and Lydia might soon be joining them at Stutthof.

From that moment on, Henry was obsessed with thoughts of how close he was to reuniting with Lydia. He imagined the moment he would give her the gift he kept hidden in the heel of his shoe. It was a beautiful pearl necklace, for which he had bartered three rations of bread and five cigarettes, and then paid a shoemaker one ration of bread to hide it in the heel together with a photo of his parents.

But their paths did not cross. The day after Lydia arrived at Stutthof, Henry was taken to the Dautmergen concentration camp in Germany, where he spent the winter of 1944. In March 1945 he was taken to Dachau concentration camp.

On 29 April 1945, Henry was liberated from Dachau. When the American commander of the camp learned that Henry could speak German and English, he sent him to Munich to work in the Denazification Branch of the United States government. He was the first DP, or displaced person, to work there. Slowly, he began to put the shattered pieces of his physical life back together, but he couldn't rebuild his emotional life without his wife. By this time, Henry had learned that everyone in his family had been killed. Without confirmation that Lydia had perished, Henry clung to the possibility that she might have survived. He forced himself to search for his wife, despite the odds being against him. With the help of an American major who gave him a pass to travel throughout the American, French and British zones in Germany, he set off in search of Lydia.

Henry travelled through city after city in Germany, passing through villages that had been completely destroyed, reduced to rubble. He learned little about Lydia's whereabouts and understood all too well the pain, loss and despair in the eyes of his fellow survivors. He returned to Munich, clinging to the hope that Lydia was alive.

In the months after the war, survivors reached out to one another to share stories and exchange information, trying to piece together what had happened to their loved ones, their family, their friends. They asked each other about the camps in which they were imprisoned, the people they knew, the things they had seen. Henry crossed paths with a female survivor who knew Lydia in Magdeburg, Germany. Lydia had told this woman that after the war she was going directly to Warsaw to find her husband. With this information, Henry resumed his search in Warsaw.

It had been six years since Henry was last in his hometown among the streets, and memories of his childhood. He was astonished to see the city he once knew so well was now a barely recognisable pile of rubble and twisted metal. Despite his best efforts, he found no trace of Lydia. Henry wrote in his journal:

> I suffer more now than in the hell of the concentration camps. Then I could hope that the suffering would end, and a new life would begin. Then I knew I would never see my family again, except, I hoped, my wife. Now I will be absolutely alone.

Depressed and losing hope, he returned to Munich. As the months passed and reunions among survivors became less frequent, the thought of finding Lydia seemed like a fairy tale. Survivors began to remarry and start new lives, creating the next generation. But Henry lived only in the past, unable to move forward.

When all hope was nearly lost, a miracle happened. Henry received a letter that had been forwarded to his government employer through the committee in Munich created to search for lost relatives. He opened the letter and read a request for information on Henry Lilienheim. It was from Lydia!

Lydia pleaded for someone to let Henry know that his wife was alive and now working for the United Nations Relief and Rehabilitation (UNRRA) team in Hildesheim, Germany. After years of worry, uncertainty and dwindling hope, Henry could hardly believe he would finally be reunited with his beloved Lydia. Wasting no time, he boarded the next train to Hildesheim with a triumphant heart.

In Hildesheim, Henry leapt off the train and hurried to the UNRRA building. He barged through the entrance and searched the room for someone who might know where he could find her. A few steps away, he noticed a woman hunched over a desk reviewing a stack of papers. He rushed over to her.

'Excuse me, does Lydia Lilienheim work here?' The woman looked up, startled. She froze for a moment, absorbing the face of the man standing before her and matching it to the face of her husband, the face she had dreamed of for the past three years. Lydia jumped out of her chair and flung herself into Henry's arms. The couple embraced, overwhelmed by the love they feared might be lost; and relishing the bittersweet realisation that, despite all they had been taken from them, they still had each other.

That afternoon, as they rode back to Munich, Henry gave Lydia a ring he had purchased from another survivor, hoping he would one day be able to give it to her. He also told her about the pearls he had hidden in his shoe, which had been lost in the chaos of selection before his transport to Dachau. Lydia assured him that their reunion was far more valuable than any jewelry. They spoke about what they had been through during the three years they had been apart.

After Lydia and Henry were separated, Lydia worked in a series of work camps, her days filled with hunger, cruelty and murder. As the end of the war neared, she was taken to a labour camp attached to a factory at Magdeburg. For weeks, she heard rumours that the Americans were close. Then, one day, the Nazi soldiers assembled them into lines and began walking them away from the camp in small groups. Lydia decided to run. If she was killed trying to escape, her fate would be no worse than if she followed the Nazis to what she presumed would have been her death. But if she ran, she would have a chance to survive. She and her friend sprinted out of the line and away from the Nazis. The women ran into a laundry room, where they hid for hours until they were sure the search was over. The two women ventured out into the night, across a bridge, and straight into a group of American soldiers sitting on a tank. They were free.

After her liberation, Lydia was offered a job as a translator at UNRRA in Hildesheim, which she accepted, hoping it would help her find Henry. She sent letters to every central office, asking about Henry Lilienheim, and finally received a response. And now, finally, Henry, thirty-seven years old, and Lydia, twenty-nine, were together again.

The couple settled into daily life in Munich and began to rebuild their relationship. Immediately after the war, Henry wrote a memoir detailing his experience of searching for Lydia. Then he set it aside and moved forward with his new life.

Henry and Lydia soon had a daughter, Irene, who forged a link between the families they had lost, and the family and future they were building. Despite the relative normalcy of their new lives, they dreamed of leaving Germany and moving away from the painful reminders of their past and the ever-present anti-Semitism still simmering. In 1949, Henry and Lydia emigrated to the United States and settled in New York City with Irene, now two years old. They struggled to adjust to their new life.

Henry got a job working for a patent attorney as a technical draftsman and translator. It was a position for which he was well suited, having earned a degree in France as a textile engineer. Lydia worked in a medical laboratory as a bacteriologist. In 1959, Henry's company transferred him to Chicago, Illinois. That same year, they added a son, Michael, to their family. Henry worked during the day and attended law school at night, becoming a patent attorney and ultimately establishing his own international company.

Henry and Lydia experienced a dramatic transformation in their lives. They came to New York with no money, no friends, and only a basic knowledge of English. From this beginning, they lived the 'American Dream'. They were a vibrant couple who adored their children and lived a fulfilling life. Despite their happiness and success, however, the shadow of the Holocaust lingered. They didn't speak about it directly but, as with many children of survivors, their children internalised the experience of their parents through whispers, bits of overheard conversation, and a few scattered facts. After years of avoiding anything related to the

Holocaust, Irene watched a documentary, *The Memory of Justice*, which ignited her curiosity and drove her to learn more.

Though Irene knew about the memoir her father had drafted right after the war, she didn't read it until nearly thirty years after it was written. Moved by her parents' story, she was compelled to try to ascertain the effects of the Holocaust on the children and grandchildren of survivors. Determined to dig deeper, she made her own documentary, *Dark Lullabies*, to better understand the legacy of the Holocaust by speaking with children and grandchildren of survivors and the new generation of Germans. Despite her father's early reservations, both of her parents loved and embraced the movie. After the release of her film, Irene convinced her father to publish his writing in a book, *The Aftermath: A Survivor's Odyssey Through War-Torn Europe*. In 1996, for his Bar Mitzvah project, Henry and Lydia's grandson, Toben, created a graphic memoir based on *The Aftermath*.

After sixty-three years of marriage, Henry passed away in 2002 and Lydia followed in 2012. Their story lives on in their two children, their grandson, and their legacy of bravery, resilience and love.

Adapted from the original book The Aftermath: A Survivor's Odyssey Through War-Torn Europe *by Henry Lilienheim and interviews with Irene Lilienheim Angelico by Mindelle Pierce and Robin Lorell Davison on 12 May 2016.*

18

MANYA HARTMAYER AND ERNST BREUER

This love story began when Manya Hartmayer and Ernst Breuer met and fell madly in love in the late summer of 1943. It happened after they left the small town of St Martin Vésubie, France, when it became known that the Nazis were re-occupying the Maritime Alps after losing North Africa to the Allied forces. The couple dreamed of freedom as they continued their hair-raising series of escapes from the Nazis and experienced multiple near-death encounters.

She was twenty-one; he was twenty-six. Manya looked younger than her years, tall and painfully thin. Her green eyes were sunk in her delicately boned face. She walked with flowing grace, and her sun-streaked golden hair was shoulder-length. When Ernst first saw her, she was standing there, a young woman in a man's shirt far too large for her. Manya explained the shirt was given to her by her father before he was deported by the Nazis.

Ernst looked older than his age, born in 1914 in Austria. He had high cheekbones and a pencil-moustache. His mature looks were enhanced by a strong chin that made him look like a Roman warrior. His haunted eyes often looked like they were raging. For years he survived in the French underground as a resistance fighter. When he was hunted by Nazis in Paris, he escaped to Nice. They tracked him to his hideout and he managed to escape again. When he met Manya, he was travelling with his sister, Lisa (Liselle).

St Martin Vésubie was in the Maritime Alps, high on the French side of the mountains, about a two-hour train ride from Nice and the French Riviera. It was a safe haven for thousands of Jewish refugees, a place where Italian authorities relocated them among the local peasants. It became an instant *shtetl*, a small town, with synagogues and Jewish schools. Food was scarce, but the peasants shared whatever they had with the Jewish refugees.

Hitler assigned the region to the Italians and it was occupied by the Italian Fourth Army in November 1942, a reward for Italy's attack on France just before the French surrendered to Germany. Some say Italian sympathy for the Jewish refugees was due mainly to the work of the Italian-Jewish banker Angelo Donati, who was living in Nice. He is said to have convinced the Italians to protect the Jews from French and German persecutions.

The war ended for the Italians on 8 September 1943 when they surrendered to the Allies, and the Nazis took back the Italian occupation zones. The Germans knew the Italians were giving false papers to protect their Jews; and they began to go after them.

Manya Begleiter, later Hartmayer, was born in Berlin in 1922. Her father, Hermann, was from Galicia. Her mother, Adele, was born in Oswiecim, Poland, which was called Auschwitz by the Germans. Manya had two younger brothers, Ziggy and Willie. They lived in a comfortable two-bedroom apartment in the Jewish section of central Berlin.

In January 1933, when Hitler became Chancellor of Germany, life changed for the Jews. Later that year, the Nazis began an unofficial campaign of violence, removing them from their professions, including the civil service, and from social life as well. That was when, for safety, Adele moved Manya and her two brothers back to her hometown in Poland, where they stayed for about a year. By then, the situation for the Jews in Germany appeared to improve, and in late 1934 Hermann asked them to return.

In 1935, Manya's parents were ordered to get re-married in the City Hall, as Jewish marriages in synagogues were no longer recognised by the Nazi government. That was when they were ordered to 'Germanize' their name and change it to Hartmayer. By 1936, while the Olympic Games were going on in Germany, things got better for the Jews, but that did not last long. As the dangers for the Jews escalated, by 1938 Hermann was desperate to get his family out of Germany. They were constantly on the run, sometimes as a family, and at other times Manya was left to her own devices.

The first time they escaped was right after the *Kristallnacht* pogrom of 9/10 November 1938. The pogrom was the Nazi response to a Polish teenager, Herschel Grynszpan, shooting a low-level German diplomat in Paris. Manya's mother saved her father by hiding him in the bedroom in their Berlin apartment when the Nazis were arresting and deporting '*Ost Juden*' – non-German Jews.

Fearing reprisals, the next day they made a pact as a family to stay together no matter what would happen. They walked to the police station where, by luck, they were met by an officer who knew her father. He advised them to get out of Germany and stay with German Jews who were not yet affected by Hitler's edicts. Her father escaped across the border to Belgium. Her mother and two brothers escaped on the same route, but Manya and her younger brother were intercepted. Amazingly, sixteen-year-old Manya had the presence of mind to contact a Jewish agency that arranged to pay for her very young brother to go to a safe place for children under twelve in Belgium. Soon after that, he was back in his parents' arms. Manya was out there, alone, fending for herself. In February 1939 she tried to cross the German border into Belgium alone and failed. She succeeded on her second try with the help of a smuggler her father had hired. Once in Belgium, she was put on a train in the middle of the night and eventually found her way to her parents.

In 1940, when the war broke out in Belgium, many of the Jewish refugees fled to southern France, and so did Manya and her family; but that year, the French began detaining Jewish foreigners.

The family was interned in several concentration camps, where her father managed to keep them safe, until they arrived in Rivesaltes, in the Pyrenees-Orientales, near France's border with Spain. There she watched as her father was sent on a transport, one of many in operation daily, destination unknown. Rivesaltes functioned as a regional centre where 2,300 Jews were sent to Auschwitz after a stopover in Drancy, a detention camp in north-eastern Paris. As he left Rivesaltes, he removed his shirt and gave it to Manya, telling her it would keep her warm at night. Somehow, on the way to Drancy, Manya's father escaped and found his way to St Martin Vésubie, 60 kilometres from Nice, in the mountains near the Italian border.

Manya and her mother remained at the Riversaltes camp. Then, in November 1942, they were placed on a transport to the infamous Gurs detention camp. Gurs was one of the first and largest camps established in France. It was a place where, every day, truck transports came and went. The prisoners would all rush to see who was arriving and they cried for those who were leaving. As the French Vichy and Nazi governments accelerated the deportations, Manya would sing songs to the inmates to relieve their depression.

A French woman in the camp who appreciated Manya's singing offered her the last permit for transfer to an orphanage in Cantal, an administrative province in south-central France. It was understood that the orphanage was funded by wealthy Jews around the world. Manya wanted to stay with her mother in Gurs, but was convinced that if she left, her mother would find it easier to escape. Manya boarded a truck with the other children, crying and shaking because she was leaving her mother behind. Later her mother, Adele, fell ill and did not survive.

Alone, with no news at the orphanage, Manya worried until finally she received a postcard from her father. He warned it was dangerous for her to remain there, as the Nazis were planning to take the town. He instructed her to leave immediately and join him and her two brothers in St Martin Vésubie.

Early the next morning, Manya disguised herself as an old lady and caught the train without documents or permissions and got off in Marseille. She waited overnight for the next train to Nice, hiding in dark corners of the station with her heart pounding. She boarded the train to Nice in the morning, where the Nazis were asking for everyone's papers. She locked herself in the toilet. Suddenly there was banging on the door and shouts of "*Aufmachen*!" – open up! She thought of jumping out the window – but the noises suddenly stopped. Miraculously, Manya made it to Nice and into the arms of her father and two brothers, who took her to their apartment in St Martin Vésubie, where Monte Carlo joins the Cote d'Azur. In general, the Italian people were kind to Jews, although the Italian government showed two faces toward Jewish citizens and refugees just before and during the war. Interred by the Italians in that little town, they had to check in with the Italian police twice a day and felt very protected.

After General Rommel's loss in North Africa, the Nazis re-occupied the Maritime Alps. Manya's father realised they had to leave. They began climbing the Alps right after they heard the Nazis were on their way, or might already be there. The Italians also feared the Nazis.

It was then that Manya met her true love, Ernst. Manya and her family, and Ernst and his sister, Lisa, were part of a contingent of 1,000 to 1,200 Jews, fleeing to what they thought was safety across the Italian border, at the peak of the Alps, more than 6,000 feet above sea level.

Ernst and Lisa, who spoke Italian, stayed with Hermann's family as they fled. They tied baskets, knapsacks and suitcases around themselves with rope, and started their climb through La Madonna della Finestra Pass. It was an incredible feat that challenged even professional climbers. The fear of the Nazis was sufficient to enable pregnant women, seventy- and eighty-year-olds, some with canes and crutches, and little children to make it to the top. They were a long, straggly line of people who, from a distance, looked like a string of ants scrambling up the mountain.

Manya was wearing only summer clothing, including the shirt her father gave her in Rivesaltes. She looked at the peaks high above her and was freezing. She questioned whether they ever would make it to the top. Her brothers assisted young and old in need of assistance up the mountain, pulling them as best they could. Manya felt that with each step up, she was moving further away from her mother, Adele. Every stone she touched was wet with tears for her mother. As she climbed further, there were fewer trees, and when she looked back, she saw a beautiful lake, glistening like a jewel in the greenery, and wondered that God gave the world so much beauty – but she could not share in it.

Hermann knew the Italian border with France was on top of the forested mountain, with a large military outpost. They were with the lead climbers who managed to be among the first to be greeted by the *Carabiniere*, the Italian national police. The cold and exhausted climbers were jammed into the military barracks and learned the Italian soldiers were also running from the Nazis. Descending into the valley, which was in some ways more difficult than climbing, they came upon the Italian Alpine village of Valdieri, in the province of Cuneo. All Italy was in chaos after 8 September 1943, as Nazis already in the country were disarming their former allies; and those who resisted were shot on the spot. The village filled with refugees, who were trading valuables for a place to stay. After the local hotels filled, others found themselves staying in peasants' homes.

Deciding that there were too many Jewish refugees in Valdieri, Hermann managed to stay in the nearby woods with others, but not before they gathered supplies. Manya's family and Ernst and Lisa Breuer were asleep in a barn when the Nazis attacked Valdieri and 500 Jews were arrested by the SS, as were those caught by Nazi patrols in other small villages. Immediately, Hermann rushed them deeper into the woods. There, with no food or blankets, he traded his gold wedding band for canvas drop cloths to cover them from the rain.

Manya stayed close to her father, two brothers, Ernst, and Lisa who acted as interpreter. When they came upon several Italian peasants, Lisa learned from them that several villages had been burned because they were hiding Jews.

In February they came upon a group of Italian partisans. Speaking on behalf of Hermann, Lisa said her group wanted to join up with them. The request was denied because the partisans did not have enough food and ammunition to share, and because, with the exception of Lisa, none could speak Italian.

When the Nazis approached where they were staying, Manya separated from her father and her two brothers. She, Ernst, Lisa and a few of the partisans ended up in Rome at the beautiful French Catholic convent of Notre Dame in Via Garibaldi. A French noblewoman, in charge of the convent, took in all of them.

Ernst organised a hiding place for the few partisans who brought them to the convent. He hid them in the cellar and pushed heavy furniture against the door so that the Nazis would have trouble finding them. Manya and Lisa were taken to the dormitory where the nuns had small cells. Lisa stayed with Manya in one cell and a nun gave them clothing, including nightgowns and socks that were knitted for them. The convent was very cold as the interior was marble. Manya fell ill with tonsillitis. She was also exhausted emotionally. The nuns were forced to take her to the hospital to remove her infected tonsils – an operation done with no anesthesia or medication. It was a painful ordeal.

Without realising it, the nuns gave hospital administrators Manya's real name, though she had been using a false name, Myna Bershe, for years. After the operation, the fascists found out that Manya was born in Berlin and tried to arrest her on the spot. Manya recalled seeing the fascists in black uniforms standing in front of her hospital bed asking her who she was and why she was in Italy. She could not talk and feared her last moments had come. One of the nuns wasn't having it. She argued that the fascists should return in the morning when Manya could answer their questions. The patient, she pointed out, was covered with icepacks and couldn't speak. When the fascists left, the nuns rushed Manya, unconscious, out of the hospital and hid her. When she woke up, she was back in the convent.

On 5 June 1944, Allied troops landed at Anzio-Cassino in Caserno and the liberation of Rome began. When she was liberated, Manya went to the synagogue to give thanks for her survival and to pray for her father, mother and brothers. She thought the building would be closed, but to her surprise it was open. It was located near the Coliseum where, hundreds of years before, Christians were hunted with lions; and she knew exactly how they must have felt because she felt that way in Rome, too. It was there that she was told to provide her name to the American authorities – some of them happened to be there with Manya, and they would help her to come to America.

Manya gave her name and Ernst's name, and a few days later, they found themselves on an American army truck with Ernst's sister, Lisa, that took them to a pier where they boarded the Liberty Ship, the USS *Henry Gibbons*. They joined 978 other refugees, destination America.

The order to rescue them came from President Roosevelt in June 1944. He established the War Refuge Board (WRB) by Executive Order, to find havens for 'all victims of oppression'. These refugees were joined on the ship by wounded returning American soldiers, housed separately.

US Secretary of the Interior Harold Ickes chose the Jewish American writer and journalist Ruth Gruber, then his special assistant, to go on a secret mission to shepherd the first (and only) shipload of Second World War refugees to be sheltered in the United States. He appointed her to the rank of general of the US Army for the duration of the journey, to protect her from the potential danger of being captured by the Nazis in Italy, where fighting was still intense. Under the Geneva Convention, high-ranking officers are supposed to get special treatment; Gruber's mother scoffed at that pretence while trying to talk Ruth out of taking on the mission.

Their ship took them through the Mediterranean and then across the Atlantic Ocean, both infested with U-boats and Nazi bombers out to destroy them. The *Henry Gibbons* was surrounded by a flotilla of other American transport and war ships.

The ship left Naples on 21 July 1944 and arrived in New York Harbor on 3 August. Tensions between the refugees and wounded soldiers ran high because too many of the soldiers felt that Roosevelt was fighting a war for the Jews. (The Jews certainly did not think so, and it was definitely not the case – but Jew hatred was everywhere.) Tensions between the two groups were reduced significantly when Ruth Gruber decided to put on a show highlighting the acting and comedic abilities of the passengers on board. Soon, soldiers were flirting with the young refugee women.

There were 525 male and 457 female refugees aboard, representing eighteen nations. They signed away their rights to stay in America permanently. They would have to leave when the time came, because their arrival fell outside the bounds of the immigration quotas. The State Department, under Breckinridge Long, was determined not to let a single Jewish refugee into the country before, during or after the war. To thwart him, Roosevelt established the War Refuge Board at the behest of the Treasury Secretary and his good friend Henry Morgenthau.

There were 874 Jews and 108 Christians on board, including doctors, pharmacists, opticians, artisans, merchants, bookkeepers, tailors, teachers, lawyers, writers, actors, painters, sculptors, musicians, engineers and rabbis. They were outside the strict quotas. Historians say that even as late as 1944, another 100,000 Jews and many others could have been rescued as well, had Long's policy been more humane.

The journey took thirteen days, while Gruber's reports of the atrocities they escaped made it into the front pages of national newspapers. In New York, the refugees waved at the Statue of Liberty and once docked crossed the Hudson on a ferry to Hoboken. There, they boarded the train to Oswego, a small town in upstate New York.

Ernst and Manya wanted to marry when they boarded the ship. They petitioned the captain, who refused them, saying they should wait until they got to America. Ernst wanted to protect Manya and take care of her for the rest of her life. He thought that she was all alone, and that Hermann, Adele and her two brothers were gone, just like his whole family, except Lisa.

When Ruth Gruber met Manya, she told the writer she was Polish and did not know what had happened to her Polish parents. She told Gruber her story of escape and survival, including the weeks it took to recover from a brutal beating in the Rivesaltes camp. Gruber learned that Hermann wrote postcards to Manya in code. When he warned her that Nazis were coming for her, he wrote, 'The *lecht* (Yiddish for candles) are coming for you.'

In Oswego, Manya was brought back to sunshine and life. She was grateful forever for the beautiful country that took her in. She was with her love, Ernst, and his sister, Lisa. Their final destination was a former army camp, Fort Ontario, on the banks of the lake, that had been decommissioned just months before. Entering the camp was traumatic for some of the refugees, because they had to march past armed soldiers under glaring spotlights. The place looked like a concentration camp, behind chain link fences and rusted barbed wire. That worry evaporated when they were escorted into their homes in two-storey wooden barracks painted white. They were issued towels and soap, mattresses, cotton bedsheets, blankets and pillows: bedding they hadn't seen in years.

Manya's first American breakfast consisted of seven eggs and all the bananas she could eat. She realised that she could look up and not be afraid that someone was going to grab and murder her. She had come a long way and was young enough and old enough to remember and realise how lucky she was to be in Fort Ontario. Although it was not exactly what they thought it would be – it was just another camp in which they were interned – she didn't mind because she felt she was starting to live again.

Manya and Ernst were very much in love but could not get permission from the government to get married because of their undefined status in the camp. Ernst was particularly upset, and they begged Ruth Gruber for assistance. Ruth tried everything to accomplish that, continuously writing and phoning her superiors in Washington, DC, to get a permit for the couple to leave the camp. Only then could they go to Oswego City Hall during the quarantine period to obtain their wedding licence after their blood tests, so that the wedding could proceed. Finally, that did happen – with a police escort. That day, Manya realised that she had nothing appropriate to wear on her wedding day, but she did have her father's shirt. Gruber called her mother in New York City the day before the wedding and asked her to bring one of Ruth's dresses for Manya to wear. Manya tried it on; it fit, and she got married in it. Ruth's mother also brought pearls for Manya to wear, and they added a glow to her skin. While they took the train back to Fort Ontario, Gruber's mother crocheted a veil for Manya to wear at the wedding. On the balmy August morning of the wedding, Manya and her survivor friends raced around the camp picking wildflowers for her bridal bouquet.

Manya and Ernst were married under a *Chuppah,* a wedding canopy, by three rabbis, two from Europe and an American rabbi who came as an honoured guest and gave them away at the wedding. At that time, Manya did not know whether any of her family members had survived, and she prayed for them.

The couple was in the camp long enough for Manya to give birth to a baby girl they named Diane. Her status as an American was in question, as it was for the rest of the refugees. They were uncertain if they were going to be sent back after the war was over, an eventuality they all had to promise to honour prior to boarding the *Henry Gibbons*.

In their hearts, none of them believed they would be sent back to the hell that they came from. It took the House of Representatives to decide the status of citizenship for their daughter, Diane. In the end, because of the 14th Amendment in the Constitution, Diane was declared an American citizen.

The couple and their fellow refugees lived in the Fort Ontario military camp for eighteen months. Their stay in Oswego was an emotional event for the local community and a political conundrum for the nation. On 22 December 1945, President Harry Truman announced that the refugees would be allowed to stay in the US. It was not until 17 January the next year that the gates of the War Refugee Center, as it was known, were opened, and the refugees were truly free. That was eight months after Germany surrendered and five months after the Second World War ended.

Manya Breuer, known as Fort Ontario's first bride, went on to sing with the Los Angeles Opera Company, the American Opera Company, and the Beverly Hills Symphony. She found out much later that her father and brothers survived the war, and finally they reunited in the 1960s.

Phone interview with Manya Hartmayer by Mindelle Pierce, and video interviews with Ruth Gruber, 17 December 2012.

19

JACOB AND REISEL NAJMAN

This tale includes five weddings. My mother, Reisel Lieberman, was born in south-eastern Poland, in the Carpathian town of Nowy Sacz (Yiddish: Sanz) on 7 July 1912. Her impoverished family lived in a sylvan setting in a tiny two-room apartment above the court of Rabbi Aron Halberstam, son of the famous Divrei Chaim and descendant of the Sanzer Rebbe, founder of many Chassidic dynasties, including Satmar, Bobov, Munkacs and others. The house stood high on the banks of the Dunajec and Kamienica rivers, near the Royal Castle, a military training base. During the winter, my mother and her five siblings would slide down the hill on my grandmother's wooden cutting board and sometimes be given a sleigh ride to school. In the summer, they would cool off with a swim in the river.

Alte Mindelle, my maternal grandmother, was tall and elegant with piercing black eyes. She was the talk of the town, friendly and joyful. When Emperor Franz Josef came to Sanz, she was chosen to accompany him in his carriage as the town's ambassador. My maternal grandfather, Mendel Shaya, was born in Oswiecim (later Auschwitz), in central Poland. Short and stern-looking, he was a Talmudic scholar at the local yeshiva. Raizel remembered his one weekly sign of affection – a kiss on her hand and a cube of sugar offered every *Shabbos*.

When Mendel Shaya's mother died in childbirth, his forty-year-old father married a sixteen-year-old girl. Within weeks, she had banned ten of his children, aged over ten, from their home. Mendel Shaya's twelve-year-old sister, Anna Hirsh, walked all the way to Vienna from Oscwiecim and became an apprentice to a pastry chef. By the time she was eighteen, she was able to buy passage to America.

The marriage of Mendel Shaya and Alte Mindelle was arranged. They met for the first time on their wedding day under a wedding canopy. Like many other families in Nowy Sacz, they suffered from grinding poverty. During the early years of her marriage, Alte Mindelle earned extra money by making candles, assisted by all her children. They did so secretly, in the darkness of night, to avoid paying the local mercantile tax. Reisel said Alte Mindelle was determined and strong. She kept her husband employed at the local Yeshiva even when he was disgruntled because of his pitiful salary. He threatened to quit, leaving the family at risk. Brazenly, Alte Mindelle pleaded with the head rabbi to use money from her candle making to augment his salary, while convincing him to praise her husband. When Reisel was in her twenties, she moved to Krakow, where she worked as an embroiderer, specialising in flat tapestries used for covering and decorating grand pianos.

Jacob Najman was born in January 1910 in Praszka, a picturesque small Polish town on the German border with a population of 900. His maternal grandmother, Miriam, was known as *Bubba*, and famous for being from a most distinguished family. She headed the Burial Society and lived to be the oldest person in the village, at 104. Bubba Miriam had five sons and five daughters, eight of whom emigrated to America. The sons were *Kohanim*, Jewish priests, patrilineal descendants of Aaron, the brother of Moses and the first high priest of the Israelites in the desert.

Jacob's mother, Rachel, died of complications during childbirth when Jacob was ten years old. She left five children. His oldest sister Helen, at thirteen had to drop out of school to care for her siblings. Distressed over the loss of his mother, Jacob recalled often skipping classes to sneak into the cemetery, climbing its high wall to cry on his mother's grave. Mordechai, Jacob's father, got Jacob a position as a tailor's apprentice with his older brother, Shmeila, a tailor with exceptional skills. In no time, Jacob became a master tailor.

At eighteen, Jacob was conscripted into the Polish Armed Forces and was discharged in July 1929. He used his superb sewing skills to become head of the tailoring arm of the Supplies Division. After he was discharged, Jacob became captain of the local Maccabee (Jewish) soccer team. To keep the family going, Mordechai worked long hours as head butcher for the Butcher Co-op in Praszka. He wanted Jacob to make money as a tailor, and not waste his energy on soccer games. When the team played non-Jewish teams and Jacob's team won, the losers would throw rocks at the Jewish players and once Jacob was hit in the ear by a rock that impaired his hearing.

Shmeila and his girlfriend, Nachama, had been close since they were children. When Jacob and Shmeila partnered to establish their own thriving tailoring business, Nachama invested in them. The brothers travelled from village to village on market day, selling men's suits off the rack and made-to-measure suits for wealthier clients. Nachama met privately with Jacob to convince him that they had sufficient profits for her to use her boyfriend's share to 'establish themselves' in an apartment.

That was when Jacob decided to use his share to visit Helen and her family in Paris. She had been living there for eight years and had a third child that Jacob had not yet seen. In preparing for his trip, he created his own plus-fours with matching socks in Parisian *haute couture* style. Mordechai begged him not to leave. 'Show me one boy in Praszka,' he said, 'who has such a successful business.' He added, 'I found a nice girl for you, too.' His father cried because by then he was too old to work, and Jacob had been supporting him. Jacob left anyway, and often said, 'Thank God I did not listen to my father!'

The day before his departure, the two of them went to visit his mother's grave. Jacob told his father that the nice girl he had in mind for him would wait for his return. Before he left, Jacob arranged for his sister's wedding and asked his brother to give his father his share of the profits every week. He sent additional money home to his father, too. Jacob would often ask rhetorically, 'How could I eat if I was not sure that my father had enough to eat?' Jacob kept on sending money home even after his father was murdered in Auschwitz, because he did not find out until after the war.

Jacob arrived in Paris in spring 1937 and rented a room at the Hotel Lafayette in the Marais, the Jewish quarter. The very next day, he found work as a tailor in a makeshift clothing factory. They did piecework, making separate components of garments. His brother-in-law helped him get the job.

Jacob was a fast worker, producing twice as much as his co-workers. He was paid at half the going rate per piece, because his tourist visa was stamped *sans profession*, which meant he was 'not permitted to work'. His boss told him it was risky to hire him and arranged a hiding place in case inspectors showed up to hunt down illegal workers. Jacob did not work on *Shabbos*, but broke local laws by working on Sundays.

After Reisel's mother died in early 1937, she returned to Nowy Sacz from Krakow to care for her father and four siblings. Though it was comforting to be home, she was stifled by restrictions imposed upon her by her ultra-orthodox community. She longed to explore the world. In July 1937, she and two girlfriends left for Paris to visit the *Exposition Internationale des Arts et Techniques dans la Vie Moderne* (International Exposition of Art and Technology in Modern Life). En route, she met Jack Rhineberg, a friend's brother from Nowy Sacz. He fell for Reisel, but the feeling was not mutual. Reisel befriended Jack's other sister, Gutsha Rhineberg, as well. She also lived in Paris.

Though Reisel's tourist visa did not permit her to work, she found several small jobs, hand-sewing tapestries for wealthy patrons. The three girls were delighted to live in a leaky two-room flat in a dilapidated building, so long as they could visit the Exposition. There, they and 31 million other visitors viewed the greatest art and architectural achievements of their age, including Pablo Picasso's famous anti-war oil painting, *Guernica*, which depicts the horrors of the devastating bombing by the Nazis of the Basque town during the Spanish Civil War.

Sitting in Gutsha's second-floor apartment in 1938, Reisel lamented that her tourist visa was about to expire. She felt that she had to return to Poland. Jack planted the idea of emigrating to America in her head. He, too, was living in Paris on a tourist visa, and had been to New York to spend time with his mother.

While in New York, because he loved Reisel, Jack visited Reisel's uncle Aaron and petitioned him to sponsor her in America. He asked Aaron to mail Reisel an 'Affidavit of Support', a document to assure authorities that she met the requirements for immigration and would not become a burden on the state. Jack told him, 'There's a war going on, and what is she doing going back to Poland?' Very quickly, Aaron arranged for his son-in-law, Dr Max Blacker, to prepare the support document and mail it to Reisel.

Reisel's sisters in Nowy Sacz implored her not to return to Poland, where life for Jews was becoming increasingly dangerous. 'Do anything, but do not come home!' Both of Reisel's two girlfriends went back. One of them, Edja Cesla, was deported to Auschwitz, but managed, miraculously, to survive and emigrated to America after the war. The fate of her other girlfriend remains unknown.

In mid-1938, the Nazis intensified their assault on European Jews, and Jacob was glad he had applied for a visa to emigrate to the US. He had gotten engaged to his boss's daughter Rose, who was as determined to stay in Paris as Jacob was to leave it. Complicating their relationship further, Rose resented Jacob's sending money to his father. When she insisted that he stop supporting him, Jacob ended their engagement. He refused to give his life and love to a woman who would not share his commitment to his family. Rose did not return the diamond ring Jacob gave her. She gave him a cheap copy instead.

Meanwhile, Reisel wrote to her father, Mendel Shaya, asking him to petition uncle Aaron for a loan to come to America. Mendel Shaya wrote an impassioned letter to Aaron, pleading that he advance monies for his daughter's ship's passage to New York. He added, mistakenly, that Reisel had romantic feelings for Jack, and that those feelings were reciprocated. He added that Jack would be a good provider who would repay him for the passage in short order; and that Reisel would pay him back as well, with gratitude, because she was a 'good girl'.

A few weeks later, Reisel received the affidavit from Aaron but did not know how to navigate the complex system of the US Embassy to issue a visa and quota number. Gutsha advised Reisel to speak with her good friend and neighbour, Helen. She was thinking about Helen's brother, Jacob Najman, who completed and filed his own required paperwork for the embassy. Gutsha's brother, Jack, was in New York at the time, and Jacob had been gracious enough to translate Yiddish letters she received from her family. His kindness convinced her that Jacob would be willing to help Reisel with her visa.

Gutsha knew that Jacob liked visiting his sister Helen and her family on the fourth floor. She invited him to come down to her second-floor flat to meet Reisel. Just before they met, Jacob was shocked to learn that he should have submitted his affidavit from his uncle Jake to the US Embassy along with his original papers. He was keeping them carefully tucked in a secret pocket in the lining of his jacket and waited for his visa quota number to come up. But because the document expired, Jacob lost three years. He had to start the entire immigration process from scratch.

Reisel and Jacob were attracted to each other from the moment they met. Freed from his engagement to Rose, Jacob invited Reisel to a local café where they sat for hours at a small round table, sipping coffee. Jacob assured her that with his assistance she would prepare and file the required papers for emigration and get it right the first time.

Jacob registered her at the embassy with her affidavit from Jack Rhineberg and Aaron's son-in-law, Dr Max Blacker. Then Jacob escorted her to the Hebrew Immigrant Aid Society, HIAS, the Jewish refuge agency, for advice on how to prepare the paperwork. By then, Reisel and Jacob were 'going steady'. In the year that followed, the couple spent most of their free time together, talking about their dreams and hopes for the future. Typically, Reisel would wait on the street outside his tailor's shop for Jacob to finish work. Then they would go off, arm-in-arm, to eat the dinner she prepared for them. While courting, they went to the Paris Opera twice a month. On Sunday evenings they would go to a Yiddish club to enjoy coffee and mini pastries. They would sing songs in rounds, with men singing one stanza and women answering. Their favourite song was Gerbertig's popular love ballad, *Mein Liebe Reisela* (Reisel, My Love). They dreamed of a religious wedding ceremony and a meaningful celebration. That meant putting off the wedding until they could celebrate with their families.

On the night of 9 November 1938, *Kristallnacht,* Nazis in Germany and Austria torched synagogues, vandalized Jewish shops, homes and schools and arrested tens of thousands of Jewish men. It was a harbinger to the world of terrible things to come.

That was when Jacob was pulled out of bed and arrested by the French police in the middle of the night. He lived in the same small Yiddish-speaking, Orthodox Jewish neighbourhood in Paris at the same time that seventeen-year-old Herschel Grynszpan assassinated a low-level German diplomat in Paris. As mentioned in an earlier story, that assassination was the Nazis' excuse for the *Kristallnacht* pogroms. Grynszpan was motivated by the way Jews, including his parents, had been dumped on the Polish border and murdered.

After interrogation, Jacob was released because he was able to prove he was in the process of emigrating to America. The police ordered him to leave France within twenty-four hours and return to Poland or be deported to Ghana, Africa, to serve in the French Foreign Legion. He turned to Reisel for advice. Reisel arranged with a concierge, for a price, to hide Jacob in his rooming house. Jacob offered him twice the usual amount per month, and it was implied that this sweetener would encourage the concierge to protect him. He hid safely in that room for almost ten months, anxiously awaiting his visa/quota from the US Embassy.

On 1 September 1939, Hitler stormed into Poland. From newspaper reports, Jacob and Reisel assumed that their hometowns had been decimated. That crushing news left them unaware of the fates of their families and unsure of their future. That same day, announcements were made on the radio that all foreigners residing in France must report immediately to the Prefecture of Police. Jacob arrived at the police station as late as he could on a Friday afternoon.

Jacob always was hyper-vigilant. Staring out of the station's window, he saw trucks down below loading young men who raised their hands when their names were called. They did not know whether they were being expelled from France or being conscripted into the army or the French Foreign Legion. Jacob assumed it was the latter. Still in the station, as he heard the police officer call out his name, he had a vision of his mother, Rachel.

He imagined she was caring for him by holding his left hand and would not let it go. That was why Jacob ignored the police officer's call. The left hand, frozen to his side, had his mother's rose-gold, ruby-encrusted engagement ring on it. His father had brought it back for her after he left the Russian Army at the turn of the century. Jacob was given that ring in spring 1937 as he departed Lodz for Paris to visit his older sister, Helen. It was wrapped carefully in a folded white handkerchief and was slipped into his hand through the window of the moving train by his youngest brother, Vovala. A family treasure, it was meant to serve as a symbol of protection.

Hours later, the trucks were full and those left behind, including Jacob, were instructed to return the next day, on Saturday 2 September. Jacob found Reisel nervously waiting for him outside the Prefecture of Police, and they realised that they had just twenty-four hours to figure out how to remain safely in Paris.

As a Polish Army veteran, Jacob thought reenlisting in the Polish Armed Forces would enable him to stay in Paris. He would not be bothered by the police during the war until the volunteer Polish Army in France needed him. Early the next day, they took his papers to the Polish Consul and he said that he wished to enlist in the Polish Army in France to fight the Nazis with other Polish expatriates. He received a document from them and was told to present it to the Prefecture of Police. He returned to the prefecture and said he was signed up with the Polish Army in France, if and when it was formed. The policeman said, 'You were supposed to be here at twelve o'clock.'

'I couldn't make it,' said Jacob, and showed him the Polish Consul's letter. The police threw it back in his face, saying, 'It's no good!' Then French police interrogated Jacob about his whereabouts for those ten months after he was ordered to leave France. He gave them the name of the concierge who hid him, who was charged but released the next day. That enabled Jacob to evade arrest.

Across the street from the Polish Consul's office was the office of the Polish Military Attaché, who reported to the Polish Ambassador to France. Jacob walked into his office, saluted smartly, explained the whole situation in Polish and added, 'The Prefecture of Police doesn't want to recognise the document (from the Polish Military Attaché) and I'm Polish, and they want to send me back.'

Then and there, the Military Attaché drafted another document for the police, stamped it and told Jacob to show it to the prefecture. He also told him that the paper entitled him to ride free on the Metro.

After returning to the police with the stamped paper, he was told by them to return in a week. The couple were ecstatic. Jacob declared, 'A week! A miracle! A diamond!' Exactly one week later, on 8 September, the French military issued Jacob a provisional certificate. It meant Jacob could stay in Paris safely until the Polish Army in France was organised and he was called to duty. Every four weeks he had to report to the Prefecture of Police.

Reisel knew that spouses of members of the Polish Army in France were entitled to a government stipend. If they married, Reisel would be entitled to one, too. A quick marriage was a practical matter instead of the romantic experience they imagined sharing with their families. On 26 October 1939, they were married with ten other couples in a civil ceremony at the mayor's office in Paris. The Town Hall itself, like many public buildings in France, was an exquisite eighteenth-century building. Despite its beauty and elegance, the experience was drab. Jacob's rooming-house concierge and his wife, accompanied by their dog, served as their witnesses. Jacob hated dogs! Reisel and Jacob did not stand under a *Chuppah*; no ceremonial glass was broken; and no *ketubah,* the religious marriage contract, was signed. After the businesslike exchange of vows uttered in French, a language they did not understand very well, they were declared husband and wife.

Jacob and Reisel treated their witnesses to a shot of whiskey as a show of appreciation. The newly married couple then walked down the boulevard to start their new lives together. Though happy to be married, they missed their families and their religious traditions. As they walked, Jacob noticed a pious-looking older man coming toward them, carrying a book under his arm. He wore a black three-quarter length wool coat and a worn black hat tilted slightly forward, just grazing his thin, gold wire-rimmed spectacles. It was obvious to Jacob that he was an Orthodox Jew.

Hoping to inject a sense of religious tradition and meaning into their wedding day, Jacob whispered to the stranger, '*Bist du a Yid*? (Are you a Jew?) May we bother you for a moment? You see, we too, are Jewish. We just got married in the mayor's chambers.'

Jacob explained their deep longing to have their new marriage blessed, and he asked if the man would be so kind as to sanctify it. How comforting a simple blessing in their native tongue would feel to them. The old man seemed touched by Jacob's heartfelt plea and the urgent look in his bride's blue eyes. He agreed, and Jacob and Reisel lowered their heads. The man first asked Reisel and Jacob to remove their wedding rings, as he considered their civil wedding invalid; and then he placed his wrinkled hands gently above their heads and chanted, in Hebrew, the complete *Sheva Brachot*, the seven traditional Jewish wedding blessings. After asking Jack to place the ring back on Reisel's finger, he proclaimed her his bride according to the laws of Moses and the Jewish people. His blessings filled a void inside the young couple, of love, tradition and optimism.

As they walked on, their evening was interrupted by the discordant sound of a siren warning them that they must take cover in the basement of Jacob's building. Despite the danger that surrounded them, when the air raid was over they slept soundly for the first time as husband and wife with renewed hope in their hearts.

They called Jacob to the Polish Army in France much later than most, as he was born in 1910 and was older than most of the other volunteers. He reported for duty in April 1940, under the command of General Wladyslaw Sikorski, First Prime Minister of the Polish Government in Exile. He was posted to Camp Coetquedan in Brittany, France, and assumed Reisel would be safe in Paris with her allotment from the army.

Soon thereafter, Reisel received a postcard addressed to Jacob from the American Embassy via the International Red Cross, which she forwarded to him at Camp Coetquedan. Jacob's visa quota number was waiting for him in Paris but would not be activated for at least another year. He needed to file a new Affidavit of Support. He had to petition his uncle Jake Niesner in America to re-send it and buy his passage to America. By that time, Reisel had received all of her documents to emigrate, thanks to Jacob's guidance.

On 10 May 1940, six weeks into his service and seven months after their wedding, the Nazis attacked France and on 14 June defeated the French Army. The commanding officer of Camp Coetquedan gathered his troops and advised them that they would be evacuating to England to regroup and join the British war effort. As with the Dunkirk evacuation, a flotilla of ships, fishing and pleasure boats was dispatched to save them. All told, 20,000 soldiers from the Polish Army in France were evacuated to England.

The soldiers could choose to leave the Polish Army in France and remain there, but were warned: 'Men, if you leave, you're on your own. You will have no money, food, transportation or military discharge papers.' The officer added that anyone who wanted to leave the army should step forward. Jacob and a small group of men stepped forward. The commander, who knew Jacob well, walked over to him and asked, 'Are you crazy? You are Jewish. You will surely come in contact with the invading Nazi army if you leave us and go to Paris!'

The Nazis were monitoring all roads leading to Paris. Despite the risk, Jacob was determined to return to Reisel and to retrieve his visa from the US Embassy. As he walked back to Paris, the Wehrmacht captured him four times, and four times he escaped.

The third time Jacob was arrested, he was sure his luck had run out. He and other prisoners were ordered to line up, hands up against a stone wall. A Nazi soldier walked behind the row of prisoners, pausing to press the barrel of his gun into the backs of each man's head. As Jacob stood, waiting for death, his thoughts were of Reisel and the plans they had made together. After thirty minutes of silence, he turned around and realised the soldiers were gone, leaving them all unharmed.

Jacob continued to walk toward Paris and was shocked when he heard it was about to fall into Nazi hands. Desperate and determined, Jacob walked for nine days, using a tree limb as a walking stick to support his weakened body and his blistered, rag-wrapped feet. He never considered the possibility that Reisel might not be there waiting for him.

Following his military-issued map, Jacob was confident he was on the right road, when, for the fourth time, he was picked up by a Nazi patrol. This time, however, the Nazis drove him to their headquarters in Versailles. Jacob did not utter a word during the drive, fearing his accent would betray him as a Polish refugee. The soldiers ordered Jacob into the basement of the Nazi Military Police Headquarters, intending to interrogate him the following day. At dawn, Jacob escaped through a window, walked the short distance to the Versailles train station and bought a ticket to Paris.

Once in Paris, Jacob rushed to No. 11 Bonoird Street looking for Reisel. It was where they had first met. But it was empty. Next, he headed to Reisel's leaky flat, where he met the wife of the concierge on the street. She said that she had a letter from Reisel, and so Jacob had her new address in the countryside. Next, he went to the Red Cross in Paris and they arranged for a letter to be delivered to Reisel advising her that he had returned to Paris.

The week beginning 9 June saw 2 million Parisians flee their homes by car, horse-drawn carts, bicycles and on foot via the roads heading south. They were running from the Nazi army, approaching from the north with tanks and dive-bombers. Hundreds of thousands of others fled from northern France, and from the towns and cities along the escape routes. As many as 6 million French men, women and children abandoned their homes in mid-June 1940.

The French government evacuated Paris the next day, which was when Jacob went to the US Embassy with his nephew, Charles Hersh, who spoke fluent French, to obtain his visa and quota number. They both wore berets to blend in as Frenchmen. When they arrived, they expected to join the usual crowds of people there, all desperate to apply for, or pick up, their visas to come to America. They found the area almost deserted, except for many trucks lined up and down the street in back of the embassy.

They got to the embassy early. Jacob showed the postcard to a porter standing in the doorway. 'What happened?' his nephew asked the porter in French. The porter said that Jacob was too late. The embassy had just been evacuated, with its files loaded onto trucks that were headed for Vichy France, along with the French government. The porter added that Nazi troops were poised to invade Paris.

'Wait,' the porter declared. 'I think there are some papers laying on the table ... maybe they are for you.' And, with that, he jotted down Jacob's name and he went in, checked it, and he came out asking, 'Is this you?' He was holding Jacob's documents. It was a miracle. Jacob slipped a few francs into the porter's hand. But he still had problems to overcome. He had to wait a year for his number to come up. On the morning of 14 June, Hitler's army occupied Paris and an 8 p.m. curfew was imposed on the city.

As soon as Reisel got Jacob's letter telling her that he had arrived back home from his posting in Camp Coetquedan, she set out for Paris, hitching rides. 'A truck picked me up here and dropped me off there ... several truck drivers, and they dropped me at the Metro where I happened to meet Helen's mutual friend.' In a few hours, she was at Helen's apartment. Jacob was soaking his blistered feet in a pail of saltwater when he heard a knock on the door. The friend said, 'I have a present for you!'

Standing behind him was Reisel and in a moment, they were in each other's arms. Jacob and Reisel remained legally in Helen's apartment until Helen's family returned from the countryside, and then they stayed in a Paris rooming house for more than a year.

Paris was ruled by the Nazi military and by French officials approved by them. During the occupation, food, tobacco and clothing were rationed. Jacob was able to find work, and the loving couple spent their time contemplating their future, planning their immigration to America as soon as they could.

In mid-July 1940, Reisel put herself at risk by crossing the demarcation line from Occupied France into Vichy in order to post a second letter to Jacob's uncle Jake in America. That letter implored him to mail back a new Affidavit of Support for Jacob. Mail out of occupied Paris was erratic and unreliable, and they decided it was prudent to proceed by mailing the letter from Vichy. The American Embassy had already moved to Vichy, the capital of Free France.

They agreed that women would do better on such a mission, and by then, Jacob was working as a tailor. Reisel came up with her own brazen plan to get across the border. Standing on the 'occupied' side of the border, she and her girlfriend, Rifka Wein, watched as a group of Nazi soldiers practised their morning drills. Seeing that Rifka was nervous, Reisel said, 'Rifka, say nothing. I will do the talking.' Summoning up her courage and resolve, she batted her bright blue eyes, flipped her blond hair over her shoulder and charmed one of them into helping her. Strategically, she placed her thumb over the red *Juif*, Jew, stamp on her documents, and told the guards that her father was German, as she proceeded across the demarcation line.

After crossing into Vichy France safely, Reisel was ready to mail the letter to Jacob's uncle Jake in New York. But she needed a return mailing address in Vichy where he could send the signed form. From there it could be delivered to the embassy, as required.

Taking another risk while sitting at a coffee shop nearby the demarcation line, Reisel approached the first woman she met, who happened to be the owner of a rooming house in Vichy. After explaining her situation over a cup of coffee, she asked the woman if she would permit her to use her house as a return address. The woman agreed, and Reisel mailed the letter, but not before she asked the woman if she and her friend could stay in the boarding house overnight. The woman let them sleep there, and the next morning, Reisel and her friend returned to Paris, sneaking back across the demarcation line. Several weeks later, the woman from the boarding house in Vichy received a letter from Jacob's uncle that included the Affidavit of Support. She kindly brought it to the US Embassy in Vichy, where it was filed.

A year later, on 14 May 1941, Jewish men between the ages of eighteen and forty were called to present themselves to the Paris police. They were summoned via green postcards, and that wave of arrests became known as the *billet vert*, or 'green note'. More than 5,000 Parisian Jews, mostly of Polish extraction, were taken into custody in this wave of arrests. The prisoners were sent to the detention camps of Pithiviers and Beaune-la-Rolande. Jacob ignored the summons, because he was just a few days away from receiving his final visa and quota number.

The following day, Jacob was leaving his fourth-floor flat on 11 Bonoird Street for work very early in the morning when he was intercepted by two French police officers on the second floor of the dark, narrow, winding staircase. They asked him if he knew Jacob Najman. Jacob responded immediately, 'Yes, I know him.' They responded, 'Good. Where does he live?' Jacob responded, pointing his finger upward, 'On the fourth floor.' The police marched up to the fourth floor just as Jacob made his way out of the building. He headed to the Metro, which he rode back and forth for the whole day.

That evening, he devised a plan to stay with his cousin, whose husband was arrested on a previous roundup. He was sure the police would not return to his cousin's flat. He hid there for twenty-one days, until 4 June 1941, the assigned date for picking up his visa quota card at the American Consulate in Paris. At 4 p.m., he went to the Visa Section of the American Consulate and picked up his visa and quota number. His visa made it legal for him to emigrate to America, assuming all his other papers were in order. But they weren't!

For the privilege of leaving France legally, Jacob did not have his final exit visa or the required additional stamps on his passport. The stamps represented the twenty-one days he was hiding when he was required to make monthly registration visits to the Prefecture of Police.

Reisel had her necessary documents to emigrate to America, thanks to Jacob's loving guidance before the war broke out. Several months after Reisel returned from her successful mission in Vichy, Jacob arranged for a *macher*, an illegal 'maker' or expediter, to smuggle her over the demarcation line for the last time, from Paris to Toulouse in Vichy France. They dreaded another month-long separation, but Jacob was determined to assure her safety by insisting that she leave occupied France. In Toulouse, Reisel waited in a local rooming house for Jacob's coded telegram. If all went as planned, Jacob would meet Reisel in Toulouse, and they would travel to America together via Spain and Portugal.

Jacob feared for his safety and left Paris to reunite with Reisel the day after he received his visa and quota number. He knew he risked arrest for not having the required stamps on his passport. On his way to the train station, he sent a coded cable to Reisel: 'Dr. Miller will be performing the operation on Thursday morning,' which meant that Jacob would arrive in Toulouse on 5 June.

Before he left Paris, he gave his nephew, Charles, a one-week crash course on how to be a tailor, including tough love by slapping him on the hand whenever he erred. With his newly acquired trade, Charles supported his family, Helen and her three children, and did so successfully for the rest of his life.

On 4 June, Jacob boarded the night train from Paris to Toulouse after saying a tearful farewell to Helen on the station platform. There were Nazi soldiers all over, and Jacob was careful to blend into the crowd as much as possible. Once aboard, Jacob sat with a group of three men at a table hoping for the best. He tried not to arouse suspicion as the Nazi patrol boarded the train and went from passenger to passenger, demanding to see their papers. A burly soldier ('Like a horse,' recalled Jacob) approached him and grabbed his papers, as Helen and her children were watching from the train's platform. From his seat near the window, Jacob could see Helen and her children crying, as they were certain he would be arrested. Then, just as the soldier began to examine Jacob's papers, the train's whistle blew. The burly soldier threw them at Jacob and jumped off the train.

Jacob said that he left the train at a station before Toulouse, where he met the same *macher* they used for Reisel to cross the border. The *macher* took Jacob through the woods and crossed a river in a rowboat to Vichy. There, Jacob caught a train bound for Toulouse. Part of Jacob's plan was to jump off the moving train just before he arrived in Toulouse. However, the train was going too fast, and he disembarked in the city. There, he spotted Reisel standing just beyond the Nazi checkpoint. As soon as she saw Jacob, she propelled herself past the Nazi soldiers, threw herself around Jacob and kissed him passionately, causing a backup all the way to the railroad platform. To keep the line moving, the Nazis barely glanced at Jacob's papers and waved him through the line.

Through the Toulouse immigrant community, Jacob was advised it would be easier to obtain his *Exit de Sortie* in Marseille. He and Reisel traveled to Marseille on 11 June to find another *macher*. Jacob heard it would cost 2,000 francs and struck a deal with a Mr Debalt, who owned a shipyard in Marseille; but forty-eight hours later, Jacob still had not received his exit document. Reisel had her *Exit de Sortie* on 13 June, but they were worried because it had a thirty-day expiration date. Meanwhile, Jacob still did not have his exit document, and these were two dilemmas that had to be solved quickly.

On 22 June, Germany began Operation Barbarossa, attacking Russia. Jacob became even more concerned about his safety, as his passport was issued by Russia because his home city, Praszka, was under Russian rule when he obtained it. Nazis and their French collaborators were everywhere, looking for Jews, Poles and Russian foreigners, all of them considered possible 'fifth columnnists'.

On 12 July (the fast day known as the Fast of the 17th of Tamuz), Jacob decided to find a local *shul*, a synagogue, to pray on his mother's *yahrtzeit*, the anniversary her demise. He never had missed praying for her in a synagogue on that date.

Jacob felt that Reisel had to leave France for her safety, because he worried her *Exit de Sortie* would expire. He arranged for her to depart by train from Marseille to the port city of Balboa in northern Spain on 16 July. Jacob thought he would meet her there, where ships might be sailing to America. Upon arrival in Balboa, Reisel stopped by the office of the Spanish Telegraph Company and returned daily to keep in touch with Jacob.

He learned that a fellow refugee from his town in Praszka obtained his *Exit de Sortie* in only two days. Desperate, he sought out Mr Debalt again and struck another deal with him. For triple the original deal, 6,000 francs, he would receive the said document the next day. In front of Jacob, Debalt called the Chief of Police. 'I know them all,' said Debalt. Then he told Jacob, 'Tell the police that I sent you and show them this card at 5 p.m., and they will give you your document.' Jacob told Mr Debalt, 'My wife will be waiting for me all alone in Balboa and does not know what to do. I will kill myself tomorrow if I don't have it; but I will turn you in first, because the French police are looking to arrest me.'

At 5 p.m. the next day, Jacob went to the Prefecture of Police and told the clerk that Mr Debalt sent him. The police gave him his *Exit de Sortie,* as promised. On the way back to Hotel Le Bar to get his things, he ran into Reisel's friend outside the rooming house, who told him the French police had just rushed inside. They were looking for Jacob because he should not have received his exit document, as he never showed up for the previous roundup on 14 May.

Upon hearing that, Jacob went straight to the train station. He always said, 'That's why I came to America with one pair of pants.' He cabled Reisel in Balboa, having learned from HIAS, the Hebrew Immigrant Aid Society, that a ship heading for the US was due in the port of Seville. His telegram to Reisel said that 'Dr Miller will be operating in Seville, Spain on Tuesday' and that she was to leave Balboa by train and meet him there.

On 18 July, Jacob met Reisel in Seville. Miraculously, they were on the same train.

On 2 August, the Jewish fast day of *Tisha B'Av*, the 9th day of Av, Nazi SS Commander Heinrich Himmler formally received approval from the Nazi Party for the Final Solution.

The Najmans lived for several weeks in a hotel in Seville, waiting anxiously for information about the ship's arrival in port. Their hotel bill was paid by HIAS. On 6 August, they boarded the SS *Navemar*, a cargo ship charted privately by the 'American Jewish Joint Distribution Committee', the 'Joint'. It is an international Jewish welfare organisation that continues to do its good work to the present day, as does HIAS. On this barely seaworthy ship, a freighter designed to carry cargo plus fifteen passengers in seven rooms, they packed 1,200 passengers in cargo holds. They slept on wooden crates formerly packed with Seville oranges, on decks and in lifeboats, with everyone fighting for limited food, drink and sleep. Tickets for the few passenger cabins sold at exorbitant prices. The captain vacated his cabin and charged $2,000 to anyone who could fit themselves into the small space. It was one of the last ships carrying refugees from Europe to the United States during the Second World War. Along with the Najmans were Marc Chagall's daughter and son-in-law, who brought over Chagall artworks worth a thousand pounds. The art was stored on deck, rather than in the holds of the ship, to avoid possible flooding.

On board, at the suggestion of HIAS, Jacob became acquainted with a rabbi with several yeshiva boys he had rescued. Jacob and Reisel shared their meals with them. He told the rabbi about their secular wedding in City Hall and about the compassionate old man who blessed their marriage on the street. Moved by their story, the rabbi offered to marry them in a traditional Jewish wedding ceremony. Without their relatives, but surrounded by their new family of yeshiva boys, they were married again, in the steerage section of the ship. It was not the wedding of their dreams, but it made them feel optimistic about their future as a couple in America. The honeymoon was another adventure. There were no private quarters on the ship, and the only places to be intimate without an audience were in the empty lifeboats. Reisel and Jacob waited their turn for a lifeboat and consummated their 'Jewish' marriage in the balmy ocean air with deep darkness enveloping them.

For six weeks, the *Navemare* zig-zagged across the Atlantic, manoeuvring to avoid aerial attacks from the Luftwaffe and torpedoes from U-boats. Its arrival in New York Harbor on Saturday, 12 September 1941 made news. Arriving with typhoid-ridden passengers under a yellow flag of quarantine, the *New York Times* called it 'the Ship Packed Like a Cattle Boat'.

Jacob and Reisel were met on the Brooklyn dock by a family friend. Their relatives had gotten tired of waiting for the ship, constantly delayed, and they relied on their friend to bring them 'home'. After greeting them and learning they were married, Uncle Aaron asked Reisel for her *ketubah* (the Jewish marriage contract). The only document the couple could produce was their secular marriage licence from Paris. For Uncle Aaron, this did not suffice. The next morning, on 14 September, he took the couple to a rabbi in the Bronx. He presided over yet another wedding ceremony, their fourth (if you count the street wedding in Paris). This time Reisel was given a *ketubah*.

After the war, they found out that Reisel's father, Mendel Shaya, died of a heart attack when he was ordered to walk down the hill from his home to the round-up of the Jews in the town square. The rest were taken to the Belzec death camp. Only Reisel's brother, Lazar, survived; and Reisel said she was glad her father did not have to suffer. After Lazar was imprisoned in a Soviet labour camp for several years, Reisel found him via the International Red Cross Tracing Services.

Jacob and Reisel worked hard to live the American dream. While working double shifts, sixteen hours day as a tailor and foreman in the needle trades, Jacob invested his money in real estate. Reisel was a homemaker and the force who led Jacob into real estate. Later, he opened his own factory, manufacturing children's coats. Jacob also became involved in Jewish causes, including his Orthodox synagogue in the Bronx. They had two children, a girl and a boy, shortly after coming to America.

The couple was blessed with long lives: Jacob lived ninety-eight years and Reisel ninety-nine. As a result, they enjoyed many years with their grandchildren and great-grandchildren. Reisel was a master at giving marital advice. Most memorable was a mantra she would often share on how she dealt with Jacob. It was clear and simple: 'When he is up, I can be down; and when he is down, I can be up.' It worked!

Finally, two weeks after their fiftieth (golden) wedding anniversary on 26 October 1989, Jacob and Reisel had their dream wedding on 9 November, enveloped by the love of their family and friends. That also was the day, fifty-one years earlier, that Jacob was arrested in Paris and went into hiding after *Kristallnacht*.

Helen, sponsored by Jacob to come to America with her children, walked him down the aisle. Reisel was escorted by Lazar. Eight of Jacob and Reisel's grandchildren participated in the ceremony, each chanting one of the seven traditional wedding blessings. (One granddaughter, Bess, chanted remotely from Israel, where she served in the Israeli Army.) The senior couple renewed their vows under a beautiful, custom-designed *Chuppah* made of a 5-foot-square piece of white silk, hand-painted with a tree of life. Reisel and Jacob's names were the tree's roots, and their children's and grandchildren's names were on the branches. As the years passed, the names of the Najmans' grandchildren's spouses and the next generation of children were added to the branches. The Najman grandchildren were married under that same *Chuppah*.

After a remarkable life together, they separated for the last time on 6 January 2008. Months before Jacob's passing, he sang his favorite Yiddish song, *Mein Liebe Reisela*, to his beloved wife with increased frequency. When he passed into the next life, his hand was tucked safely in Reisel's.

Two years earlier, Reisel lost the ability to speak and remained behind her veil of silence for the rest of her life, even at her beloved Jacob's funeral – but for one exception.

One day, as Reisel and her daughter, Mindelle Najman Pierce, drove through the gates of the cemetery to visit her husband's grave, Reisel tugged excitedly on her shoulder and said quietly, 'Mindelle ... Mindelle! You know he loved me very much.'

She remained silent for three more years, until the first day of *Rosh Hashanah*, 2011, when she was reunited with her beloved Jacob in the Garden of Eden.

Reisel My Love
In a street, in the attic of a little house,
Lives my dear Raisele.
I pass under her window every evening
Whistle and call out,
Raisel, come, come, come.
A window opens, the old little house awakes,
And a sweet voice rings out
In the quiet street—It's Raisele speaking.
Wait a little longer, my dear,
I shall soon be free
Walk around the street awhile,
One, two, three.
I walk cheerfully, singing and cracking nuts,
Then I hear her little feet
Skipping down the steps.
As she comes down the last step
I embrace her.
Quietly I kiss her head,
come, come, come.
I'll ask you, Dovidl,
Don't whistle any more.

Story by Mindelle and Ira Pierce after decades of interviews with her parents and their few surviving relatives and friends.

20

ERNEST AND SARA PAUL

With anti-Semitism growing in our little town of Beregu Falu (Nove Selo), Czechoslovakia, and the war coming, my parents sent me, Ernest Paul, to live with my father's brother and his family in Budapest. I joined a Zionist youth movement with my cousin, and we went to the meetings in the basement of his synagogue. I remember very clearly one particular teacher we had, a leader in the Zionist movement, who taught us about Zionism and Eretz Yisrael.

Her name was Hannah Senesh. She was from Budapest and she said the Jewish people must go to Mandate Palestine to survive. She called it our true homeland. I never heard anyone talk about Eretz Yisrael like that before. Listening to her share her ideas and her ideals ignited a spark and a flame that burned in me throughout my life. My greatest desire from that moment on was to survive the coming war and live in Israel. Senesh was a great idealist, and she challenged us to join her. I became a true Zionist the first and only time I heard her speak. I was a member of *Dror Habonim* (Hebrew for Builders of Freedom), a Zionist socialist youth movement. We met regularly to make plans to secure our homeland.

Hannah Senesh moved to Palestine in 1939, and soon European Jews were being herded into ghettos, labour camps and concentration camps from which few would return. Joining the resistance as a fighter, I lived in underground bunkers, was captured many times, and beaten and tortured each time. I tried to save others and narrowly evaded death on several occasions, escaping the horrible fate of most of my family.

After joining the British Army in Mandate Palestine, Senesh trained and volunteered to parachute into Europe. She landed in Yugoslavia, and her mission was to share her idealism with those behind enemy lines. She bolstered the spirits of partisan fighters by reaching out to me and others fighting against the Nazis in her native Budapest. She arrived in Hungary when the deportation of the Jews was at its height and immediately was caught by the Hungarian fascists, the Arrow Cross. Over a period of months, she was imprisoned in the Conti Street Prison, beaten and tortured – because she was a Jew – and then she was shot.

At the time, I also was imprisoned in the Conti Street Prison with forty others rounded up from underground bunkers. We all were members of the same Zionist movement because of Senesh. She instilled in us the dream of a place that would accept all Jews and redeem our sorrows. Though I was helpless, I was willing in spirit and heart. Senesh's self-sacrifice was an experience I vowed never to forget, and I resolved more than ever to live in Israel if we were fortunate enough to be liberated, so that I could defend the right of Jews to live in freedom. I stuck to that decision.

From my cell, I had a distant view of her execution. I was just sixteen and it had a deep impact on me. I gained strength from watching that experience and decided, like Senesh, I would not waver. All of us in the group became stronger from her example. A small window in my cell faced the courtyard through which Senesh walked, without flinching, toward her death. Though I could not tell her I respected her courage and ideals, I tried to emulate her behaviour with bravery and silence whenever I was beaten and tortured for information.

Then we escaped from Conti Street. Our own people came for us wearing Nazi uniforms and carrying false documents that directed the head of the jail to transfer us to their guard. Once we were away, our people took some of us to the Swiss Embassy in Budapest, and others went to the Swedish Embassy. We were emotionally and physically in bad shape. Once I found myself in a safe haven, I tried to regain some inner emotional understanding and outer physical strength, as I needed both very badly. The Russians liberated Budapest on 13 February 1945, and I stayed at the Swiss Embassy only a few more weeks.

The leadership of *Dror Habonim* appointed six of us to go to Bucharest, Romania. We were to take over ex-Nazi headquarters and set up a centre to receive refugees. We were the leaders of a 'self-managed' unit and we did the cooking and cleaning. We were caring for survivors of the concentration camps, some young, some old. Among them was Sara, who would become my wife.

The first time I saw her, I felt destiny had brought us together. I took one look at her and my heart melted. I thought, I'm going to take care of this young girl and do whatever it takes to help her.

Sara had just arrived in Bucharest to live in Kibbutz Frumpka at Maria Rosetti. Sara described the place as a magnificent villa, with high iron gates. When she got there, about 100 people were standing around outside. They had come to see her and gaze upon the first survivor to arrive there. They all had survived the war in underground bunkers, and they all looked normal, while Sara said she looked like a circus freak.

I saw more than the frail, sick young woman who appeared before our group that first day. I saw beyond what she had endured and what she had survived, to what she could and would become. I believed I could help her to triumph over whatever circumstances and experiences had caused her to be in such a miserable state. I appointed myself her special guardian. My heart had been captured at first glance; and I took my desire to nurture and nourish her as a serious commitment. Truly, I had no idea what the future had in store for us.

From the beginning, Sara was showered with special attention and lots of fresh food. Emaciated and having lost her hair from typhus, it was difficult for her to understand what I saw in her. She told me, 'Outside I was nothing. I had no hair. I looked terrible. I was still coughing up blood. But you saw more of what was inside. You were so kind and caring, always trying to help me. You saw more in me than I did!'

It took a long time for the beautiful, vibrant woman that I knew was buried within to begin to heal and emerge. She drew my attention with her shining brown eyes; and more so, with her sense of humour and strength in facing a new life. When we got to know one another better, I was at her side constantly, taking her for short walks as soon as she was able. The sunlight shone on her face, reflecting warmth and affection.

We both had suffered during the war, but in separate and very different ways. I understood it might take a long time until Sara regained her strength and returned to good health. I was up to the job of seeing to it that everything imaginable and possible be done to help her recover. It was not a responsibility I took lightly, because, while finally she was safe from physical harm, from the Nazis, exactly how much more was wrong with Sara had not yet been determined.

Sara weighed a mere 68 pounds. She needed encouragement to eat as much as possible. Even seeing simple natural foods like fresh fruits and vegetables amazed and surprised her. She imagined that part of the world that produced such wonderful foods had been destroyed. The women around her counted each bite of food she took as though she was a little child, all with the goal of trying to coerce her to eat just a few more bites at mealtimes.

Our love was born of great compassion that I was eager to give to her. Sara never gave up her fight to live. Our abundance of gratitude for one another was based on my aching to see her recover and know I had done what I could to save her; and she always was so thankful for the kindness she received. I was jubilant when I could fulfil any request where Sara was concerned. Her first such request after she came to the kibbutz was for scrambled eggs and a sour pickle.

She was sixteen, and I was seventeen. She couldn't walk without someone holding her up, but we were able to get her medical care and medicine and expected her to make a big turnaround. It was a real challenge to build up her strength, and it took us about a year to do that. Whenever I looked at her, I felt a lot of pain at how sick and how weak she was, at how badly she was treated and how much she had suffered.

Jumping on my old, battered motorcycle, I raced through the town, scouring the countryside to find a farm with a freshly laid egg to purchase. That done, I found a sour pickle at a delicatessen. No task was too small or too large for me, and, as she got better and stronger, her beautiful face and smile strongly captured my attention. I shined shoes for extra money to buy Sara luxuries like eggs and butter to helped her regain her appetite, slowly gain weight and, even more slowly, show signs of recovery. Among other things, she was suffering from tuberculosis. Sara was very ill. She had a cousin, named Sarah, who was in the underground with me. 'Sara, Sarah', they called to one another, and I thought they had gone crazy, until we understood they were cousins and fate had brought the two of them together.

Where my Sara was concerned, while it took a year for us to get her on her feet, personally, as time passed week-to-week, month-to-month, my relationship with her began to grow. I gave her the idea that we as survivors should get together, but she didn't jump at the idea. She wanted to go back to her village to see if anyone in her family survived, and to finish her education. Sara told her cousin that I had asked her to marry me. Sara said, 'I thought he takes good care of me, we feel good together. But still, I don't know.' Sarah, her cousin, responded with, 'He saved me from two Nazis who were going to kill me; he saved my life; and if you're not going to marry him, I am!'

The next answer Sara gave her cousin was that she had thought about that, and realised she was in love with me. 'I had a warm, amazing feeling about Ernest and decided to marry him.'

Finally, Sara agreed to marry me. Our wedding and another couple's wedding took place at the same time in the basement of our kibbutz. It was built to hold 100 people, but now had 300 living there; and of course, all 300 members were crowded into the basement for the weddings. Zvi, the so-called captain of our ship and the family friend who bought Sara to us, was in charge of *Dror Habonim*. He performed the marriage ceremonies for both couples. Sara and I sat next to the other couple, and our closest friends sat near us. The other couple had their closest friends sitting near them. There was a bottle of water on each table, plus a bottle of red wine on ours.

Sara remembered a few gladiolas on the table. I wore a blue shirt, with white embroidery; Sara wore a white shirt. The dancing and drinking of water and the one bottle of wine was shared by all 300 guests and the festivities went on until 4 a.m. Music was provided by one of the members who had an accordion. Neither of us ever had been at a wedding before, and after the ceremony and celebration, they had nothing in writing – no marriage certificate, no *ketubah*, wedding contract, or licence.

A few weeks later, I got an order sending us to Budapest to take charge of an orphanage. Soon, that orphanage was responsible for fifty children, which was too much for us to handle. Professionals were bought in to run the place, and we were sent to Italy to lead a youth group to prepare them for *Aliyah* (immigration to Israel).

Being in Italy was a great opportunity, because Sara's tuberculosis was not cured, and I hoped to find medical treatments for her there. I told the Italian health authorities about the illnesses and problems my wife suffered, and they picked up the bill to put her in a well-known hospital. She remained there for about eight months as they tried to get her lungs working. Other survivors from the camps also were there, many of them children. When they died, Sara felt very depressed and hopeless.

Soon, I felt I was running out of recovery options for Sara. But I never gave up on her – even when they told me there was no hope. The last hope, I felt, was a sanatorium on the Italian–Swiss border, at the highest altitude in Switzerland. The transfer was approved, and I was given a budget to keep her there. I told the doctors that she was all that I wanted in life. To see my wife, I travelled from Rome to the border every month. The train rides lasted two or three days. I stuck to that routine for a year. I saw progress from month to month when I was there, and in 1945, we went back to Rome together. Sara remembered:

> I felt good, and I began to grow. My hair grew, I gained weight, I did things like go swimming in the ocean that are bad for people with TB, but I got well. I became a pretty girl. I was working in our kibbutz, and my husband worked in the Central Committee, meeting with survivors about making *Aliyah*. He was a big Zionist. He wanted to go to Israel and live on a kibbutz, like all his friends were doing.

In 1947, we got permission to make *Aliyah*. Fake documents were issued, saying we were brother and sister, since we were too young to be a married couple. But until we got there, Sara never told me she didn't want to live on a kibbutz. My wife had suffered so much. For Sara, the idea of a kibbutz felt like another confinement, and after such a long time of being closed in, she could not go along with the idea. As Sara put it, 'I knew how much Ernest wanted us to be in Israel. There we were part of the new State of Israel when it was created. I danced the hora in the streets. He gave up his dreams for me, his love for me was that strong.'

We lived in an apartment in Haifa. Soon I volunteered to join the *Haganah*, the Israeli defence organisation. I carried a rifle on my shoulder to protect the Jews in downtown Haifa against the Arabs, who were being armed by the British. I was issued a serial number, as were all soldiers – 1513. I had been hoping and dreaming of joining the army, and they accepted me.

Sara said, 'I remembered I, too, had a profession. I could use the experience I had gotten in Germany making grenades and bullets for the Nazis. I volunteered to make ammunition in a secret factory (the now famous Ayalon Bullet Factory that doubled as a laundry facility). We were defending our own people. We supplied the soldiers with our ammunition. I stayed up all night, being extra cautious in its preparation.'

After the army, I became an officer in the *Histradrut*, Israel's national trade union, a prestigious political job in Israel. Sara remembers:

> Every three months, I visited the doctor so he could check my lungs. The doctor said, 'Go home and make a baby,' and Ernest didn't believe it. He didn't want me to risk my life to have a child, not after all we'd been through, but sure enough we had our daughter, who was truly our miracle baby, and then a second miracle, a son was born to us. Little Ben Gurion, my husband called our son.

I heard that my older brother was alive and living in the United States. He wanted to see me. I had lost contact with him ten years before, when I heard he had been killed. I visited him after I got permission for a three-month leave. After six weeks, I missed Sara and our kids. When I told my brother that I wanted to go home to my family, he insisted I stay longer and offered to send airline tickets to bring my wife and kids to the States. My brother said, 'I want you to stay.' I asked for a longer extension from my job, and my family arrived two weeks later. My brother and his wife had a supermarket on Marshall Street, in Philadelphia. They had an apartment over the store, and we stayed with them. Sara was happy there. The food was good, and it was plentiful. When Sara saw all the food in my brother's place, she really enjoyed it. In the camps, she nearly starved to death, and that isn't something you can forget. In Israel, in the early days – 1948 and 1949 – the government had food rationing, so of course, most of what we received we gave to our children. Sara did not want our kids to experience hunger the way she had. Hunger made my wife's experience in Israel difficult.

In the US, she started to enjoy the freedom and the abundant food that was available and was having nightmares about going back. We stayed in America for a year, and after that I wanted to return to Israel, but Sara didn't want to go back. That's when my brother intervened and said I should do what's best for my family. I knew he was right. Then I received notice to return to Israel in 1956, reporting to my military unit to help Israel during the crisis following the nationalisation of the Suez Canal, and to fight infiltrators who were crossing Israel's borders.

'He wanted to be in Israel, and I wanted to be in America. His pain was my pain,' Sara explained. 'After the camps, whatever I went through was paradise,' she said. 'He'd done everything for me, so I did as he wished,' and we returned to Israel.

Our return was temporary. Eventually we settled in America and would remain there throughout our married life. We also had another child, a son. Sarah said, 'Our three wonderful children all are caring, giving people; the kind of people who would happily break open their piggy banks to give their money away whenever someone needed help. And they have given us six wonderful grandchildren.'

Fifty years after our modest wedding at Kibbutz Frumpka Maria Rosetti in Bucharest, Romania, we were legally married with a 'real' rabbi in a very moving religious ceremony in elegant surroundings, with hundreds of family members and friends in attendance.

A month later, when our granddaughter got married, she gave a speech. According to Sara, 'Our granddaughter said there was no better gift grandparents could give their grandchildren than showing them how happily married we were after 50 years.' Another new generation from our union increased our happiness as we welcomed five great-grandchildren.

Sara passed from this world in 2007. I, who once had been able to help rouse Sara's spirits and restore her health at a time when she was barely alive, felt hopeless to help her at the end of her days. But I was inspired by Sara's remarkable outlook, one she maintained throughout our lives together. Rather than dwell on the horrors and atrocities that had befallen her and claimed almost her entire family, she chose a path of gratitude to illuminate her life, my life and the lives of our wonderful descendants. I always said to God, 'You took everything from me, but you have also given me so much joy.'

Interviews with Ernest Paul in his apartment house lobby in Atlantic City, New Jersey, by Mindelle and Ira Pierce, in 2015.

21

RABBI SALOMON AND HENRIETTA RODRIGUES PEREIRA

Rabbi Salomon Rodrigues Pereira was the Sephardic chief Rabbi of the Netherlands. He was referred to as the *Chacham*, the Brilliant One, a rare and distinguished title referring to the highest level of scholarship in Jewish law, liturgy and the Jewish canon. Prior to the Nazi invasion of Holland, he served as the Chief Rabbi of The Hague, the second-largest Sephardic Jewish community in the Netherlands, behind Amsterdam. Both Ashkenazic and Sephardic communities in the Netherlands were decimated by the Nazi Holocaust, and the Dutch Jewish population sustained one of the highest levels of loss in Europe. After the war, Chacham Pereira was elected to serve as the chief Rabbi of both Sephardic and Ashkenazic communities. The Ashkenazi community had no rabbi left alive of the required stature.

The grand Spanish-Portuguese Synagogue in Amsterdam, also known as the *Esnoga*, was built in 1675, and has served as the architectural template for many other Sephardic synagogues built in Europe, the Americas and South America. It was itself fashioned after Solomon's Temple. Over the centuries after the Spanish Inquisition, the Dutch Sephardic Jewish community thrived in the atmosphere of extraordinary religious tolerance set by the government and royalty in the Netherlands.

The Pereira family immigrated to Holland in 1609 and began a long lineage of scholarship, with rabbis and chief rabbis counted amongst the ancestors of Rabbi Pereira. Rabbi Salomon Rodrigues Pereira chose an area of secular scholarship, teaching the Classics, Roman and Greek, in the gymnasium (high school) of a town in the very north-east of Holland named, Windschoten. This provided him with a modest income. He married one of his students, a young woman named Henrietta Hart, from Windschoten, in Groningen, the northernmost province in Holland. Some years later, when they had moved to Hilversum, he was appointed as Chief Rabbi of The Hague. Each weekend he and the family travelled there to stay in the rectory of the ancient and impressive synagogue. That she came from a wealthy family was fortunate, for it allowed them to buy a proper house, accommodating their five children and the many guests they hosted. The Hart Wool concern was a family business begun 200 years prior, trading in wool, with offices around the globe.

The Nazis invaded the Netherlands on 1 May 1940. As luck would have it, Henrietta's two brothers were out of the country on business at that time, visiting the United States. Understanding the imminent existential threat to all Jews in Holland, they not only remained in the US, but used their influence to establish contact with Nazi leaders in Germany and arranged for wire transfers to Nazi accounts in Zürich in order to forestall the deportation of their sister and her family.

As a psychological method of subjugating the Jewish population, it was common for Nazi officers to place soldiers in the homes of community leaders. My mother's home thus was forced to host SS soldiers. My mother was twelve years old and quite sensitive to the fear, bewilderment and turmoil around her. She was very afraid of the soldiers stationed in her home. They took up residence on the third floor of their large home. My mother remembers one SS soldier as sullen, distant and quite threatening, while the other was more mild-mannered and polite. In fact, he would regularly offer provisions that were in short supply, such as large tubs of butter or sugar. When those SS soldiers were deployed elsewhere, one left a full uniform hanging in the closet. My mother suspects this was the latter's attempt to help the Jewish resistance. Not knowing if this was a trap, the uniform was returned to the local Nazi headquarters.

Immediately following the Nazi invasion, Jewish children were prohibited from attending public school. Schools were established in various homes to educate the children that were no longer allowed to attend state schools.

Eventually, the Jews from all corners of Holland were deported to the Jewish ghetto in central Amsterdam, an area surrounded by barbed wire. From there, Jews were transported each week to Westerbork, a concentration camp which served as a transit hub. (The Nazis imprisoned Anne Frank and her family at Westerbork between their arrest in August 1944 and their transfer to Auschwitz the following month.)

My uncle Martin (Martinus) told me that the Nazis would drive around the streets in military vehicles and take pot shots with their rifles at Jews walking on the sidewalk. He remembered several occasions when, while wearing the yellow Star of David, he was forced to dive into vestibules and alleyways to avoid the bullets.

The payments to Zürich from the brothers in the US continued for approximately two years and culminated in one large payment made to the German Embassy in Buenos Aires, in the late spring of 1942. That ransom of approximately $1.9 million was delivered by my mother's cousin, Fritz Hart, in a large satchel delivered to a German diplomat.

Shortly after that, my mother's family received eleven tickets on a freighter bound from Spain to Montevideo, Uruguay, in August 1942. They were escorted personally by two SS officers on a train from the Jewish ghetto, through Holland, then across Belgium and France, and they were unceremoniously given their papers at the Spanish border along with the tickets for the voyage.

My mother's eldest brother, Arnold, a wool trader, married one of the orphan children my grandparents saved and carried with them to freedom. She, Trudi Katzenstein, her mother, father and her sister, Marianne, had come to Holland with their parents from Germany in the late 1930s.

While escaping by train to Switzerland, Trudi, her younger sister and their mother and father encountered resistance fighters, who left suddenly when they saw SS soldiers boarding. The fighters left a rifle in the train. Trudi's father told his wife and daughters to flee the train and he remained, so that the SS were distracted from chasing them. They focused on him instead, arresting him and sending him to Westerbork and then to Auschwitz to be murdered. Trudi's father sacrificed himself by accepting responsibility for the rifle so that his wife and two daughters would live.

Trudi, nineteen, and Arnold, twenty-three, were married on the boat by my grandfather. They chose to remain in Buenos Aires, while the remainder of my mother's family and Marianne continued their search for visas to gain entry to the United Kingdom. Why my grandfather wanted to go to Britain while it was still seriously threatened with invasion by the Nazis can only be answered with an historical perspective. First of all, he had a brother in Ramsgate, in the south of England. Secondly, he was uneasy having left the Jewish ghetto and his community. Thirdly, he wanted to join the expatriate Dutch army, the Orange Brigade, which fought under the British command.

Arnold was a wool trader, acting as a zone representative of the Hart Wool Company. He visited sheep ranchers all over the South American continent. Trudi and Arnold had three boys, Mario who now lives in Spain, Eddie in Buenos Aires, and Miguel in Amsterdam.

My mother's other older brother, Martin, joined my grandfather, landing at Normandy and advancing with the Allied front line across Europe, into Germany. My uncle was fond of joking that as bad as the Nazis were, the mosquitoes on Normandy beach were worse. Among other notable occurrences was their attendance at Bergen-Belsen concentration camp as it was liberated.

Another relative, Hans Werthauer, whom I refer to as an uncle, was raised secularly in a small German town, Lage, near Detmild. After he saw his parents arrested and sent to their death, he and his younger sister spent most of the war hiding in a monastery and nunnery, respectively. He ended up wearing a British uniform and served as a translator for the liberating British and US forces. He also was at the liberation of Bergen-Belsen where he met my uncle and grandfather. Ultimately, he was given a train by Allied commanders, a German engineer, a rifle and a large group of Dutch Jews in the camp, and was instructed to shepherd them back to Holland. Believe it or not, after a journey of several days, those of the reconstituted (and anti-Semitic) Dutch armed forces stationed at the northern German border would not allow them to cross the border. He circled the train to the south and entered through Belgium, where he encountered more sympathetic Dutch soldiers.

Fritz Hart, son of one of Henriette's brothers, biding his time in Boston during the war, served as the courier of the ransom to the German Embassy in Buenos Aires. He had lost a brother early in the war, who had left Holland in an attempt to escape to England. He was a physician and was caught boarding a boat on the Normandy coast to cross the Channel. He was arrested and brought to the local police station, which the Nazis had commandeered. His family was informed that he was executed, but over the subsequent decades they could not find out where he was shot or the location of his grave. His mother, who lived in Buenos Aires, would return to Holland and France each summer to sequentially search towns and graveyards for his remains. She spent weeks every summer unsuccessfully pursuing this goal over decades. After his mother's death, Fritz continued the annual summer search for his brother's grave.

There is an extraordinary and highly improbable encounter and consequent discovery that took place in 1998, in which Fritz visited my uncle Arnold (who still was married to Trudi, the orphan he betrothed on the transatlantic voyage to freedom). Arnold informed Fritz that a friend had visited several days before and happened to mention seeing the grave of Fritz's brother in a small cemetery in Central Holland, about an hour outside of Amsterdam. Arnold knew of the perennial efforts by Fritz and his mother, so he asked his friend for the particular details of where the graveyard was and where the grave was within it. Arnold drove Fritz to the cemetery the next day. They found the grave easily, following the detailed instructions of Arnold's friend. Afterwards, they rested in the coolness of the small stone mausoleum at the edge of the cemetery. Fritz had much to contemplate, having finally attained the goal he and his mother had pursued for decades.

Inside the small, long, single room were three objects. To the left, upon entering was a small wooden bench on which two or three people could sit. Across from it was a glass-topped display case with a single open book inside. Along the far short wall was a bookcase, with approximately thirty volumes on it. It was one of a set of two hand-written compendiums, cataloguing the names of all the Jews in Holland and Belgium who were killed by the Nazis in the war. Each book contained approximately 300 pages, each with a column of names in alphabetical order of those murdered. These books were sequentially displayed in the adjacent case. Every day, a page was turned, and the book returned to the display case. When all pages had been turned and each page displayed for one day, the book would be returned to the shelves and the next volume would begin its turn in the case.

They sat on the bench for some time in silence, Fritz considering his good fortune and his mother's endless and unsuccessful search. Arnold, his cousin, my uncle, respected the solemnity of the day. After some time, they got up and looked in the case across from them. The book on display was coincidentally opened to the name Hart. Both pages were filled with the names of close and distant relatives who were murdered a few decades before in the land they had just driven through. The name of his brother was written at the top of the visible list.

By my calculation, the number of pages in each book multiplied by the number of volumes, when divided by the forty-four years since the war ended suggested that there could not have been two complete cycles of display. What are the odds that the correct volume would be opened to the correct page on the very day that Arnold and Fritz found the cemetery, not to mention that his brother's name would be at the top of that page? There were approximately 300 people (relatives) with the last name 'Hart' in that volume. There was an equal or greater number of Pereiras killed by the Nazis.

After the war, my mother and her family returned to Holland. They found their house in ruins. The furniture had been broken apart and the floorboards torn up and burned for heat during the severely cold winters and the infamous shortages of food and fuel.

Several pieces of the family furniture had been given to non-Jewish friends and placed into storage, including the dining room table and chairs. These were made in the capital city of Groningen, in 1917, for Henriette's parents for the imminent wedding of their daughter to the young rabbi. (The furniture carries the label of the maker in Groningen. After the war, they were reupholstered in a muted green mohair fabric, which had been the curtains of the living room.) In 1989, after the death of my grandmother, Henriette, I had her furnishings shipped from Amsterdam to Boston. The shipment also included her Passover Wedgwood dishes, many knick-knacks, antiques and family heirlooms, and three large armoires, the oldest dating to the late 1600s.

I still light my grandfather's *Chanukiah* candles, utilise the silver, a Victorian egg timer, and the beautiful bone-white dishes on Friday evenings while celebrating *Shabbat* around the same dining room table and chairs made for them in 1917. My children are well educated and will carry on these important traditions; and will continue to honour the memory of my righteous grandparents.

Dr Jonathan Kramer, the grandson of Rabbi Salomon Rodrigues and Henrietta Hart Pereira, worked with Mindelle Pierce in researching and writing this story.

22

JACK AND INA SOEP POLLACK

'I am writing with a pencil stub. Darling, try to steal a pencil for me somewhere.'

So said Jack Pollack, secretly, to his lover, Ina Soep, in the winter of 1943. Manya, Jack's wife, was known to be difficult, flirtatious and moody. In 1941, they both decided that they needed to divorce after the war. Jack became infatuated with Ina before the war when they met briefly at a birthday party. During the war, their love matured when Jack was incarcerated in the same barracks as his wife, in Westerbork, a transit camp in Holland. Love was sustained throughout the horrors of the war as they increased their note writing to one another in the Bergen-Belsen concentration camp. Afterward, they married and came to America. 'I was in a camp with my wife and my girlfriend,' said Jack. 'Believe me, it was not easy.'

Steal a Pencil for Me became a book, an award-winning documentary film and an opera, all with the same name. They were based on the love notes Jack and Ina wrote to each other. Jack decided to do the film after being married to Ina for fifty years.

On 10 May 1940, Holland was invaded by the Nazis. The Dutch Army held up for only five days, and surrendered after the Nazis razed the centre of the city of Rotterdam and threatened to go further if there was no capitulation.

Queen Beatrice left for London and that was the beginning of the end for the Jews in Holland. They were allowed no bicycles, radios or valuables and could shop only between 4 and 6 p.m. They were not allowed to teach at universities and public schools, and so they taught their children in Jewish schools and at home. The first year of the occupation, Jews could go to the seashore, but after that they could not.

At night, the Nazis raided Jewish homes, removing the residents from the cities and deporting them to Westerbork, then a transit camp. They took the poorer families first, followed by the middle class and then, last, the wealthy. After deportation, vans removed their furniture and valuables and shipped them to Germany. According to Jack, the Nazis fooled 90 per cent of the inmates into thinking that their living in Westerbork was temporary, as it gave them amenities such as sports fields for soccer matches, a hospital, schools and entertainment. In fact, everyone there was earmarked for extermination.

The Dutch built Westerbork in the summer of 1939 as a refugee camp, mostly for German Jews who entered the Netherlands illegally. Westerbork was actually administered by German Jews.

Just prior to being shipped to Westerbork, at a birthday party of a friend on 6 June 1943, Ina was introduced to Jack and his wife, Manya. Ina felt that Manya was beautiful, with 'orangey curly blond hair', but was certain she was not for Jack. She was too flirtatious, sitting on the knee of the birthday boy's father. Immediately upon their introduction, Jack lost his heart to Ina, a twenty-year-old beauty whose father was an extremely wealthy diamond merchant, the second largest in Holland. Their family had a chauffeur, and two cleaning ladies, while Jack lived in a lower middle-class neighborhood. While Jack fell in love with Ina, he did not expect to see her again. Jack thought at the time, 'She is *The Girl* I should have married!'

One day, the Nazis took Jack and his father, both accountants, to the square in the city, and made them believe they would be shot. They weren't; the Nazis simply thought it was a funny joke.

Ina told her father that she wished to go into hiding and join the Dutch resistance to the Nazi occupation of the Netherlands, but her father said no. Ina had a boyfriend, Rudy Cohen, who was murdered shortly after he was selected and shipped by the Nazis to Auschwitz.

In Westerbork, 2,000 people were selected in the middle of each Monday night – it didn't matter who – for transport in cattle cars to Auschwitz. They were old, young and of working age. That they would be murdered there was unknown to them.

The saddest moment in Ina's life was when she learned that her closest neighbours invited her boyfriend to go to America with them prior to the war. Of course, because they were in love with each other, he rejected the offer.

Manya and Jack arrived in Westerbork in July 1943, and Ina and her family arrived two months later, in September. When Jack heard that Ina's family was arriving at Westerbork, he went to the authorities and asked that Ina be housed in his barracks, Number 46. As a board member of the Jewish Council and wealthy, Ina's father was able to transfer her to the camp's laundry from her earlier job dismantling batteries. That is where she met Jack again.

Ina said that Jack won her heart by sheer persistence. In the pitch dark, Ina and Jack, together with other couples, would walk, talk and neck. They could not see each other in the barracks. Ina said, however, that she could view Manya's bed from her bed, with an 'evil eye'! They were both on the third level. It was when Manya forbade Jack to talk to Ina, that the note writing began. Jack wrote to Ina, 'I am happier in the five weeks we are in the barracks together than in the seven years I was married to Manya.'

Westerbork's schools, sports facilities and entertainment served as a show camp for the International Red Cross to visit and examine. Jack was made a principal of one of the schools. Cabaret night was Tuesday nights 'Of course, in the end, no more cabaret and no more people, because everyone destined to the work camp was meant eventually to be exterminated,' said Jack.

On Friday, 3 December 1943, Jack listened with pleasure to Beethoven played by the Westerbork Orchestra, with Ina in the audience. He wrote how he loved her. By then, Ina had also fallen in love with Jack. They gained a sense of peace which Jack said he never felt with another woman. What kept Ina going was the optimistic nature of Jack's notes. They wrote their notes in shorthand to one another.

The comings and goings of the transports were unnerving, and on 12 February 1944 Jack was selected to be shipped to Bergen

Belsen. Three months later, Ina was slated to go to Auschwitz, an extermination camp; but at the last moment, her father was able to transfer her to a transport destined to Bergen Belsen, where she rejoined Jack.

Life became much more difficult for both of them, working for twelve hours of hard labour under Nazi SS supervision. Ina noted that conditions were abominable. They slept on a board, and sanitation were indescribable as they could not keep anything clean. The soup they served was terrible, and everyone was hungry all the time. They had lice all over their bodies and people were dying from them. Nonetheless, Ina and Jack kept writing to one another.

When the Nazis tried to start a diamond business in Bergen Belsen, Ina volunteered to do German shorthand for them. Her father's friend assisted her, and she said that diamonds saved her life. Upon Ina becoming a secretary, at least they had more paper on which to write to one another. It made their lives easier. Manya had a boyfriend, a doctor, in the camp, and yet people were snitching about Ina walking out with Jack.

Typhus was breaking out in the camps. Many of the inmates, including Ina, could not eat, suffering for nausea that lasted for 3-4 days. After that condition, they became ravenous, and Ina's sister went around asking for extra bread for Ina. Manya gave her bread after Ina's illness broke. That was one of the nicest things that Manya ever did for them.

On Passover in the camps, Ina went looking for a symbol of the Passover. She found a darning device that looked like an egg, which they used to help maintain their sanity during the holiday.

In the concentration camp, Jack was able to exchange a piece of clothing for a piece of bread that he wanted to keep for the 'last emergency'. He realised that his hunger would require him to exercise tremendous willpower not to eat it straight off. His sister knew about the saved piece of bread and one day she got very sick and said she needed it. Jack refused her wish. Another good friend of Jack's also knew about the piece of bread that he had hidden, and he asked for it for his son who, too, was ill. Again, Jack refused; and after the war, the friend did not speak to him for a whole year. As Jack testified with tears, the friend did forgive him, but it was difficult, emotionally for Jack to explain what had happened, over a piece of bread!

As time went on, both Jack and Ina seemed optimistic in their continuing love notes to each other. Ina remembered that at the end of each evening, the diamond cutter women would chant, 'Still, we are a day closer to liberation.'

An adjacent, huge woman's camp had a makeshift dental office within it. The woman dentist was from Poland, and Ina went to her for treatment of a terrible toothache. She described the camp, which had inmates in striped uniforms from Auschwitz. Ina saw dead people lying everywhere. They were being loaded onto carts that were made to be horse-drawn, but were pulled instead by people. They were no longer burying the bodies; they were incinerating them in the crematorium. Jack wrote:

> My dear little lady, I think about my future life if I make it. I think about being together in a little quiet house in the winter by a hearth with a delicious meal. I almost can't imagine that there will be such happiness in store for us... Going back to my barbed wire. These are only dreams of the future.

Ina spoke about her uncle's death. She said that they threw his body onto a cart. She believed the greatest tragedy of her father's life was when his son, Ina's brother, died. He was stoned to death in a rock quarry in the Mauthausen concentration camp. At his funeral, Jack wrote a tender poem, ending in 'It must be God's will... How can we understand... Till we come close to you again.'

The camp soon was to be liberated by the Allies, but Jack and Ina were not certain whether they could continue to stay together or whether one of both of them would survive. Ina asked, 'What will happen if we are not liberated together? Everything is so vague.' Jack fretted that Ina might go with her family to America and that he would despair around Amsterdam, 'while my one and only love is meeting more interesting and charming men. My always dearest Ina.'

On 7 April 1945 a Nazi transport arrived that sent 8,000 camp prisoners away from Mauthausen on three trains. Jack wrote, 'I want not to say goodbye, just see you soon.' Jack's train was sent to the east; Ina's to the west.

Leaving Bergen Belsen, Jack said, cannot be described. Whole transports of prisoners suffered terrible typhus. He and Manya were on the verge of death. Jack remembers pulling dead prisoners out of the cattle cars and digging their graves and then saying the Kaddish.

On 23 April their transport came upon the Russians; they could see their army uniforms. Jack went into a coma for two days and his weight went down to 75 lbs.

The British 11th Armoured Division liberated Bergen Belsen on 15 April 1945 They found 60,000 prisoners and over 13,000 corpses, including those of Anne and Margot Frank. The corpses were lying around the camp, unburied. Jack said, 'How many times can you say how good God is after losing parents, so much family and friends. But we did survive.'

Ina's transport train finally rolled into the front-line and was liberated by US armed forces who had never seen or heard of a concentration camp. Ina was impressed by their straight teeth. At that time, all of her collection of love notes to Jack were lost, except for twelve, when she was lifted up onto a truck by the American soldiers.

At the time of their sixty-first wedding anniversary, Jack made a presentation to the United Nations International Day of Commemoration of Holocaust Liberation, on 27 January 2006, where they viewed movies of the concentration camp's liberation, and read the Universal Declaration of Human Rights, Articles 18 and 19 on freedoms of thoughts, conscience and religion.

After the war, all of the survivors of course aimed to find what happened to their families. Ina had no knowledge that Jack had survived. It still was difficult to travel at that time. Jack's sister, Betty, just happened to hitch a ride on an American army truck, wearing a nurse's outfit that she borrowed for the purpose of getting that ride. Then, they came upon an accident. Betty was called to help treat the victims, which she could not do, because she was not a nurse. She said that doctors must be called. Thereupon, she saw a long line of skeletons, one of whom called out 'Betty. It's you.' She looked and saw her brother, Jack, and her nephew.

Jack prepared yet another letter to give to Ina. What a surprise, Ina wrote back! The letter was accompanied by roses. Ina wrote that she was panicked that she hadn't heard from him.

When he came back to Ina, Jack was dreadfully thin. He looked as old at thirty-two as he would look sixty years later. His first order of business was to obtain a Jewish divorce, the *Get*. Manya stayed in touch with Jack and Ina but burned all of her war memorabilia. She never remarried and died in a Dutch nursing home in 2005.

Of the 110,000 Jews who were forced out of the Netherlands by the Nazis, only 5,450 returned. Jack Pollack was a founder and served as president and chairman of the Anne Frank Center-USA for many years and had been the keynote speaker nationwide for over 100 openings of the Anne Frank travelling exhibitions. On Jack's eightieth birthday, he was knighted by Queen Beatrix of the Netherlands for his work for the Ann Frank Center-USA and for speaking about the decimated Jewish population of the Netherlands at universities and a myriad of other organisations in the US.

Jack's parents Frederick and Grietje and sister, Juul, perished in the Holocaust. He returned to Amsterdam to start what he called his 'second life' as a certified tax consultant. He married Catharina (Ina) Soep (1923–2014). He emigrated to the US in 1951 with his wife and two small sons and he began his 'third life', building an investment firm and working for many organisations to teach the lessons of the Holocaust through his own experiences. He was a founding board member of the Westchester Holocaust Education Center, in Purchase, NY, and a member of the NYS Commission on the Holocaust. In 2004, Mr Pollack received an honorary doctorate from Hofstra University, and he has received the Louis E. Yavner Award, an honour for a New York State resident who has made distinguished contributions to teaching about the Holocaust and human rights.

There is an afterword to this story, Ina and Jack's daughter Margrit was told by her cousin one day that she was the daughter of survivors and that she should read her parents' collection of love notes from the camps. Her interest was piqued: love in the Holocaust?

'The notes blew me away,' said Margrit. With the help of her father, she found 130 of them:

> The daily, precise details of struggling to keep one's dignity, the willpower that it took to get up in the morning and face the grim reality of their existence, relying on slivers of hope for the future – all were deeply moving. The notion that even under these horrendous circumstances there was still love, jealousy and passion – basic emotions that proved the human spirit cannot be easily broken, that the power of love is measurable in life and in death.

The love notes were an eye opener and an inspiration. They haunted her and she decided it was a story worth telling, a quilt worth weaving, a heart worth exposing. Daughter Margrit Pollak Shield translated their love notes. Jack Pollack died on 9 January 2015 at the age of 102. Margrit smiles, remembering, 'I spent a lot of time in my childhood trying to figure out escape routes from our house. I had a million hiding places. And I still dream about the Nazis.'

Margrit Pollak Shield, daughter of Jack and Ina Soep Pollack, was interviewed by Mindelle Pierce in 2017.

23

ROSI AND FRITZ SCHLEIERMACHER

This is the story of Rosi Wronker Schleiermacher and her husband, Fritz Schleiermacher, as told by their daughter, Sabine Schgleiermacher Seidler.

Rosi Wronker was born in Berlin in 1905, the second of two children. The affluent Wronker family was well integrated both into the Jewish and secular communities of Berlin and, like many Jews living in the larger German cities at that time, the family was not observant. Rosi`s mother, Emmy, born Berliner, was the youngest of twelve children.

Rosi`s Uncle Alfred, her mother's oldest brother, was an admired and accomplished engineer and physicist with a distinguished record of service as a highly decorated officer in the First World War. In 1903, Dr Alfred Berliner became Chairman of Siemens, one of the world's largest and most powerful companies, later serving as a member of its Supervisory Board.

Initially, her Uncle Alfred supported Hitler, as did several other high-ranking Jewish industrialists of that time. As a political conservative, Alfred and other well-respected Jewish businessmen thought that they could work with Hitler. Of course, they were very wrong!

Rosi was an intellectually curious, bright, accomplished student. Rosie's parents valued education and sent Rosi and her siblings to Jewish schools that provided the best education in secular subjects. Rosi planned to study architecture after high school graduation. Unfortunately, she graduated in 1924, a year in which terrible economic conditions cast the middle class of Germany into poverty, including her family. They no longer could afford to send her to university. The family struggled to make ends meet, dealing with food shortages and rationing as the economy worsened.

In the spring of 1929, Rosi's older brother, Franz, was working for Akkumulatorenfabrik AG, AFA, a company that produced batteries, especially for cars, ships and trains. Franz introduced Rosi to his engineer colleague, Fritz Schgleiermacher, and immediately the two were attracted to one another. They were an unlikely pair for this time. Fritz was a thirty-three-year-old, Protestant Aryan and Rosi Wronker was a Jew. However, both of them were secular. In 1929, marriage between Jews and non-Jews had not yet been banned; and laws to marginalise and ostracise Jews had not yet been passed. In July 1929, shortly after they first met, Rosi and Fritz were married.

Their wedding was attended by Rosi's mother and a few family and friends. It was a small civil affair devoid of religious tradition and symbolism, lacking even the popular convention of a white dress for the bride. The bride and groom opted to wear chic, stylish clothing, rather than traditional wedding attire. The couple spent their honeymoon hiking and skiing in the Austrian mountains, oblivious to what the future would bring.

The society in Berlin was highly liberal and intellectual, which suited Rosi and Fritz perfectly. Rosi worked in a school for actors and loved her job. Fritz, unable to fight in the Second World War because of an injury sustained in in the first, was recruited to work as an engineer where his brother-in-law, Franz, worked. Producing batteries, his company in the late 1930s became important for the Nazi war effort. At that time, his company helped the Nazi military voluntarily, because the people did not know about Hitler's real plans.

In the early 1930s, interfaith marriages such as Fritz and Rosi's were accepted in cities like Berlin, where Jews and non-Jews blended into a common culture. That is in stark contrast to the small towns and villages outside those cities, where such relationships still were uncommon.

Fritz and Rosi had many good friends who opposed Hitler and the Nazi regime. Right after 1933, they lived in a 'bubble' of friends they could trust, and they avoided Nazis. In fact, *Mischlinge* (intermarriages) were tolerated for quite a long time, likely due to the many well-known celebrities, including artists and actors, with Jewish partners. Also important in their lives was their Uncle Alfred, who still maintained excellent relations with the head of Fritz`s company.

Rosi and Fritz were very much in love, committed to one another and to starting a family of their own. Within a year, they began trying to conceive a child, but as the months passed and Rosi did not get pregnant, their disappointment and frustration grew. Compounding their emotions were the changes in Berlin society that changed the way Jews were treated and how mixed marriages were viewed. Following the Wannsee conference in 1942, the Nazis moved forward with their plans to murder the Jews in Germany and in Nazi-occupied Europe. Intermarriages between Jews and non-Jews were no longer accepted in society, placing both partners at risk. When a marriage between a Jew and non-Jew ended, whether by divorce or death, usually the arrest and deportation of the Jewish spouse occurred immediately.

It was in 1943, in the midst of these restrictions, that Rosi realised she was pregnant. The joy of finally expecting a baby was dampened by her fear of an uncertain future for their unborn child. That was in addition to the stress of living in a city besieged by war, surrounded by exploding bombs, and permeated by Nazi brutality. Rosi and Fritz lived in a state of constant fear.

While some of Fritz's friends and neighbours encouraged him repeatedly to end his marriage to Rosi, Fritz refused to divorce her. Soon, their Jewish friends and relatives began to disappear. Fritz's life became more difficult and dangerous each day. His marriage to a Jew, his personal and political beliefs in opposition to those of the Nazi government, and his failure to embrace the ruling party when asked, placed him, his wife and unborn child at risk.

Fritz continued to work under the hidden sponsorship of his company's CEO, who liked him a lot. By then, Rosi and Fritz lived in hiding and rarely left their home. Their days and nights were spent running to the cellar for shelter from the bomb attacks, or they stayed hidden at home. Though she would not have dared to leave the safety of the house without her husband, Rosi wore her yellow star on the rare instances when she went out of the house with Fritz. On Saturday, 27 February 1943, the *Fabrik Aktion* began, when all remaining Jews in Berlin were to be arrested.

In early March 1943, there occurred the 'Rosenstrasse Protest'. It was the only collective street mass demonstration against the Nazi party or the government, conducted by the separated Gentile wives of Jewish men. The unarmed women decided that they would not leave their street demonstration, and the authorities were astonished that the women would not relent when ordered to go home by the SS and local police reinforcements – even when the SS ordered that their machine guns be aimed at the demonstrators. Certainly, never before had there been a public protest against the Nazis treatment of the Jews. During that episode, the Gestapo relented. and they released the Jewish husbands after Goebbels, Reich Minister of Propaganda of Nazi Germany, decided that the demonstration was not against the Nazi government, but it was for reuniting families.

In early May 1944, as Rosi neared the end of her pregnancy, she left Berlin. Acting on the advice of a trusted friend, Rosi travelled to a small hospital in Gablonz, Germany (today Jablonec in the Czech Republic). Though it was a hospital for older people, Rosi's friend told her about a doctor there who could be trusted. Despite the risk, this kind and honourable doctor was willing to care for Jewish patients.

On 20 May 1944, baby Sabine was born. Rosi stayed in Gablonz for several weeks before returning to Berlin with her new baby. She was eager to be with Fritz and looked forward to the end of the war, expecting the Russian Army or the Allied troops to defeat the Nazis after the invasion of Normandy in June. Fritz, however, had hoped Rosi and Sabine would stay safely out of Berlin until the war was over.

In October 1944, after his continued refusal to divorce his Jewish wife, the Gestapo arrested him. Fritz's crime was that he was married to a Jew; and compounding that crime, he declined to endorse the policies and actions of the government and refused to join the Nazi party. Fritz was placed in a camp in Halle, eastern Germany, where non-Jews who refused to divorce their Jewish spouses or refused to join the Nazi party were incarcerated. Here, Fritz was forced to use his engineering skills to further the Nazi war efforts.

After Fritz's arrest, Rosi felt afraid and vulnerable. She was alone with their newborn daughter, unsure of how she would survive. With few options, she travelled to her Uncle Alfred's villa outside Berlin, possessing a key to his mansion. Alfred had believed his position, power, and connections would keep him safe. When Hitler's rage against the Jews escalated and his plan became clear, Alfred could not avoid the reality that his prestige and wealth could not protect him. When Rosi arrived at Alfred's mansion with her baby daughter in late 1944, Alfred had already committed suicide. She did not know that, and she assumed that her Uncle Alfred and his wife were staying at their rural mansion in Brandenburg. In reality, the Russian soldiers had invaded their wealthy property and murdered Aunt Clara, Alfred's widow. Probably they suspected her of being a rich Nazi.

Aunt Clara was in fact an Aryan woman from a very influential family, and thus the Nazis had left the mansion in Berlin-Dahlem alone. Rosi and her baby hid in a room in the basement of the villa. She spent her days in the dark; lonely and sick with fear, wondering what would become of her beloved Fritz. Only when searching for something to eat did she leave the house without the yellow star, hoping that nobody would know her in that part of Berlin.

In April 1945, Russian troops arrived in Berlin. Russian soldiers had a reputation for drinking and prowling around in the basements of houses in Berlin looking for wine, whiskey and women, adding a new element of fear to Rosi's days. Her worst fears almost were realised one day when two Russian soldiers entered her basement hiding place. Rosi feared the soldiers would have their way with her, then kill her and her baby. But baby Sabine smiled and cooed at the soldiers as Rosi stood there, paralysed with fear. Remarkably, the soldiers began to play with Sabine, tossing her into the air. Then, without taking anything or harming anyone, they left the house.

Shortly thereafter, one evening Rosi left the house and walked to a nearby meadow, hoping to find greens she could cook for her daughter. Suddenly she came upon an American tank, and then she knew the war was over. It was one of the happiest moments in her life.

When the American troops crossed the River Elbe in April 1945, Fritz escaped, managing to walk during the nights and hide during the days until he reached Berlin. Knowing that it was the safest option for Rosi, Fritz went right to Alfred's villa to find her. When he arrived, he reunited with his wife and daughter with much relief and joy. That eclipsed even her happiness when she came upon the American tank. A few days later, on 8 May, the Nazi troops surrendered and the war was over.

Rosi and Fritz were able to return to their apartment in another part of Berlin which, fortunately, had escaped damage during the war. Fritz could return to work as an engineer for his old company, because the allied occupying powers needed batteries for their military equipment as well. The couple began receiving packages from relatives who had managed to escape Europe to America, England and to Thailand, where Rosi's brother, Franz, had found shelter. But many other relatives did not escape and had been murdered.

Years later, after the war, Fritz provided assistance to his company's CEO as a witness for his defence, when industrial leaders were accused of collaborating with the Nazis. Later, Fritz became the chief manager of the automotive giant, BMW, with the family becoming a main shareholder of that company.

Sabine was raised in a loving, happy home. There was no religion in their home, except perhaps for a Christmas tree, but Sabine was raised with a humanistic set of values and ideals. Although Sabine went to a Protestant school, she always was told about her Jewish heritage. The family remained in Germany.

Later, in 1952, they moved to Essen, a big town in the industrial area of Ruhrgebiet, where Fritz continued to work for his company. Sabine finished high school in 1963 and returned to Berlin, studying law and married Hans Seidler, who later became president of a large, prestigious engineering school.

In 1946, Rosi learned of her mother, Emmy's, fate. It was from a woman who had been with her during the war. She learned that in 1942, her mother had been deported to Theresienstadt, where she died of typhus three months later. It took years for Rosi to overcome her depression, after learning of the deaths of her mother, her other relatives and their best friends. Fritz never spoke about this time in his life, suppressing the pain and fear of those years, but the memories returned as flashbacks during the last days of his life. While he was in the hospital, his mind forced him to relive his darkest days in the Nazi prison. Only Rosi's presence was able to calm him. Fritz died in 1968, some weeks after the birth of his granddaughter, Sabine's first child.

Sabine and her husband, Hans Schleiermacher Seidler, were interviewed on video by Mindelle Pierce as they were about to leave the US for home after their visit. The interview took place in the Bedding Department of Macy's, on 34th St., in New York City.

24

SALA AND SIDNEY GARNCARZ

Ann Kirschner knew only two things about her mother, Sala Garncarz's history: that she was born in Sosnowiec, Poland, and had survived a Nazi camp. Even as an adult, Ann knew no more than that about her mother's experiences during the Second World War. Her mother never spoke about those years. When the topic did arise occasionally, Sala would turn her head and without a word end the conversation before it began.

Then, when Sala was sixty-seven years old, forty-six years after her liberation and preparing for triple bypass surgery, Sala handed her daughter a faded red, cardboard box. 'You should have this,' she whispered. Nestled in the box was a small brown leather portfolio containing hundreds of letters, postcards, notes, scribbled-on scraps of paper, some in Polish and some in German, and a few old, creased photographs, collected during her five years as a Nazi prisoner. Ann also found Sala's diary. The first entry was dated 28 October 1940, the day her mother boarded a train to the first of seven camps. Sala's journal recounted her first year as a sixteen-year-old prisoner of the Nazis. 'These are my letters from camp.' And with this gift, she invited Ann into the years of her life that had until that time been inaccessible. Ann was introduced to young Sala – brave and daring, scared and lonely, strong-willed and passionate.

Sala Garncarz was born in Poland, the youngest of eleven children. By 1940, four of the children had died and four had started their own families. Only Sala and her two unmarried sisters, Raizel and Blima, still lived at home with their parents in Sosnowiec, Poland. One day, the Garncarz family received a letter:

'By order of the Jewish Council of the Elders, Raizel Garncarz will report on October 28, 1940 for six weeks of work at a labour camp...'

Sala, older and stronger than Reizel, reported for work in her place. She felt she could handle the work, and the wages she earned would help her struggling family. She thought it was only for six weeks. But Sala also had an ulterior motive. At sixteen, she was yearning to experience more than their small city had to offer. She was curious and adventurous, but unaware of the Nazis' plans for the Jews. Sala saw this as an exciting opportunity to peek at the world beyond Sosnowiec.

Three days after the letter arrived, Sala reported to the train station, accompanied by her family and friends. A woman standing nearby watched Sala's mother hugging her daughter goodbye, overcome with sadness and dread. This woman walked over, put her arm around them and said, 'My name is Ala Gertner and I will be with her. I will take care of her.' And with that, Ala and Sala boarded the train to the Nazi forced labour camp in Geppersdorf, Germany.

In the months that followed, Sala continued to document her experiences almost daily through letters to her family and friends, and in her diary entries. She wrote of the people, activities, and routines of Geppersdorf. She chronicled her experience of navigating the camp among the Nazi officers, the Jewish Council, and the other workers. She documented the mystery and dread surrounding the influx of new labourers and the removal of the weak and sick. But she also wrote of love, attraction, and romance among the prisoners.

Despite the hardships the prisoners experienced, they were allowed to send and receive mail. Sala received letters from family and friends, informing her of the worsening conditions outside the camp: deportations, arrests and the increase in anti-Semitic violence. These letters were Sala's only connection to her old life and to the outside world, and she clung to them for strength and hope. Every letter she received was added to her collection, carefully and discreetly concealed in whatever hiding spaces she could find. As weeks turned into months, Sala managed to keep her secret letters hidden.

Sala's diary and her letters clearly articulate that, despite the hardships of the camp – the unforgiving cold, the crowded barracks, the persistent hunger, the inhumane treatment, the lack of the basic human dignities, that the loneliness of being away from home and family were her worst hardships. To fill this void, some prisoners reached out to others with the hope of creating a sense of belonging and some semblance of security. Courtships among the workers were common. Some snuck notes to each other, others stole meaningful glances, and the most brazen men crept into the women's barracks, risking a beating, or worse, for just a touch.

This may have been what Ala, Sala's protector since that first day at the train station, and Bernhard Holtz, a man with whom Ala worked in the camp, were seeking when they fell in love. Nicknaming their swift-moving messenger *Sarenka*, Polish for 'little deer,' Sala was tapped to exchange secret love notes between Ala and Bernhard. In one note, Ala wrote, 'There is so much longing, a tremendous yearning for love. A deep silent love is flowing between us. He knows, I know, we both know, this love is hopeless.' And yet they continued their relationship.

Sala, too, had suitors. One in particular was Chaim Kaufman, a handsome young shoemaker. He committed himself to making sure Sala's feet were warm and dry, a luxury in the labour camp. Their paths crossed in the camp not long after they arrived, and they grew fond of each other. Chaim was familiar as he knew her family. In a strange and unpredictable environment, his presence was a source of comfort. However, Chaim's feelings quickly grew more serious than Sala's. Though grateful for and appreciative of this attention, Sala was ambivalent. Chaim, however, was quite sure of his love for Sala and passed her notes in which he expressed his adoration and his intention to marry her. With each letter, Sala's uncertainty grew. After six months of courting her, Chaim demanded an answer, clinging to the possibility of love, commitment, and a chance for a future.

To Sala, unable to see the possibility of love under these conditions, this was a ridiculous aspiration. Though loath to hurt his feelings, she knew she wasn't in love with him. She had to be true to herself, and she blamed her unwillingness to commit on her youth, her inexperience, and fear for her family's safety. Chaim, hurt and rejected, became enraged and hostile, the exact opposite of all that he had been before. However, by this time, Sala was facing greater upheavals.

Deportations were becoming more frequent and violence continued to escalate. After two years at the Geppersdorf work camp, Sala spent the next several months being shuttled from camp to camp – first to Gross Sarne, then to Laurahutte, back to Gross Sarne, then on to Brande. Through it all, she clung to her letters, concealing them from the Nazis and fellow prisoners alike. Finally, she was moved to Gross Paniow, where a severe typhus outbreak resulted in a six-week quarantine. The Nazis suspended work to give the prisoners time to recover, fearing they would be unable to find healthier Jews to take over the workload. During the relative calm of the quarantine, Sala fell in love.

One day, at ration distribution, Sala met Harry Haubenstock, a handsome Czech businessman ten years her senior; and she was quite taken by this older, sophisticated man. Harry began sending her love notes, passing them through friends or leaving them at a designated spot, and their romance blossomed. To Sala, Harry was so different from everyone she had known before. He was Czech, spoke German, instead of Polish, was not from a religious family, and had no connection to her old life. Being with Harry felt like a huge leap from the world she had known, and this may be what appealed to Sala's curious, adventurous side.

In his love notes, Harry called her 'my little bride', and for the first time, the thought of marriage felt exciting and full of possibility to Sala. As their feelings deepened, Harry assured Sala that one day they would be liberated and would be together forever. Despite their horrendous circumstances, his optimism was contagious and she, too, looked forward to sharing their lives together. His words increased her appetite for life and made her more determined to survive.

Sala continued to correspond with her family and friends. Her sisters' letters discussed who was sick, who had been deported and who was unaccounted for. These letters continued to be her only connection to her family, and she clung to them for strength.

When the quarantine ended, the prisoners were sent on to another camp where security was tighter. Sala and Harry saw little of each other. One day, Sala received a letter from Ala, who was now in the Bedzin ghetto, announcing that finally she had married Bernhard. She wished Sala the same happiness with Harry. Despite their attempts to stay together, one morning Sala and a group of women suddenly were taken to Zacler/Schatzler, a labour camp in Czechoslovakia. Though Sala initially received a few letters from Harry, the flow of mail quickly ended. Still, she continued to write unsent letters to Harry, holding on to them and their plan to reunite in Prague after the war, when they would marry and begin a new life together.

As the end of the war drew nearer, the Nazis marched Sala and her group to the outskirts of their camp to dig trenches. After several weeks of backbreaking work, Sala and the other prisoners were finally liberated by the Russians in May 1945, as they marched between camps on a dirt road. After liberation, life moved very quickly for Sala.

The days after liberation were chaotic. Sala, now twenty-one, and her friends began searching for their families. Sala took her cache of letters that she had protected for the past five years and set off to her hometown. When she arrived, she went to her sister's apartment, hoping to find members of her family. Instead, she found someone else living in the apartment with her sister's furniture and belongings. She had the devastating realisation that this was no longer her home, and she headed to Prague to search for Harry. She arrived in July 1945 and entered a boarding house for refugees.

Networks had been set up throughout Europe for Jews searching for family and friends who may have survived. It was through this network that she learned of her family's fate. Two of her sisters, Raizel and Blima, were quite sick, but miraculously had survived and were in Sweden receiving medical attention. Her mother, father, brothers, other sisters, their spouses and all of their children had been killed.

It was through this European network that Sala obtained Harry's address. Excitedly she sent him a telegram telling him that she had arrived in Prague, as they had planned. In response, Harry sent a relative to tell Sala to forget about him and leave Prague. Harry, as it turned out, had been hedging his bets, igniting a romance with a girl in each camp. Ultimately, he married a woman from his hometown, with whom he had suffered and endured a three-month death march through the freezing winter and whom he had promised to marry if they survived. They married right after the war and had two daughters.

Sala felt devastated and betrayed. With Harry no longer part of her future, Sala began her trip to Sweden to reunite with her sisters, stopping in the German town of Ansbach along the way. During what she had anticipated would be a brief stop, Sala began to feel the effects of the physical and emotional exhaustion of her experiences. She was still reeling from the loss of her family, friends, and her old life and had been on the move since her liberation, frantically searching for her family. While in Ansbach, she realised she needed to take a break to mourn her losses, process her wartime experience, and regroup so she could move forward with her life. Sala decided to stay there until she felt strong enough to go on to her sisters.

On 8 September 1945, shortly after she arrived in Ansbach, the town's 200-year-old synagogue reopened just in time for *Rosh Hashanah* services. It had been used as a Nazi stable during the war, but the American Army's Fourth Infantry had cleaned and renovated it for the High Holidays. *Rosh Hashanah* services were packed, the first holiday gathering since the end of the war. During the service, Sala contemplated her new life. Her family was gone. Her relationship with Harry was over. Her sisters were sick and far away. She was alone.

Unbeknownst to Sala, she had captured the attention of an American soldier, Sidney Kirschner, who noticed her during *Rosh Hashanah* services. Sidney wrangled an introduction and he and Sala began spending time together. Sidney's family had emigrated from Poland to the United States in 1918, and he had been sent to Dachau with the United States military after its liberation. Sala was cautious, having suffered tremendous loss during the past five years, but Sidney's foreignness was exciting and enticing, and the couple soon fell deeply in love.

In Sidney, Sala found a man of great warmth, optimism, and compassion. His innate curiosity about the world and his insatiable interest in everything appealed to her. She was attracted to his strength and determination, and Sala appreciated his romantic streak, all of which suggested that he would be a loving, faithful husband. In Sala, Sidney found a woman of immense strength, intelligence, courage, and resilience. He appreciated not just her outer beauty, but also the beautiful person she was on the inside. Her self-awareness, honesty and integrity impressed him, and he was in awe of all Sala had been able to endure and overcome.

They decided to marry. Sidney's mother, however, was sceptical about her son's choice of a bride and suggested they postpone their marriage until Sidney returned to the United States. Sidney refused, threatening to reenlist and stay in Ansbach rather than wait to marry Sala. In an effort to change Sidney's mother's mind, Sala sent her future mother-in-law an eloquent letter, recounting her experience during the war and professing her love for her son. After reading Sala's beautiful letter, Sidney's mother relented and four months later, in March 1946, Sala and Sidney were married in a civil ceremony in Ansbach, paving the way for her entry to the US.

Sidney left for New York, determined to expedite the paperwork required to bring Sala to join him. A few weeks later, she was on a ship headed to the States and just one week after her arrival, on 8 June 1946, Sala and Sidney were married in a religious ceremony in New York. The couple settled into an apartment in East Harlem, where Sala hid her box of letters deep in her closet, and even deeper in her heart.

Sala and Sidney had three children. Not wanting to burden her family with the pain and loss she endured during her five years as a Nazi prisoner, Sala kept her secret from her husband and children. For fifty years, the most painful and heartbreaking years of Sala's life remained locked away.

Shortly after Sala arrived in New York, her sisters followed, living close by. Blima, who had married in Sweden, died shortly after her arrival, the result of years of illness and abuse during the war. Raizel married and became a beloved teacher in Brooklyn, but was unable to have children. It would be years before Sala learned of the fate of her dear friend, Ala. She and Bernhard had been among the hundreds of thousands of Jews sent to Monowitz, a sub-camp of Auschwitz, as the end of the war drew near. There is no record of what happened to Bernhard. As for Ala, she befriended some members of the underground resistance and joined a successful plot to bomb the crematoria. They destroyed a portion of the camp's electric fence, enabling approximately eighty Jews to escape. Ultimately, Ala was caught, tortured, and hanged for her participation. In 1991 a memorial in the sculpture garden of Yad Vashem, Jerusalem, was dedicated in her honour as one of four women who made possible the only armed uprising at Auschwitz.

Sala's story is actually the confluence of two love stories – that of Sala and Sidney, but also of Sala and those with whom she corresponded during the war. The letters from her sisters, friends, and family sustained her through her darkest days, and Sala credits them with saving her life. When the world around her fell into chaos and violence, her letters were a reminder that she was loved, that she was special, and that she was needed. They enabled her to see into a world in which love, hope, and the possibility of liberation endured.

Sidney's love inspired Sala to move forward, to rebuild her life, and look to the future. Sidney's affection, warmth, and optimism encouraged her to start over and imagine a meaningful life with family, security, and happiness. Together, they created a strong family bond and embraced their Jewish life together.

In 2016, Sala and Sidney celebrated the 70th anniversary of their civil wedding and danced at their grandson's wedding a few weeks later, on the 70th anniversary of their religious ceremony, along with their children, seven grandchildren, and eight great-grandchildren.

Years after Sala invited Ann into her box of letters, Ann asked her mother what she expected when she gave them to her. 'Nothing in particular,' she answered. 'I wanted you to have the letters from me with my blessing.'

Based on video interviews with Sala and Sidney Garncarz, with Ann Kirschner, Sala's daughter, at the home of Ms Kirchner by Mindelle and Ira Pierce on 17 December 2014.

25

LUNIA AND LEO WEISS

It has been said that the war was the great *shadchan* (matchmaker), because couples who otherwise never would have met often married one another right after the war. In Lunia Gartner's and Leo Weiss's case, they did know each other before the war, but tradition and circumstances would have prevented them from ever marrying – had the war not intervened and changed everything.

Lunia and Leo met as teenagers in Stryj, Poland, on the left bank of the Stryi river in the foothills of the Carpathian Mountains in the Lviv Oblast, now western Ukraine. They had friends in common – Leo's former girlfriend was Lunia's close friend – but their lives were vastly different. Lunia came from a deeply religious Hasidic family, one of the most prominent, richest, and most philanthropic families in the city. She learned what it meant to help others simply by watching her parents and grandparents help others, both individually and collectively.

Leo's life was tough. He was only thirteen when his father died of tuberculosis and his mother struggled to support her two young sons when she took over her husband's furrier business. When he was a young teen, Leo discovered the reason money was so tight, because his father's business partner was cheating his widow. As the 'man of the household', he confronted the swindler and told him, 'I won't call the police if you leave now and never come back.' The partner disappeared quickly and quietly.

Still in high school, Leo set to work as a furrier, helping his mother raise his younger brother, Mucyk, who was eleven. He excelled in his studies without much effort and was one of the most popular boys at school. At his funeral, an entire lifetime later, Leo's friend said, 'Girls wanted to be with him, and boys wanted to be like him.'

Like Leo, Lunia was an excellent student. She was beautiful and deeply compassionate, living a happy life that revolved around her family and girlfriends. And coming from a very religious family, Lunia's modesty was as natural as breathing. She would never chase a boy. Leo admired Lunia from afar, for he understood she never could be his girlfriend. As he succinctly expressed it, 'She was beautiful. She was smart. She was modest, but she was much too rich!'

Lunia's parents married in 1921, and Lunia was born in April 1922. Her mother, Chana, was a descendant of the legendary Backenroth family, from Schodnica in the Carpathian Mountains. The family-owned crude oil reserves were extensive enough to support the entire Backenroth family, worldwide, for generations. Michael Karpin wrote *Tightrope*, a book about this illustrious family – and the subtitle says it all: *Six Centuries of a Jewish Dynasty*.

Lunia's father, Naftali, and the Gartner family, owned large lumber and steel enterprises in Stryj. They were recognised as great Torah scholars (especially Naftali and his father, Shammai) and were generous philanthropists. The Gartners financed large municipal projects, including building an extension to the local hospital and a first-class theatre/opera house in Stryj. This performance space was so beautiful, and acoustically so advanced, that travelling troupes performing in London, Paris, Vienna, Berlin, and Rome, regularly performed in Stryj.

When Chana married Naftali, she helped women and children by providing dowries so poor girls could marry, and she granted financial assistance to widows. Her labour-intensive philanthropic project was the Stryj Orphanage, and she raised virtually all the money for its operating budget.

In addition to Torah, helping others, and loving each other, life in the Gartner home was filled with love for Eretz Yisrael, the ancestral Land of Israel. Lunia's father, Naftali, and his father Shammai, were *farbrente* (passionate) Zionists. But none of them was leaving for Eretz Yisrael unless all of them left, and by the time the war broke out, it was too late to run, and the dream became a nightmare.

Once the war began and the ghetto was closed in Stryj, Shammai, Lunia's grandfather, asked each grandchild to come to him separately. Lunia remembers it well:

> We were always together, the whole family on holidays and on Shabbat, so it was something very unusual that grandfather called me in alone. I will always remember what he said to me. My grandfather had sparkling eyes and a beautiful long, flowing, white beard. To me, I imagined this must be what Moses looked like! Grandfather told me: 'Child, these are terrible times. I hid many valuables – gold, silver, diamonds – under our factory. There is enough hidden, so whoever in our family survives can start a new life. Here, I also bought for every member of our family, a cyanide pill. Only when there is no hope to live, only then should you take this pill, to prevent your suffering. And here are a few diamonds. Use them for anything that can help you live. Child, think a hundred times before you touch the cyanide, but don't think even twice before you use the diamonds to help you.'

Shammai's words gave Lunia strength to continue later in the war, when all she wanted was to take the cyanide and end the pain.

The Stryj Ghetto was established initially as an open ghetto, with easy access in and out, but soon it was locked. Lunia remembers: 'The Nazis pushed us out of our beautiful villa and forced us into the ghetto, located in the worst part of town. Before the soup was even cold on the table, our Polish neighbours took over our house!'

In those first days of the ghetto, with her habitual sense of optimism, Lunia saw it as a bit of an adventure. The outbreak of war, 1 September 1939, was supposed to be Lunia's first day of her last year of high school. On that September morning, Lunia's first thought was about extra days of summer vacation. At first, she was even happy, as she still was living with her nuclear and extended families. Coming from a religious family, suddenly she found more freedom. For adults, survival was paramount, but for kids, especially sheltered teenagers like Lunia, those first ghetto days seemed almost carefree. They were not yet starving, rules were loose, but no one could imagine the horrors ahead.

Lunia remembers: 'All of a sudden, it seemed like every boy in the ghetto discovered me! Before, I was never alone talking to a boy without a chaperone, but now the grownups were too busy to bother about who was talking to me! It was such a big difference. Now, wherever I went, a whole group of boys would follow me. Each one was trying to outdo the other to impress me. I felt almost like a movie star.'

While all the other boys were chasing Lunia, Leo had another plan. He didn't join the crowd of boys trying to get her attention. Instead, he visited with her parents while she strolled around the ghetto, flirting with the boys. He played cards with her mother, who was a good card player, and played chess with her father.

Lunia remembered that it was funny. At the time, she thought that Leo was stupid for not trying to impress her like the other boys. But, she said, 'Later, when I was alone and I was an orphan, it mattered a lot to me that Leo knew my parents, but even more important to me, was that my parents had known Leo.'

Leo's strategy of 'courting' Chana and Naftali instead of Lunia became the foundation of their relationship. As Lunia affirmed, 'When I was alone at the end of the war, this mattered more to me than anything else. I think it's one of the main reasons I married him.'

Leo seemed to adjust to adversity better than most people. His strategic thinking, natural charm and innate courage stood him in good stead during the war and throughout his life. He managed to escape from the ghetto, and describes it in his own words:

When the Nazi commander wanted a volunteer, I stepped forward right away. I didn't know what he wanted, but I figured it would give me more freedom, and I would have a better chance to escape the ghetto. Then the Nazi said, 'We had big German and Polish engineers come to look, and they could not fix it (a lighting problem). We sent them away, but you, Jew, if you fail, we won't send you away. You, we will kill!' Now, I saw my idea was not so good. The Nazi leader showed us the building with the problem, one of the tallest in the city – six storeys! I looked up and decided, if I'm going to die, who needs to climb up so high? So, I started in the basement. I walked from one light fixture to another. I'm not an electrician. I'm a student, so what hope did I have? I did not expect to live, but I walked around, looking up at the lights, trying to buy time to plan another escape – this time, not just to escape the ghetto. It was to escape death. Suddenly I found the light with the problem – just some loose wires. Because all the other engineers must have started at the top, they gave up before they reached the basement. One, two, three! I fixed it! I found the Nazi leader and, in front of him, I clicked my heels and saluted him like a soldier. I reported that the problem was fixed! He was shocked, but also very pleased. He turned to me, and gave the biggest compliment: 'Weiss, if you weren't a Jew, you could be my friend!'

Leo would always laugh at this point in his story and ask, 'With such friends, who needs enemies?'

Leo was given more freedom, better work, and a measure of respect. When he learned about the devastatingly hard work Lunia was assigned to do, he intervened. Lunia continues their story:

The Nazis liked to give hard manual labour to women and others who looked weak. I was assigned to carry heavy lead pipes – like huge sewer pipes – one girl at each end. Leo found a way to help. The best job in the ghetto was to work in the garden. He went to the office to talk to the Polish secretary. He came every day until he convinced her that his 'cousin' (me, Lunia) would be a good gardener. He bragged so much about my knowledge of plants and gardens that they decided to make me the manager of the whole ghetto garden! The good news: Now I had the best job in the ghetto! It was not hard work, and I could eat some of the vegetables we were growing. The bad news: I didn't know anything about gardening! I never pulled a weed in my life! But we had gardeners who worked at our villa before the war, so I tried to remember everything our gardeners did, and that's what I did too. It worked! The vegetable plots grew big, and I planted pretty flowers around them. I had a team of girls working under me. Best of all, I let everyone eat as much as they wanted; and none of us was starving anymore. I did one more thing: I borrowed the bra of a big woman and wore it under my rag clothes. During the day at work, I ate as much as possible so I would not be hungry at night. Then, when the Nazis were not looking, I stuffed big quantities of vegetables into my empty bra, so much I could feed my whole family, including my grandparents, aunts, uncles and cousins too. I did this for months. It was the only time during the war when my family was not starving!

Then the Nazis began deporting Jews in *aktions*, and the goal was not to get caught. Lunia explains.

You could not let them get their hands on you. That was the most important thing. Because even if you had the best papers in the ghetto, when the Nazis caught you, they took you. That's why so many people in the ghetto prepared a hiding place, a bunker, where you could hide during the *aktions*. It was imperative no one knew the location. That's why my family hired an architect to design it in the ghetto; but only our family built it. That way, no one except our family knew the bunker's location. Our bunker was hidden behind a fake brick wall, and one person [the Gartner man who drew the short straw] closed it up and put cauldrons of water in front, to make it look like a cooking hearth. Then he hid above, in the exposed rafters. During one aktion, when my family was running, a young man was running nearby. My grandfather Shammai said, 'We must take him into the bunker with us!' One of his daughters, running beside him, begged, 'No, it would be too dangerous.' Grandfather Shammai did not argue. He simply said, 'The Nazis have taken away everything from us, but they cannot take away our *menschlichtkeit* (humanity). If he does not come into the bunker, then I will not come in.' His daughter had no choice. She could not leave her beloved father outside the secret bunker, so everyone was huddled safely inside the bunker, including the young man. When the next *aktion* came, virtually the whole Gartner family hid in the bunker – but Lunia and her little brother, Zvi. were too far away and had to find alternative hiding places.

The uncle, who drew the short straw, watched from the rafter and later described to Lunia what he saw. The young man grandfather Shammai had rescued led Nazis directly to the bunker and offered to show them 'a bunch of rich Jews'. That is how Lunia's family lived and died. Shammai's heart of gold saved the man who betrayed them all.

The news spread throughout the Ghetto: 'The Gartner's are taken! The Gartner's are taken!' Lunia ran with Leo to the barbed wire, trying to reach them. Wherever her family was going, she wanted to be there, too, but she could not join them. Neither could anyone remove her hands from the barbed wire fence she grabbed so fiercely – not Leo, not anyone. She held onto the fence, with the barbs going through her hands, motionless. She remained fixed to the barbed wire, watching, watching, until she could see them no more. On 21 May 1943, naked and defenceless, in a pit near Janowska, the Gartner family was shot, and together, they died.

Leo was now a slave labourer. It was considered smart not to look directly into the oppressor's eyes – better to look down, as a sign of subordination – but Leo was not a 'look down' type of person: 'You treat everyone the same – kings and beggars – because all people were equal, no better, no worse.' Even during the Nazi years, Leo never acted like a slave, and he never ran away from what he felt was right, regardless of the consequences.

The day following her family's murder, Lunia tried to reach her little brother in the neighbouring slave labour camp, to tell him in person of the tragedy. Spotted by two Ukrainian policemen, she was caught and attacked viciously. 'I was beaten so badly with their clubs and their whips that my skin was cut to shreds. I was bleeding a lot; I must have fainted. When I regained consciousness, they were carrying me, by my head (down) and by my legs. I could see my bloody trail (I didn't let on that I regained consciousness). They tossed me back into the ghetto and left.'

The next day, 23 May, two days after her family's murder, battered and bruised as she was, a Jewish policeman, a *Kapo*, tried to drag her to his room to rape her, mumbling that he had had his eye on her for quite some time. Leo saw what was happening. Enraged, he grabbed the *Kapo*, and beat him to a bloody pulp. The *Kapo* crawled away, humiliated and hissed, 'Weiss, tomorrow you will be dead.'

Leo has to decide: He either waits for the next day when the Nazis surely would kill him, or tries to escape immediately. Waiting meant certain death. But where could he go? The local population was virulently anti-Semitic. But Leo had an idea.

From the time of the first *aktion*, Leo knew his frail mother, Julia, could never outrun the Nazis. In the last *aktion*, with the Nazis close behind, Leo – always a quick thinker – shoved his mother to the ground, put a tin cup in her hand and pushed her head down. The Nazis ran right past her, believing she was an old beggar woman, but Leo knew he needed a more permanent plan to keep his mother safe. He secured the cooperation of a Ukrainian school friend to find her a hiding place and, in case of extreme emergencies, prepared one for himself and Lunia. He paid the Ukrainian a lot of money, including gold and a diamond contributed by Lunia, to hire a man to give them food in the hiding place. Leo and his Ukrainian friend dug a hole under a pigsty, where Leo's mother, Julia, hid for the duration of the war.

Now, with death imminent, Leo planned to run there and take Lunia with him; but she would not leave without Zvi, and wanted Leo to beg his friend for an additional hiding space for Zvi. But it was impossible. Leo already had tried to get space for his own brother, Mucyk, but the Ukrainian had refused. Lunia describes their hasty goodbye: 'Leo wanted me to leave with him, right then and there. But I still had hopes to bring food to Zvi and I didn't want to go into hiding him. There was no time to argue. Leo had to get going. *Chutzpa* (guts) and luck – that's what you needed. He kissed me goodbye with an 'I'll send for you – don't give me any trouble, just come.' Then he was gone.

'In the middle of the day, he stole a bicycle and a shovel from the Nazi collection room. With his black wavy hair and his long Jewish nose, somehow, he made it out of the city. Of course, for a long time I didn't know if he made it at all – I thought I lost him, too.'

Months went by. When he thought it was safe, Leo sent word to Lunia via the Jewish Underground to smuggle herself out of the ghetto with his brother, Mucyk, and to look inconspicuous. He added, 'Look for a driver with a horse, jump in quickly.'

This rescue attempt did not go well. Lunia and Mucyk managed to smuggle themselves outside the locked Stryj Ghetto, but Nazis suspected something amiss and started searching the area. As they approached, Lunia shoved Mucyk onto a nearby bench and frantically whispered, 'Kiss me!' Though stunned, Mucyk complied. Lunia's quick thinking outwitted the Nazis. By pretending to be Polish teenagers passionately in love, they became invisible to the Nazis, just as Julia had been when disguised as the old beggar woman months earlier. The Nazis, searching for escaped ghetto Jews, asked the kissing couple, 'Did you see those Jews?' Lunia nodded and pointed in the opposite direction. It was now far too dangerous to escape, so Lunia and Mucyk smuggled themselves back into the locked ghetto and waited nervously.

It was a long time before Leo could convince the driver to attempt another rescue. This time, Lunia smuggled herself out alone because Mucyk was safely with a group in a protected ghetto bunker with over a hundred Jews. The Nazis knew of its existence and were desperately trying to locate it.

Lunia was proud to say that not one of the tiny handful of 'underground' Jews who knew its location, not one – including Lunia, herself – disclosed it, not even under the most severe torture. When she was tortured, Lunia explained, 'Because of my stubborn nature, the more they cut my skin to shreds, the tighter I closed my mouth!'

About eight months before the end of the war, Leo succeeded in persuading the driver with the horse and buggy to make another rescue attempt. Leo's message to Lunia was brief: 'Look for the driver and get in!'

She wondered how she would know which was the right horse and driver. She wondered how long she should wait. She wondered if she would get caught before anyone came. It was a frightening night, but finally, just as she was giving up, a driver with horse and carriage drove up and whispered, 'Get in!'

Shortly before the war's end, with love and persistence, Leo succeeded in bringing Lunia to the hiding place under the pigsty, which he shared with his mother. There the three remained – not moving, not speaking, not eating – until the end of each day when Dmitri, the Ukrainian friend, came with a few scraps of food.

Eight months later, the war ended. By that time, Lunia's legs were so weak, she could not stand, and the skin fell off the soles of her feet. Finally, Lunia, Leo and Julia crawled out of the hole below the pigsty. They found Mucyk, who with Julia, made Aliyah and lived out their lives in Eretz Yisrael.

Leo had other plans. He knew he wanted to spend his life with Lunia. First, they went back to Stryj, as did other survivors, to search for anyone alive. Lunia wanted to find Zvi. Although she knew the rest of her family was dead, she hoped, that Zvi had somehow miraculously managed to survive. He had to the end, but Lunia was devastated to learn that on the very last day of the war, the Nazis at Zvi's slave labour camp shot every prisoner dead.

Lunia and Leo searched also for the hidden crates of gold bullion, British pounds sterling, and diamonds in the corner of the Gartner factory. Lunia's grandfather, Shammai, had left enough valuables buried there for any surviving Gartner family member to start a new life. But instead of finding buried treasure, they found an empty hole. Lunia had lost her greatest treasure – her beloved family – and now also her family's monetary treasure as well. At this point, Leo said to Lunia, 'There's nothing left for you here. Come to Italy with me and start a new life.' Lunia agreed, but her Aunt Fancia, who survived the war in Siberia, raised an objection.

Following pre-war protocol, Fanica said it was not proper for Lunia to travel across national boundaries with a man who was not her husband. Although it seemed ludicrous after everything

Lunia had endured, she agreed to Fanica's stipulation. And that is how Lunia Backenroth Gartner came to marry Leo Weiss.

Leo saved Lunia and they began a new life together, first in Italy, then in America. In Italy, Lunia and Leo had nothing – except each other. Leo traded goods on the black market, so that they could eat. One day, Lunia saw a sign announcing a competition for three full scholarships to the University of Modena. She turned to Leo and said, 'Why don't we take the exam? We have nothing to lose!'

As outstanding students in a *gymnasium* (high school) before the war, and perhaps knowing a bit of Latin, they managed to understand the Italian in the qualifying exam. The results were astounding: Lunia won one full scholarship and Leo won the second one! Despite unbearable war-time losses, they were beginning life again.

One day, Leo came home from class to find Lunia despondent. When he asked why, Lunia told him she had gone to a doctor who told her she could never have a baby. Leo's response was typical: 'You want a baby? I'll give you a baby.' And nine months later I was born!

During their time in Italy, my parents earned PhDs. Leo's was in Chemistry and Lunia's in Pharmacology. Leo was active in the *Bricha*, smuggling Jews across the Alps to meet ships clandestinely headed to Eretz Yisrael. Leo was a fearless, inspiring, and courageous leader – qualities he exhibited for the rest of his life, trying to help others wherever he could. And Lunia, in quieter ways, less flamboyant, but no less effective, made a difference in other people's lives as well.

In America, Leo was chairman of the Chemistry Department at Rochester General Hospital in upstate New York, and then Head of Purchasing for all the laboratories at the hospital. Lunia worked as a pharmacist in privately owned and hospital pharmacies for many years.

Throughout their lives, they found ways to help others. And wherever they went, both together and separately, they gave love. Love of family. Love of Israel. Love of freedom. Love of life. Love. This is what they taught their children and grandchildren, and now this is what their grandchildren – now grown and parents themselves – are teaching their own little children as well. Love in Heaven and Hell, and then Heaven, once again.

Written by Ann Weiss, daughter of Leo and Lunia Weiss, with Mindelle Pierce.

26

ROSE WEISZ AND JOSKA CSEH

Rose Weisz was born in 1924 in Gyongyos, Hungary, the fourth of six children. Though the sparks of anti-Semitism were beginning to appear throughout Europe, life for Jews in Hungary was calm. The Weisz family struggled to make ends meet, it was a constant battle with only the mother working, trying to support her large family during a time of economic uncertainty in they country. During the 1930s, as each of the older Weisz siblings became old enough to leave home and find work, Rose, her sister and two brothers moved to Budapest. Rose's younger sister and brother stayed in Gyongos with their parents.

By the late 1930s, the first overt anti-Semitism became evident in Hungary and by 1940, the Hungarians, allies of the Germans, had restricted travel, segregated housing, and required Jews to wear yellow stars. Jews were no longer allowed to own businesses or hold professional licences. In Budapest, Jewish residents were forced out of their homes and into the ghetto, an area of approximately fifteen blocks, with multiple families crammed into tiny apartments. Indiscriminate beatings and murders were becoming daily occurrences.

Even in these difficult times, love emerged. Rose was a beautiful woman, warm and charismatic, who captured the attention of all those around her. She dated often and was engaged to be married several times. But Rose ended every relationship before her wedding day, leaving a trail of broken hearts in her wake. Her family had learned not to take her engagements seriously – until she walked down the aisle and married Nicholas Spitz, a handsome and charming tailor.

Conditions for Hungarian Jews continued their precipitous decline, and with each passing day, Jews began to disappear. Some were sent into forced labour, others were arrested and removed. Still others simply vanished. The Weisz family felt the impact in 1942, when several members of their family were taken in quick succession. First, Rose's two older brothers were taken into work brigades. Soon thereafter, Nicholas was forced into a work brigade. The Nazis took Rose's sister next. Rose worried about their fate and feared for the rest of her family.

As more anti-Jewish laws were passed and violence increased, Rose became desperate to save what remained of the family. By this time, Jews were forbidden to travel, so escaping Hungary was not a viable option. Hiding, while incredibly risky, was not the better option. It was the only option.

In early 1943, Rose took a dramatic risk. She approached a non-Jewish woman she knew in Budapest and offered to buy her identification papers. Rose did not know how she would react: Would she report Rose to the Nazis? Or would she accept Rose's offer? In desperate need of money, the woman agreed, and they made the exchange, money for papers. Rose examined the identification papers carefully, peeled back the woman's photo, and replaced it with her own, transforming herself into Maria Willem.

Soon after, Rose was notified that one of her brothers had died of a head injury sustained while working in forced labour. Her resolve to survive and save her family intensified, and she swore to protect her family by any means necessary. Now nineteen, she removed her wedding band, put a cross around her neck, and Rose, now Maria Willem, moved into a room in a Budapest house designated for non-Jews.

Though Rose sometimes would cross paths with the other tenants of the house, she tried to keep to herself. One of these other tenants, an imposing and intimidating Austrian shoe salesman, made Rose feel uneasy. He was tall and handsome, with slicked back hair and a military-inspired suit. With his tall, shiny black boots, dark leather trench coat and menacing motorcycle, he carried himself with the confidence and arrogance of a Nazi.

His limp, which others assumed was the result of a war injury, added to his aura; and Joska kept the real cause to himself — a childhood bout of polio. Joska Cseh looked like the prototypical Nazi monster and he frightened Rose to her core.

Joska, however, was quite taken with Rose, who he knew only as Maria. One day, the landlord asked Joska to deliver a letter to Maria's room. He climbed the steps, calling out to her. The sound of his boots on the stairs and his voice calling her name were terrifying. She met him in the hallway, retrieved the letter with a polite 'Thank you' and retreated into her room, closing the door behind her. Despite her lack of interest, or perhaps because of it, Joska was smitten. From then on, Joska tried to engage Rose in conversation at every opportunity, but she remained distant and aloof. Rose was singularly focused on saving herself and her family. Joska made her feel uneasy and vulnerable, constantly making her speculate: *Is he a Nazi? Does he know I'm a Jew? Is he going to turn me in? Is he going to go after my family?* Though polite, she kept him at a distance, always finding a reason to excuse herself from the conversation.

Then, one day, he invited her to the theatre with him. Terrified to say yes, but equally terrified to say no, she felt the panic welling inside of her. In that moment, she realised that if she could not control her fear, it would betray her. Rose turned on her charm and declined gracefully. Though it sounded lovely, she explained, she was working that evening, covering a shift for a friend. Then she excused herself and walked away. And with this, Joska Cseh fell in love.

Rose hoped that her excuse would discourage Joska from pursuing her, but it had the opposite effect — it piqued his interest. He asked Rose to join him for dinner the following week, and Rose quickly weighed her options. Say no, and the invitations would continue. Or say yes, and make it clear that there was no chance of a romantic relationship. She agreed to the date.

Josh took Rose to a lovely restaurant and acted like a perfect gentleman throughout the evening. Though they made polite conversation, Rose was riddled with anxiety and fear. She maintained a calm veneer throughout the evening and hoped that would be the end of his interest. But he invited her out to dinner again. Their second date went the same as the first, and the invitations continued. Three weeks and several dates later, Joska proposed.

Rose asked for some time to consider his marriage proposal. *How far can she take this charade? Does he know she is a Jew? Is this a trap? Or is he really in love? If he found out she was Jewish, would he still love her, or would he report her to the Nazis?*

The next time she and Joska were alone in the boarding house, Rose invited him into her room and asked him to sit down. She knew the risk involved in telling Joska the truth, but continuing the charade was more than she could bear. Despite the risk to her and to her family, Rose felt she had no choice but to reveal the truth.

'Joska, I can't marry you because I'm already married. My husband was sent to a work brigade months ago, just two weeks after we were married. I don't know if he's alive or dead.' He nodded, saying nothing. She continued, 'I'm not Maria Willem, I was born Rose Weisz. I'm Jewish.' She explained that one of her brothers had died in the work brigade and another brother and sister had been taken away. Her family meant everything to her, and she would do everything possible to keep them safe. Still, Joska was silent. When she had finished, Rose said, 'Now you know. Do you still want to marry me?' After a long pause, he answered, 'I understand. Let me think about all this and tomorrow night we'll meet again and talk. Good night, Rose.' And with that, he left.

Rose spent the next day tied in knots, worried that she had made a mistake by revealing herself to him. She knew that she had risked her life and the lives of her family by telling him the truth; and she waited for Joska to come to her room that evening, half expecting Hungarian officers to kick in her door and drag her to her death. By the time Joska arrived at 8.30 p.m., Rose was petrified.

Joska began to speak. 'When Hitler started making those speeches, saying that the Jews started the war and that everything was the Jews' fault, all I could think of was, 'Those poor people. I feel so sorry for them." Rose felt a glimmer of hope. He told her that he was in love with her and wanted to help. 'I'm going to do everything I can to help you and your entire family.' She was speechless, weeping with gratitude, relief, and hope. The intensity of her emotions made him uncomfortable, and he tried to focus on the business at hand. 'Tomorrow I'd like to meet your whole family. There's no time to lose.' Rose looked at Joska with affection. She promised that once she could determine what had happened to her husband, she would marry Joska. They both knew that it was unlikely Nicholas would return; but, for now, the marriage conversation was placed on indefinite hold.

The following day, Rose brought Joska to meet her family and explain their plan to save the forty-two members of the Weisz group, family and friends. The first order of business was to obtain false identification papers for every member of the family. Next, Joska would find them a safe place to live. Finding forty-two sets of identification papers was no small feat. Thus, Joska first asked his own family in Pecs, Hungary, who were well-established in their community. Because it was unlikely that that they would be asked to show identification, they handed over twenty-two sets of papers to save the Weisz family.

Rose soon found out that Joska wasn't a shoe salesman. He used that story as a cover for his much more lucrative job: he had been trafficking in the black market since the war began, and he knew how to find just about anything. With his connections, he purchased twenty-two additional sets of identification papers as well as counterfeit military papers that identified him as a German officer. Those saved Joska countless times throughout the war as he conducted his illegal activities.

In early 1944, Joska rented an apartment building in an industrial zone in the eastern suburbs of Budapest. He then snuck the forty-two members of the Weisz group into the apartment building, now with papers identifying them as non-Jews. Rose, her parents, grandfather, aunts, uncles, cousins, friends, and even Rose's in-laws, were safely tucked away in this out-of-the-way house.

Knowing that the Weisz clan was as safe as possible in 1944 Hungary, Joska set out on his next mission: to rescue Rose's beloved sister. Joska bribed a man with access to Nazi records for information on Rose's sister and discovered that she was imprisoned in Auschwitz-Birkenau. Despite Rose's protests that it was too dangerous, and he had done enough, Joska felt compelled to save her. It took several days of bribing, sneaking, and lying to get to the outer gate of Auschwitz, where he attempted to talk his way into the camp. He even flashed his false military papers to the SS guard, hoping to gain entry. However, the guards were not easily manipulated and, for the first time, Joska had reached the limits of his cunning and charm. Fearing that he was in danger and honouring his promise to Rose to return safely to her, he returned to Budapest alone. This failure haunted him as he continued to protect the Weisz family, living with them in the house until the end of war. When the Russians took Budapest from the Nazis and the Jews could emerge from hiding, all forty-two members of the Weisz group had survived.

After the war, Joska used charm and money to persuade the superintendent of the Weisz's old apartment building to return their home, which they reclaimed in March 1945. By this time, Rose and Joska had been living as husband and wife for almost a year and had grown close during the time they had been together. Still, after the war ended, out of respect for her legal husband, Rose waited for Nicholas to return. After three months had passed with no word of Nicholas's whereabouts, it seemed obvious to everyone that he had not survived. Though Rose was saddened by the thought of Nicholas's death, she and Joska had fallen deeply in love and the couple officially become husband and wife.

Two weeks after they were married, Nicholas returned! Nicholas had spent the past three months making his way back to Budapest, anticipating a reunion with the wife he adored. Seeing Nicholas, Rose was distraught and conflicted. While she was thrilled and relieved that Nicholas was alive, she was in love with Joska, the man who had saved her entire family and with whom she had shared the past year of her life. She explained to Nicholas all that Joska had done for them, and that he had saved Nicholas's parents. There was no way Nicholas could have prepared himself for his return to a wife who had married another man, and this was certainly not the homecoming he had expected. So much had happened since Rose and Nicholas had been together last, it seemed impossible to go back. Given the circumstances, Nicholas had no choice but to bow out gracefully and accept this turn of events. Nicholas was grateful to Joska for saving his parents and, in time, the men became friends.

In June 1945, Rose's sister, a survivor of Auschwitz, returned to her family. After walking for months from Auschwitz to Budapest, she arrived at their apartment emaciated, sick, and weak. Thanks to Joska, her family welcomed her home.

Though passionate and intense, Rose and Joska's love affair was short-lived. The couple's happiness began to wane as Joska struggled to settle into an ordinary post-war life. His black-market trade made him one of the wealthiest men in Budapest and he enjoyed the high life, driving fancy cars, expanding his fleet of motorcycles, wearing expensive suits, and dining at the finest restaurants. His thirst for excitement and adventure seemed insatiable, and he continued to expand his black-market operations as he indulged himself in drinking, partying, and the company of other women. The demise of their relationship was devastating for Rose. Heartbroken, she filed for divorce in 1947.

Shortly after the divorce, in 1948 Rose emigrated to the United States. Six months later, she met and married Martin Buchwalk in New York City. Over the next few years, Rose's parents and her younger brother, Tommy, arrived in New York City. Rose and Martin also helped Nicholas, Rose's first husband, and his new wife emigrate to Canada, providing the funding to start a business.

Despite the dissolution of Rose and Joska's marriage, the entire Weisz family was forever indebted to Joska for saving their lives. Joska spent his fortune on his lavish lifestyle in the years immediately after the war, and never again found the financial success of his earlier years. When his money ran out, Joska lived the rest of his life in Poland, destitute and lonely. Tommy, Rose's younger brother, had always viewed Joska as a hero and he maintained a relationship with Joska after the war. When Tommy was able, he began sending Joska money, continuing to support him until Joska's death in 2012. Thereafter, Tommy began sending money to Joska's relatives in Hungary, an acknowledgment of Joska's bravery, determination, and willingness to risk his life for the woman he loved and the family she loved.

From interviews with Tommy Weitz, conducted in December 2015 and August 2016, by Mindelle and Ira Pierce.

27

HENIEK GREENSPAN, MILLIE AND JACK WERBER

We were seated at a cocktail table hosted by Patti Kenner, a member of the Board of the Defiant Requiem Foundation. Next to us was a beautifully coiffeured woman at the Lincoln Center pre-concert gathering in New York City in 2013. It was prior to our attending the New York premier of *The Defiant Requiem*, a Holocaust-related concert-drama conceived and created by Maestro Murry Sidlin, with music by Verdi.

Millie glanced at the ring on my finger and asked if it was an antique, and I started to tell her the story of Jacob and Reisel, my parents (see page ***). She leaned forward and said that she, too, has a story to tell, *Two Rings*, and would gladly mail me a copy of her book. Our relationship grew and I asked if I could interview her about her love story involving two rings. Here it is.

Millie Drezner survived the Holocaust, married Jack Werber, also a survivor, and enjoyed a wonderful marriage that spanned sixty years. During their life together, they had children and grandchildren, financial success and a full and meaningful life.

But Millie had another love story she kept secret in her heart – the story of her first love as a young girl in the Radom ghetto in Poland. She didn't share this part of her heart with her friends or her children. Even her beloved husband, Jack, knew only the most basic facts. It wasn't until after Jack's death that Millie felt ready to tell her story. In her memoir *Two Rings: A Story of Love and War* by Eve Keller and Millie Werber, Millie recounts her experience throughout the war, honours those who perished, and thanks those to whom she owes her survival. (On 23 March 2015, Marty Werber, son of Millie and Jack Werber was interviewed on video by me, Mindelle Pierce, where he provided more insight into his parents' story.)

As a fourteen-year-old girl in Radom in 1941, Millie Drezner, her parents, and her brother were forced into the Radom ghetto where they lived in a one-room apartment with her aunt, uncle and two cousins. In the ghetto, hunger, starvation, sickness, and death were part of daily life. In the summer of 1942, the Germans began recruiting Jews aged between fifteen and forty to work at a nearby munitions factory. Though Millie didn't want to leave the ghetto, her uncle insisted, adamant that everyone in the family find jobs. In his words, 'If you find work, you might live.' Millie and her mother applied to work in the factory. Millie, passing for fifteen, young and healthy, was accepted without question. Her mother, at forty-three, was deemed too old to work and was sent back to the ghetto.

Millie's job at the factory was to stand at a noisy machine drilling holes to precise specifications into tiny metal slugs for twelve-hour shifts, punctuated by one fifteen-minute break. The women slept in a large structure on the cement floors with no bedding or blankets. After several weeks, they were given permission to visit the ghetto and bring back their valuables. Millie returned to her family's apartment and begged to stay, but her uncle refused.

Millie resented her uncle, thinking him cruel for forcing her to return to the factory when she so desperately wanted to stay with her family. As Millie sobbed, her mother tried to comfort her. 'You must go. It's for the best.' When Millie told her about the cold cement floor, her mother handed her their feather blanket. Alone and afraid, she returned to the factory. The next day, the Nazis began deporting the ghetto residents. Millie never saw her mother again.

Heniek Greenspan, at twenty-six years old, was a Kapo at the factory. Kapos were prisoners of Nazi concentration camps assigned by the SS guards to supervise forced labour and carry out administrative tasks in the camps. In exchange, they were given slightly better treatment and a false hope for survival. While some Kapos became power hungry and cruel to their fellow Jews in an effort to gain favour with the Nazis, Heniek was kind and charming. Most of the women were quite taken with Heniek, who was tall and thin with wavy, dark hair and warm brown eyes. He spoke kindly to the women, who constantly jockeyed for his attention. Millie, quiet and shy, was younger than most of the women and kept mostly to herself. She couldn't understand the young women who vied for his attention. What did they see in this Nazi-appointed Jewish police officer, tasked with keeping them in line? Besides, at age fourteen, she was too young to be concerned with boys. With her focus on daily survival, there was no room for romance in this life full of terror.

One day when Heniek walked by, Millie blurted out, 'Why are they doing this? Why are the women doing these things for you? I would never do you such favours!' He responded '*Smarkata*!' loosely translated as brat. 'You'll see, one day you'll want to do things for me, too.' Millie answered, 'Never.' And he walked on.

Months passed, and Millie, now fifteen, remained focused on work and survival. But one day, she found herself thinking about Heniek. She realised that when he was near, she felt a magnetic pull toward him that was as exhilarating as it was confusing. Millie hid her feelings. She knew nothing of romance and passion, and yet she was consumed by thoughts of Heniek. One day when she was alone outside the barracks, he took her hand in his and she felt desire that she had never before experienced. Over time, their relationship blossomed. After her twelve-hour factory shifts ended, Heniek would walk her back to the barracks, lavishing compliments on her. He made her feel special and loved. During wartime, age differences between couples didn't pose the same obstacle as they did before the war. Despite their age difference, they felt a natural connection. With the uncertainty of each day and the possibility that each morning could be her last, Millie craved Heniek's affection and protection. Though their entire relationship was veiled in secrecy, Millie felt liberated. The passion and attraction she felt for him grew stronger each day. Millie was in love and, for the first time in a long time, she was not alone.

Heniek had Millie reassigned from the munitions factory to the kitchen. Though life in the kitchen was not easy, it was a significant improvement. For over a year, Millie peeled what felt like thousands of potatoes each day, with cramping fingers and aching joints, using a dull knife. But she worked beside four other women near a potbellied stove that kept her warm through the winter. Heniek came to visit her in the kitchen from time to time, a signal that they had to talk.

On one of these occasions, he came to the kitchen and she discreetly met him outside. They spoke in the shadows as the sun went down. His plan was so wild and full of risk, she could barely comprehend what he was saying.

Heniek had heard that the Nazis were going to allow anyone in Poland with Argentinian citizenship to return to South America. In return, Argentina would release any German nationals living there. Though Heniek was a Polish citizen, his Argentinian brother-in-law offered to register him as his brother, enabling Heniek to leave for South America along with his family. With Millie as his wife, they could leave together.

To Millie, who had long ago accepted that she would one day die at the hands of the Nazis, the idea of a future with Heniek away from Poland filled her with hope. Could they get married and escape together? Her head was spinning with dreams of another life. But she needed to speak with her father, aunt and uncle – the only family she had left – before she could make such a momentous decision. She went back to the ghetto to talk with them.

As a Kapo, Heniek was able to arrange for Millie to go back to the ghetto for two hours, accompanied by another officer. She had only two hours to decide if she should marry Heniek, leaving behind her family and the only home she had ever known, and escape to Argentina, or stay in Poland where every day was filled with misery, hunger, and death.

Her family didn't hesitate. 'Marry Heniek!' There was no talk of love or happiness. The analysis was simple: the marriage would get Millie out of Poland. The decision was made. Millie returned to the barracks and, with excitement and fear, accepted Heinek's proposal. Heniek took her in his arms and kissed her. They pledged their love to each other and set the date for their wedding just a few days later. Despite the chaos, evil, and loss in the world around them, Millie was happy and in love.

Millie's family had a friend in the ghetto who had managed to keep operating a small, secret goldsmith business. Scraping together some money, they asked him to make a ring for Millie to give to Heinek for their wedding as a token of their appreciation for saving her.

They were married several days later in Millie's family's one-room apartment in the ghetto. The blessings were said, and a glass was broken. Millie gave Heniek the custom-made ring with his initial, 'HG', engraved on it. He gave her a simple gold band. After the wedding, a picture of the couple was taken. Then the couple returned to the barracks and resumed their duties, waiting for notice of the pending German–Argentinian exchange. But with no documents, no *ketubah*, no proof of their marriage, not even the same last name as Heniek's brother-in-law, their plan was a long shot. Nonetheless, they focused on their small chance at freedom.

By the time they received word about the Argentinian–German exchange, it was over. In the end, it wasn't an exchange at all. Those with Argentinian passports – including seventeen members of Heniek's brother-in-law's family – were gathered together in the ghetto and taken to the central square for transport. Instead of being freed, they were lined up and executed. There would be no escape for Heniek and Millie to Argentina.

Though unofficial, and despite living apart and having little time alone, Heinek and Millie felt married in their hearts. Henrik had access to a room in one of the barracks and on a few occasions, on a wooden bed with a thin mattress, they were able to be together as husband and wife.

A few months later, the Radom ghetto was liquidated and all Jews still able to work were brought to the factory, including Millie's aunt, uncle, and cousin. Any hope that work would save them vanished as conditions worsened. Food rations were cut, prisoners were forced to wear striped uniforms and a double row of barbed-wire fencing was erected around the perimeter of the barracks. The Nazis cautioned the prisoners against escape, warning that for every prisoner that escaped, twenty would be killed. The Nazis made good on their threat.

Another Kapo, David Norembursky, was, in Millie's assessment, the opposite of Heniek in every way. He was selfish, cold and heartless. He seemed to enjoy the power he held over his fellow Jews. He acted as though he was superior to the other Jews and indifferent to their fate. To Millie, it seemed his primary motivation was to gain favour with the Nazis for his own advancement, regardless of the price others would be forced to pay.

In the factory in Radom, work in the foundry was the most dreaded of all. Through the constant fire and smoke, the workers were forced to inhale soot for twelve-hour shifts, quietly and steadily blackening their lungs and wasting their bodies. Commandant Miller, a Nazi officer charged with overseeing this work, made sure that there were plenty of young, healthy, robust girls among the workers. It was no secret to the Nazis that the Commandant was sexually abusing these girls and, by doing so, breaking the law against *Rassenschande,* or 'race-shame'. Physical relations with a Jew, mixing Aryan blood with Jewish blood, thereby jeopardising the purity of the master race, was forbidden by the Nuremberg Laws.

David Norembursky knew the Nazis would disapprove of Miller's activities and reported him to Nazi officials. As punishment, Miller was reassigned to another facility. As a reward, Norembursky and his family, along with twelve other Kapos and their families, were brought to the barracks and given better working positions. These thirteen Kapos took the places of the thirteen Kapos already there, including Heniek.

Heniek understood what was happening and came to the kitchen to speak with Millie. From his pocket, he took a small stack of money and pressed it into Millie's hands. She refused to take the money, confused by his insistence. 'It's not to hold, it's to keep. The money is for you. It's a gift, for whenever you will need it.' She continued to protest, but he was insistent. He looked at her lovingly, trying to protect her the only way he could. This was his good-bye. He took off his wedding ring and placed it in her hand. They did not discuss the significance of this gesture, but they both knew. When she returned to the barracks that night, Millie tied their wedding rings together with some thread and put them in a small pocket her mother had sewn into her undergarments.

A few days later, the Nazis removed the former Kapos and their families. Millie watched as they grabbed Heniek and led him out of the compound. Norembursky watched too. As Heniek passed him, he glared at him and said, 'I know this is your doing. I know this is because of you.' Norembursky did not react. He didn't care that he and Heniek had known each other for years, had been classmates, had a history together. He cared only that he was safe.

Millie never saw Heniek again, nor did she ever learn what happened to him or how he died. Her first love, her husband, her protector, was gone in an instant. She forever blamed Norembursky for Heniek's death.

A short time later, Miller returned to Radom and sought revenge against the Kapo who had reported him. Somehow, Norembursky had obtained Polish papers for himself and his family. Norembursky knew if he didn't escape, Miller would kill him in retribution. He and his wife fled, knowing, as all the prisoners did, that their escape would lead to the executions of forty people.

Following the Nuremburskys' escape, the Nazi soldiers assembled a crowd in the yard to watch the consequences. In the yard, against a wall, they first lined up his aunt, uncle and cousin, who had been caught trying to escape, and shot them. Then they gathered his wife's mother, brother, and nephew, and added seventeen more, randomly selected prisoners, for a total of twenty. When a soldier dragged Norembursky's mother-in-law to the yard for her execution, she called out, 'If any of you make it out of here, you must find my daughter and tell her she will never be alone. The ghosts of her mother and family will haunt her always. They will swirl around her and never let her be. This is my curse!' And with that, she and nineteen others were executed. Millie never forgot those words.

After that, Millie's time at the compound was filled with loneliness and darkness. Having lost Heniek, she felt as though she had lost everything. When rumours spread that the Americans had landed in France and the Russians were already in Poland, the prisoners dared to hope they might be saved. Panicking, the Germans emptied the barracks. Nearly two years after she first arrived at the factory, she, along with hundreds, perhaps thousands of others were forced on a death march. They had no idea where they were going or how long it would take. For days they walked, under the blazing summer sun. Every day, people died of exhaustion, dehydration and gunshots. After 100 kilometres, they arrived in a small town and were loaded onto trains destined for Auschwitz.

Millie and her aunt, who had been with her since the factory, were ordered to strip off their clothes. Millie watched her aunt remove her shoe, carefully peeling back the inner lining of the insole and inserting a photo of her children. Millie asked her aunt to add her wedding photo as well. Throughout the rest of the war, Millie hid her and Heinek's wedding rings and the two photos remained hidden in her aunt's shoe. After six months in Auschwitz, Millie and her aunt were transported to a munitions factory in Lippstadt, Germany. Then several months later, as the end of the war neared, the prisoners were sent on another death march. On the third day of the march, the prisoners heard aircraft roaring above and saw American parachutists descending. The Nazi guards fled and the remaining Jews were liberated.

After liberation, Millie and her aunt travelled to Garmisch-Partenkirchen, Germany, searching for their family. There, Millie met and married Jack Werber, a fellow survivor. Jack's wife and young daughter had been killed in the Holocaust. Jack and Millie understood the anguish of each other's losses and the struggle to begin a new life in the absence of those they had loved. They eventually emigrated to the United States and moved to the Lower East Side of Manhattan where they joined a community of survivors who had come to America for a second chance at life.

Here, her path once again crossed David Norembursky and his wife. The Nuremburskys were living in the Lower East Side but under an assumed name. Millie knew no logic could explain who had survived and who had not. However, the fact that the Noremburskys had lived while so many others had been murdered weighed on her.

Millie, then nineteen years old and speaking almost no English, went to the Office of Immigration to report that a perpetrator of war crimes against Jews in Poland was living in the city under false pretences. Though there was nothing the Office of Immigration could do about crimes committed outside of the United States, they offered to pursue her claim of false identity if she could provide proof. Without any way to prove her claim, she was left frustrated.

Through word of mouth, the Noremburskys learned that Millie had reported them. One day, Mrs Norembursky came to Millie's apartment and begged her to leave them alone and let them live their new lives in America. Millie knew there was no way the couple would be held accountable for their actions officially. However, she could fulfil a dying woman's last wish. Without hesitation, Millie told Mrs Norembursky about her mother's execution, the price she paid for her daughter's escape. Millie repeated, word for word, the curse she inflicted upon her daughter just before she was murdered. As Millie explained,

> I was glad to do it. I was glad to give her this pain. It gave me satisfaction to know that she would now have to face the full weight of what she had done. She would live with the certain knowledge that, in effect, she had killed her own mother, that her mother knew this, and that her mother had cursed her for it.

Though there would be no formal action against the Nuremburskys, Millie felt empowered knowing that she had given a voice to those who died. She felt she had achieved a small measure of justice for her beloved Heinek. As she wrote in the book, *Two Rings*:

> Heniek was my first love... There was nothing normal about our love – we courted under the eyes of our enemies; we married as a means of escape. We were husband and wife for only a few months; we never had a home, never dreamed of a family. Nothing normal, but maybe for all that, nothing ordinary. I was sixteen and in love with a charming and beautiful man, a man who had chosen me out of hundreds of women, a man who made me feel vibrant and alive in the midst of war. I was alone and frightened in a dangerous place, and Heniek entered my life to protect me and love me and teach me the fullness of pleasure. He was the center of my life. His love woke me in the morning, sustained me during the hours of empty labor, and sent me to sleep at night. He cared for me and looked out for my needs... Heniek loved me with a sweet and assured warmth that I had never known

before, and with all the intensity of a young girl awakening into adulthood, I loved him back. I loved him. I did.

Millie and Jack raised two sons in Queens, NY, and built a real estate business. They remained happily married for sixty years, until Jack's death in 2006. Millie passed away in 2016 surrounded by her children, grandchildren, and great-grandchildren.

Millie Werber and Eve Keller published Two Rings: A Story of Love and War *in 2012. Marty Werber, son of Millie and Jack Werber, was interviewed by Mindelle Pierce on 23 March 2015, giving additional insight into the lives of his parents.*

ACKNOWLEDGEMENTS

I thank my husband, Ira, who worked tirelessly, interviewing survivors; and later, acted as my editor, wordsmith and IT advisor to help bring this book to life. I love you, my Ira.

Information was mostly collated from many video-taped interviews that Ira and I recorded, concentrating on the romantic love that grew out of the Holocaust, the state-sponsored mass murder of some six million European Jews and millions of others by the Nazis and their collaborators. There are twenty-seven stories of romantic love in all, a few precious rays of light that burst forth despite the unspeakable acts of terror perpetrated by the Nazis 1933–1945.

Most of our stories were composed with the help of the individuals I acknowledge here. Some of these treasures were written by the survivors themselves, and others were authored by their children and grandchildren.

A question that I am asked frequently is how I came to do these interviews in the first place. It did not come easily, and I had lots of assistance as discussed here. I must admit that my parents, to whom I dedicate this book, were not at all interested in sharing their stories. I was told that most survivors do not share them for reasons that include survivor's guilt, the undeniable pain that comes from reliving their traumas while telling their stories, and for other reasons, all understandable.

I do recall my Yiddisha Momma, Reisel, crying over the losses of her young sisters and brothers each time she kindled the

Shabbat candles, moaning, 'the kinder, the kinder' (the children, the children). In fact, for many years I was denied all but a few fragments of their stories until my children were grown sufficiently to ask questions. I knew well that grandparents almost never say no to their grandchildren, and that was how I got them to talk.

I never will forget the first time that happened. I was able to convince my son, Micah, to stand in front of our video camera after my husband invited my parents to sit in front of him. As rehearsed, Micah then asked them whether they remembered anything about their families during that awful period. What happened next shocked us all. My mother rushed into her bedroom, collected photos of her murdered family, and proceeded with tears to begin to tell her stories, starting off as usual with sighs of, 'The children, the children'. That was the book's beginning!

Unlike many survivor families' stories, which were kept from their children so as not to traumatise them, after my parents began talking I got to know so much about their lives before the war, and their many losses, hardships and challenges during their war years, and how their traumas were eclipsed by their love for one another. My husband used the video camera to capture many of them.

Besides Micah, all of our six children, Leah, Ashirah, Daniel, Bess and Alisa, and our nineteen grandchildren – some more and some less – were involved with his book. But first and foremost, I must thank my parents who inspired me more than anyone else.

Some time after my parents' revelations, we were visiting the Jewish Community Center (JCC) in Margate N.J. late one morning, where we bumped into our friend, Kirk Wisemayer, the head of the local Jewish Federation. He was shepherding two exhausted-looking women, Clila and Hadas Bau, who we learned had arrived from Israel, having deplaned from their overnight flight just a few hours earlier. They had come to present their parents' story at a community get-together that we were planning to attend that evening. We suggested that they take a nap in our house, which was just a two-minute ride from the JCC. They took us up on it, and that started our lifetime friendship with Clila and Hadas, who desperately wanted their parent's Holocaust story to be known. That's what began the idea that culminated in this book of love stories.

Not long after, we heard a great story of romantic love during the Holocaust from our neighbours, John and Iris Berkowitcz, and John's sister, Ruth Pengas. They wanted their parents' story known as well.

And so it went... as we kept finding more and more stories of unbelievable love, plus survival – we found that many had the same theme: a strong woman, and a non-Jew without whom they probably would not have survived.

Dr Viktor Frankl's 1946 psychological memoir, *Man's Search for Meaning*, goes a long way to explaining these stories. He dwelt on what the gruesome experiences of Auschwitz taught him about the primary purpose of life, namely, 'meaning'. It was the love for his wife that kept him from giving up, after suffering horrific, unspeakable pain from his Nazi tormentors.

There were several people along the way who kept me on track. They include, of course, my literary agent, Linda Langton and my Commissioning Editor, Connor Stait, at Amberley Publishing. They and their staff read my drafts and believed that enough people would wish to read this book, to make their efforts and investments worthwhile. They made it happen.

We are thankful to our dear friends, Barbara and Ron Zukin and Susan Sinek who kindly helped us find Linda Langton.

Especially, we thank Holocaust scholar Rabbi Dr Michael Berenbaum, the undisputed dean of the subject, who wrote the Foreword, the Timeline and provided the key stimulus to see the book through to publication.

Add Dr Miriam Klein Kassenoff, my educational consultant, who helped me almost daily with the book in so many ways in her capacity as founding director of the University of Miami Holocaust Teacher Institute. She is also the Education Chairperson at the Holocaust Memorial in Miami Beach, Florida, and the Education Specialist for Holocaust Studies for Miami-Dade County Public Schools.

Thank you to Dr David G. Marwell, who my husband and I met so many times at the Museum of Jewish Heritage in New York City where he was Museum Director. David is the author of *Unmasking the Angel of Death*, about Josef Mengele.

Likewise, the distinguished Baltimore Rabbi Mitchel Wohlberg, spiritual leader for forty years of Congregation Beth Tfiloh and Dean of its Community School, also reviewed our stories, and offered words of encouragement.

Ira Brenner, MD, a Clinical Professor of Psychiatry, did the same – and it was Dr Ira's father, Leo, who was instrumental in arranging the escape from the notorious Auschwitz Concentration Camp of 'Drimmer and Shine', a most remarkable story found here, Dr Ira provided significant input for this story.

Professor Mary Johnson, of the Women's Studies Department of Stockton University, also offered me support. She is among the most respected scholars on the Holocaust, is a good friend, a dedicated teacher and scholar who provided me with specific historical assistance.

Professor Gail Rosenthal and her staff at the Sara and Sam Schoffer Holocaust Resource Center at Stockton University reviewed the stories and allowed me to present them to several of their students, from whom we received excellent suggestions.

Additional hands-on assistance with this book came from Jeanette Friedman, without whom I could not have gotten to the publication stage. Jeanette is a creative wordsmith, a remarkable writer and editor who has analysed complex historical events and difficult, sensitive issues, including matters related to the Holocaust.

Robin Davidson was one of my earliest collaborators, who assisted in writing several of the stories tcreated from the video interviews.

Lori Miller was also an early collaborator, who wrote the first drafts of Bau and Groen, among others.

Gale Stanger and Jessica Levin provided editing assistance. Beryl Aaron was supportive in reading the stories.

Dr Bea Hollander, Dr Nancy Isserman and Lucy Reizman and others in my Transcending Trauma Project team, part of the Council for Relationships, reviewed several of this book's stories. In total, this team has conducted 305 in-depth interviews with ninety-eight Holocaust survivors, their children and grandchildren.

Oscar Rosenbloom, a Palo Alto attorney and Jewish community activist, provided advice on the amazing 'Drimmer and Shine' story, about their escape from Auschwitz, having met Shine in 2011.

My dear friend Patti Kenner and my treasured cousin, Judy Rock Goldman and her late husband, Manny Korman, were my cheerleaders all through this long process.

My artistic neighbour, Carole Couzens, expressed her love for and guided us to the symbol for the book's back cover. It is a barbed-wire heart over a railroad track sculpted by Ross Cohen, who we met via our dear friend and gifted artist, Stephanie Miller. Leonard Rosenthal, Senior Principal Scientist, and architect for PDF with Adobe Systems, kindly assisted uswith the cover photos for the publisher.

Our Rabbi Moshe Silver assisted us during a stay at Isabella Friedman Jewish Retreat Center where he officiated, with our earliest draft of the 'street wedding' of Reisel and Jacob Najman. Rabbi Moshe is not your average rabbi, having spent thirty years on Wall Street!

Our Rabbi Sruly Israel Lieber was helpful to us in translating from the original Yiddish letters from my grandmother, Alte Mindelle, to my Uncle Aaron Krischner in America.

We thank Valerie Geffner for introducing us to her uncle, Peter Guzzardi, an editor working with some of the wisest writers (and then, me!).

I constantly was sending drafts of the book for review to my writing group, comprised of my dear friends, Menucha Meinstein, Roz Kaplus, Marjorie Waterman.

My husband and I were so fortunate to receive kindness from the Zeldin family who allowed us to stay in their Versailles, France villa while we hunted down the places from which my father escaped.

The Arluck family showed kindness to us by allowing us to stay in their Florida apartment while we were working with our editorial helpers at the University of Miami.

Harriet Jackson helped with research on the history and background of France for my parents' story. She is a French historian/Educator from Columbia University Teachers College, having committed herself to using education to fight racism and antisemitism and transcending boundaries through interfaith and community activities.

Acknowledgements

Avner Avraham allowed me to convince him to incorporate the work of Joseph Bau into the traveling display on Adolf Eichmann. Bau forged the travel documents for the Masssad agents. Avner was a former Mossad agent himself and a renowned expert on Mossad operations who famously worked to reveal and publicize the inside story of the historic 1960 capture of Nazi war criminal Adolf Eichmann.

Thank you, Stanley Bergman, former Head of Preservation of The YIVO Institute for Jewish Research at the Center for Jewish History in New York City. He kindly gave me assistance to add to the book's depths in history, society and culture of Ashkenazic Jewry.

Thank you, Aviva Perlo, social worker, community cheerleader and writer, who was so helpful to me in reading and editing the stories in the book.

Finally, I owe a huge debt of gratitude to those relatives or friends of the subjects of our stories who contributed to the book (not already mentioned above). The relevant story titles are underlined:

Fran Shapiro, daughter of Sally and Charles Bedzo

Michael Benanov, grandson of Joshua and Isadora Szereny

Morris Berger, son of Max and Toby Berger

Ralph Berger, son of Fruma and Murry Berger

D. Eva Fogelman, daughter of Lillie Burstyn and Simcha Fogelman

Leo, Sipora and Marcel Groen, children of Nardus and Sipora Groen

Dina and Frank Kabak

Aviva Kempner assisted by her niece, Delaney Kempner and Dubek's grandson-in-law, Rose Deyer for Chaim Joseph and Hanka Kempner

Nancy and Howard Kleinberg

Ann Fristoe Stewart, Manager of the Leiber Collection (Museum) and Judith and Gus Leiber

Ida and Alvin Lewis, Children of Victor and Regina Lewis

Irene Lilienheim Angelico, daughter of Henry and Lydia Lilienheim

Ruth Gruber and her Daughter, Celia Michaels and son, David Michaels, caregivers for <u>Manya Hartmayer and Ernst Breue</u>

Dahlia Herman, daughter of <u>Ernest and Sara Paul</u>

Dr Jonathan Kramer, grandson of <u>Rabbi Salomon and Henrietta Rodrigues Pereira</u>

Margrit Pollak Shield, daughter of <u>Jack and Ina Soep Pollack</u>

Sabine Schgleiermacher Seidler (and husband, Hans Seidler) daughter and son-in-law of <u>Rosi Wronker Schleiermacher and Fritz Schleiermacher</u>

Ann Kirschner, daughter of <u>Sala and Sidney Garncarz</u>

Ann Weiss, daughter of <u>Leo and Lunia Weiss</u>

Tommy Weitz, Roses's brother, <u>Rose, and Joska Weitz</u>

Jack Werber, son of <u>Jack and Millie Drezner Werber</u>